Cultural Nationalism and Ethnic Music in Latin America

Cultural Nationalism and Ethnic Music in Latin America

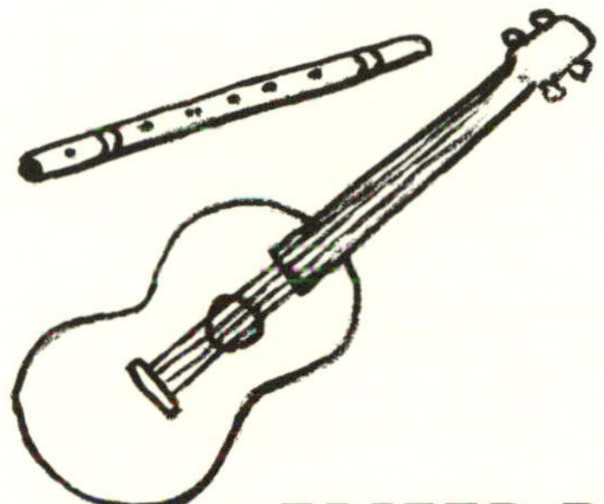

EDITED BY WILLIAM H. BEEZLEY

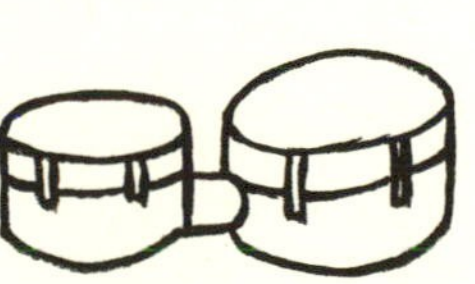

University of New Mexico Press • Albuquerque

Printed in the United States of America

Library of Congress Cataloging-in-Publication Data
Names: Beezley, William H.
Title: Cultural Nationalism and Ethnic Music in Latin America / edited by William H. Beezley.
Description: Albuquerque: University of New Mexico Press, 2018. | Includes index. |
Identifiers: LCCN 2018001023 (print) | LCCN 2018005450 (e-book) | ISBN 9780826359766 (e-book) | ISBN 9780826359759 (pbk.: alk. paper)
Subjects: LCSH: Music—Latin America—History and criticism. | Nationalism in music.
Classification: LCC ML3917.L27 (e-book) | LCC ML3917.L27 C85 2018 (print) | DDC 780.98—dc23
LC record available at https://lccn.loc.gov/2018001023

Front cover illustration: courtesy of Nicola Heindl-Watson
Back cover: used with permission of the Brazilian artist D. Souza and the Champion Folk Art collection
Title page illustrations: courtesy of Nicola Heindl-Watson
Designed by Lisa Tremaine
Composed in ITC Cushing

This volume is dedicated to

Matthew Beezley and his brother Nichols and cousins Max and Virginia

and, como siempre, to Blue

CONTENTS

ACKNOWLEDGMENTS

An anthology such as this one only comes to life from the efforts of the various contributors who trust that their efforts will result in something greater than the sum of its various parts. I am confident that these essays have resulted in something much greater than simply a collection of chapters on this theme. Together the essays provide a mosaic that offers a basic introduction to the twin themes of music and national identity and melodies and ethnic identification. Of course, they do not offer the last word on these topics, but they do provide a fascinating introduction to both. Not all of the Latin American countries are represented here, nor are all the ethnicities present, but the selections offer introductory slices of the multitude of topics on national and ethnic identity that exists in the region.

Acknowledgments must begin with recognition of the contributors. Following close after them, the executive editor of the University of New Mexico Press, Clark Whitehorn, whose general patience and positive support makes working through the publication process both a learning and a pleasurable experience.

Graduate and undergraduate students at the University of Arizona participated in this volume by listening to lectures and discussing the themes presented here. In particular, Luis Coronado, Natasha Verner, Claire Perrott, Osciel Salazar, Cristina Urias Espinosa, Allison Huntley, and Cony Marquez Sandoval have added considerably to this study of music, nationalism, and ethnicity.

The images on the back cover by the Brazilian artist D. Souza come from the Champion Folk Art collection and the photographs were taken by Cheryle Champion.

The Rise of Cultural Nationalism and its Musical Expressions

William H. Beezley

The opera *Xochicuicatl cuecuechtli* (The flowery song of mischief), sung in Nahuatl, the Aztec language, premiered in Mexico City, in September 2014. Above the stage, a screen flashed captions in Spanish of the flirtatious sexual innuendos exchanged among the singers. The performance culminated ten years of work by musicologist Gabriel Pareyón, who merged pre-Hispanic musical and legendary traditions to create the composition displaying a playful dimension of the Aztec culture. The composer chose his story from one of only two surviving *cuecuechcuicatl*, or erotic songs, from the genre called Xochicuicatl. An impish sixteenth-century Spanish evangelist, with the help of indigenous scribes, had saved them from destruction by other Franciscan missionaries determined to eliminate everything they considered lewd and impious.

The opera tells the story of the young rogue Tohuenyo, performed by Ricardo Díaz Mendoza, who attempts to seduce the *ahuianimeh*—dancers, not prostitutes—who entertained the warriors the night before battle. He and the women play an erotic game, then, much to his despair, they abandon him. Later, he receives a gift from Xochipilli, the prince of flowers, who represents love, games, beauty, and pleasure in Aztec mythology.[1]

While not the first Mexican opera to be composed in an indigenous language, it was the first to combine these lyrics with a score created for an orchestra with indigenous instruments in which a dozen musicians played pre-Columbian wooden drums, with their rhythms punctuated by rattles and flutes. This opera appropriately introduces this volume that examines music, especially operatic compositions, some with indigenous themes, and the rise of national cultural identity in Latin America. The introduction describes the first operas, their introduction into Spain's colonies, and early operas after independence in Latin America, leading to the importance of national music (including operas) in the late nineteenth century and cultural nationalism.

Opera first appeared in Florence in 1597, soon flourished across Italy, and rapidly spread throughout much of Europe. The Kingdom of Aragón ruled Naples (the Kingdom of the Two Sicilies), so Italian-style opera arrived early in Spain; nevertheless, it sputtered there because economic and political concerns caused by constant warfare with European enemies made funding nearly impossible for such an extravagant spectacle.

Rather than opera, musical drama drew on instrumental tunes, dances, and songs that were woven into both religious and secular performances. The *comedia nueva* became popular with the work of Pedro Calderón de la Barca, the father of Zarzuela, a manner of musical comedy, and other musical forms. Nevertheless, much more important were his liturgical, allegorical compositions, called *autos*, with didactic or exemplary narratives that typically ended with a song such as *villancico*, although in some autos, the composer incorporated songs within the drama.

Allegorical religious plays, or *autos sacramentales*, were performed as part of Corpus Christi feast-day processions, or adjacent to them, from roughly 1500 to the mid-1700s. Calderón composed what are now the best-known examples for the annual Corpus Christi celebrations in Madrid from 1648 to 1681. Classical mythology often inspired his religious allegories. He began with a prologue (the *loa*), followed by the one-act play, with instrumental and vocal songs as audible props, often identifying special characters, and usually concluded with either a short comic skit or a dance number. He also provided instructions for costumes, designs for elaborate scenery, and included special effects for the auto to be performed on parade floats (platforms on wheels called *carros*). The popularity of some resulted in performances for weeks in public theaters after the Corpus festival. In addition to the autos during the octave, the eight days, of Corpus, special sword and bell and other dances were performed by professionals. One scholar summed up their appeal and significance, saying, "Written in polymetric verse, they are elegant examples of Counter-Reformation religious instruction through beautiful Baroque poetry, song and spectacle."[2] Calderón's autos remained popular after his death, and composers in Madrid's royal chapels and its theaters composed additional songs for them. The tradition began to fade in the eighteenth century, and in 1765, a royal decree prohibited further performances of autos sacramentales in Spain and in the Hispanic Americas, where they had also become popular. Moreover, Calderón helped to popularize opera with two full-fledged compositions in 1659–1660, *La púrpura de la rosa* and *Celos aun del aire matan*. He inscribed the texts, and harpist–court composer Juan Hidalgo wrote the music. The two operas were performed several times over the years after their premiers.[3]

Despite prohibition against the autos, the Bourbon monarchs in the eighteenth century increased patronage of music and art. Among them, Philip V, despite his family's French origins, provided funding for numerous Italian musicians, actors, and painters in his determination to establish Italian opera firmly in Spain.

In the Americas, drama and musical traditions existed well before the Spanish arrived. Garcilazo de Vega, in his *Royal Commentaries of the Incas*, reports the people performed theater with music. This legacy throughout Spanish America has been largely lost because indigenous peoples did not develop musical notation and the Spanish colonists did not transcribe much of the music they heard. No evidence exists of sung dramas as antecedents of their introduction by Spanish colonists. Nevertheless, the significance of music in the region now called Mexico, at least for the Mexica, was clearly stated by Ixtlilxochitla in his *Historia Chichimeca*. After describing all the kinds of scribes in the city, he adds there were individuals charged with "teaching by memory all the songs in which were embodied their scientific knowledge and historical traditions."[4]

Opera's spotty development on the peninsula restrained its introduction in Spanish America. The same problems—public indifference, limited funds, no theaters designed for staging, absence of trained singers and musicians, and a lack of royal support—prevented it from flourishing in the colonies. Official opposition existed in general to profane music. Both Spanish amorous romances and urban dances might be misinterpreted or given indigenous interpretations, pre-Hispanic meanings, or magical associations when performed in public. This reflected strict oversight in an effort to counter the risk that heresies could intrude unnoticed in song or dance.

Rather, until the eighteenth century, peninsular dramatists such as Lope de Vega and Calderón remained popular. Many of Calderón's auto sacramentales, for example, featured off-stage choruses and had successful performances in Lima and other colonial cities.[5] In the eighteenth century, secular vocal music was copied and may even have circulated in Europe. Curiously, two dances that likely originated in Peru, the *zarabanda* and the *chacona*, perhaps reached Spain in the late sixteenth century. They quickly became part of the written repertoire of dances heard, danced, and cultivated by the nobility and the middle class in Spain and subsequently in Western Europe.

Opera barely appeared in Spanish America and then only during the eighteenth century. Today only three compositions are known to exist: Tomás de Torrejón's Lima production of *La púrpura de la rosa* (1701), Domenico Zipoli's *San Ignacio de Loyola* (ca. 1720), and the anonymous indigenous opera *San Francisco Xavier* (ca. 1720–1740). The Peruvian Viceroy, the Conde de la Monclova, provided funding in 1701 to Lima's choir master Tomás de Torrejón y Velasco to stage an opera in honor of the Bourbon dynasty's first year in Spain and in celebration of King Philip V's eighteenth birthday. Torrejón selected *La púrpura de la rosa*, although the original had been lost with the music of Juan Hidalgo (probably Torrejón's teacher), and he had to compose new music and a new overture for its four-hour premier performance for the viceregal court on December 19. Performances continued for other social groups, such as the cathedral dean, cabildo, and other high-ranking clerics, members of the principal religious orders, lower nobility, faculty from the university and the seminary, leading to the final performance on January 6, 1702, on the Día de los Reyes (also the anniversary of the founding of the city of Lima, called the Ciudad de los Reyes, and the Viceroy Melchor's name day), that was offered to the entire city. The cast did not include castrati or other males except for a comic tenor and an allegorical baritone, known as snub nose and disappointment. Rather females performed both the singing and acting parts. Between scenes in the opera, comic characters called *graciosos* (clowns) entertained the audience.[6]

This version preserved Calderón's original story of Venus and Adonis (probably inspired by Paolo Veronese's painting *Venus and Adonis*). Opera expert Andrew Lawrence-King describes the new libretto as "rich in complex metaphors and eloquent allusions, performed with sensual and erotic images, and spiced with lively action and hilarious comedy" in such scenes as Mars and Belna chasing Love around the stage; Adonis, while sleeping, is shot with a love dart that makes him fall in love with Venus; and the humor provided by the gardener and his wife, all displayed in the typical acting of Spanish theater. The opera also includes poetry with guitar, harp, and percussion performed with the rhythms of South American dances.[7] The overture defends Philip V's right to the throne won through the Bourbon victory over the Habsburgs during the War of Spanish Succession. The performance placed *La púrpura de la rosa* within the repertoire of available productions in Lima (restaged in 1708) and, according to some accounts, performed in Mexico City in 1728. During his career as chapel master, Torrejón had eight *villancicos* (Christmas carols) published as part of Francisco Echave y Assú's *La estrella de Lima* in Antwerp in 1688, and other compositions in Lima in 1701, 1708, and 1725; his music was sought by musicians in Cuzco and Trujillo in Peru and as far away as Guatemala and Mexico.[8]

Encouraged by these first opera performances, two other Lima residents also produced short operatic pieces in the city. Descriptions report that in 1708, Torrejón's successor Roque Ceruti—a native of Milan—composed the music for *El mejor escudo de Perseo* with a libretto by the recently arrived Viceroy, the Marquis of Castelldosríus, who had a reputation as an excellent guitarist. The opera, with an extravagant budget, became a lavish spectacle honoring the birth of Crown Prince Luis. Three years later, in 1711, Pedro Peralta Barnuevo, a Lima writer familiar with Italian-style opera, staged *Triunfos de amor y poder* over eight alternating days in the viceregal palace. This opera, another performance of political propaganda, commemorated the 1710 victory of French forces at Villaviciosa that guaranteed Philip V the Spanish throne and included an overture, dances, a satirical *Fin de Fiesta*, and a bullfight put to music. In 1724, an Opera-Seranade called *Venid, venid Deydades*, was composed by Fray Esteban Ponce de León, that was preserved in the Archive of the San Antonio Abad seminary in Cuzco. Peralta followed this with the short opera *Loa para la comedia*, that featured arias, choruses, and an imitation of Italian-style recitative. The performance displayed the use of printed scenery and mechanized staging that in South America only Lima could possibly afford and construct. None of these operas found in Peru contained indigenous musical themes, rhythms, or instruments.

In Mexico City, organist and chapel master Manuel de Zumaya composed the now-lost Italian-styled opera *Partenope* that may have been performed in Spanish.

Based on these musical works, opera had only a slender foundation in the Americas on which to build. Neither Mexico City, Lima, or any other colonial city cultivated an opera tradition despite scattered performances in various cities, nor did opera replace established forms of entertainment. Nevertheless, the operas formed part of an international circuit, with connections between Hispanic and other European centers such as Naples, Parma, and Vienna.[9]

Surprisingly, opera appeared and became somewhat common through its performance in the Jesuit missions of South America. All the missionaries—Franciscans, Dominicans, and Augustinians—occasionally used music, in the words of Louise K. Stein, as a "catechistic art" in their evangelization efforts. They regularly composed elaborate theatrical and musical pieces for feast days, especially for Corpus Christi, Epiphany, and Christmas, as part of the ceremonies celebrated. During this time, "the arts had two primary functions: when financed by the court they could proclaim the power and grandeur of the monarchy, while for the educated commoner and the nobility they were a forum for social criticism and a mirror of society. . . . Music, however, did develop its own propagandistic and nationalistic function, towards political or religious ends, especially certain forms of vernacular sacred and theatrical music."[10] Theatrical works such as *comedias* or autos sacramentales were also performed on these holidays in major colonial cities such as Lima.

The Jesuits did more than use music occasionally. They adopted a strategy that relied on music and other art forms to Christianized the pagans they found in the Americas.[11] They were most active in South America. The Jesuits in Cordoba, Argentina, went north into present-day Paraguay, and by 1732 they had established at least thirty large missions, usually called *reducciones*, with approximately 140,000 Guarani people, and pushed further to the area of the Chiquitos peoples. As part of their exertions, they taught indigenous peoples specially to sing and to play musical instruments in order to perform European church music. Accomplishing these goals, they developed instruments, adapted local tunes, and composed songs. Musical and theatrical performances celebrated church holidays and also visits of dignitaries, such as the governor and the bishop, and announcements of royal coronations, marriages, and birth of heirs. For officials, the performances were given in Spanish or Italian, but others featured in whole or in part in indigenous languages with adaptions to local customs. Throughout the reducciones, in 1640, festivals celebrated the centenary anniversary of the founding of the Jesuit Order with theatrical performances and likely musical presentations. By the 1700s, musical performances became common, reaching to the indigenous groups in

Peru.[12] The repertoire included three sacred operas, of which fragments have survived, with vocal and instrumental arrangements and use of the Chiquitos language. Even lacking the complete operas, the three can be easily recognized as distinct from European compositions.

The survival of the operas as complete scores or in fragments resulted from the conjunction of unrelated events. In 1767, the Spanish king suppressed the Jesuit order and expelled its members from all the colonies after having already exiled them from Spain. Records from various reducciones were taken to the archives of the bishop or other church authorities. The mission papers from central South America included 10,000 sheets of music that went to the archives of the Diocese of Concepción de Chiquitos in Eastern Bolivia.

The one-time Jesuit missions received international attention was only after World War II when Hans Ertl made flights over the eastern Bolivian highlands to test high-altitude photography equipment for Siemans Corporation. Ertl, a German refugee, had a good deal of experience: he had served as the official photographer for General Erwin Rommel in World War II and as the cameraman on several promotional films for Hitler's Third Reich, including *Olympia*, the documentary of the 1936 Olympic Games, recognized as a classic of filmmaking and propaganda.[13] His aerial photographs revealed that many of the sixteenth- and seventeenth-century Jesuit settlements were inhabited. Following up, he learned that residents continued to gather in churches to sing and play music, even though they had received no formal musical instruction since the Jesuit expulsion, roughly two centuries before. He took an iconic photograph of Indian men in a church playing Western-style instruments that received international attention.

In 1970, musicologist Bernardo Illari visited the church archives in Eastern Bolivia that store Jesuit records. Among the musical scores in the archive of Moxos, he discovered an untitled opera that he named *San Ignacio de Loyola*. He identified it as the work of Domenico Zipoli, Italian organ master, musical composer, Jesuit missionary, and would-be priest. Born near Florence in 1688, Zipoli studied cathedral music there and also in Naples with the famous opera composer Alessandro Scarlatti. Later he held positions in Bologna and in Rome and had cultivated a strong reputation before he disappeared, making his way to Seville then to South America, with the intention of reaching the Jesuit missions in Paraguay. He arrived in Argentina in 1717 and spent the next nine years in Córdoba studying for the priesthood and composing oratorios, masses, and cantatas for organ and harpsichord. His compositions made him well known in the Spanish colonies, especially Lima. His extensive experience in the opera centers of Florence, Naples, Bologna, and Rome as well as study with Scarlatti, no doubt, inspired him to write his only opera about the founding of the Company of Jesus (the Jesuits) by Saint Ignacio Loyola. After completing his studies and while awaiting his ordination ceremony, he died, probably of tuberculosis, in Córdoba at age thirty-eight.

Zipoli's entire score survived, with recitations (a performance that combined speech and music), arias (persuasive forms), choruses, and dances that reveal their Italian influence. These pieces did not simply mimic earlier composers (e.g., Calderón, in his opera, had the Greek gods perform the recitations and arias that presented persuasive pronouncements). Nevertheless, Zipoli, as did other composers, placed emphasis on the message, not the music. In *San Ignacio*, he "extolled Christian faith and Jesuit principles,"[14] with its recitations and arias throughout the opera sung equally by mortals, such as Ignacio, and the god-like angels. The introductory section, called *Mensajero*, has two angels who summon Loyola to battle the devil by spreading the word of God. Accompanied by angels acting as foot soldiers, Ignacio and fellow Jesuit Francisco Javier are depicted as holy warriors, contrary to their common characterization, in Christian militancy as expressed in the Crusades to the Middle East and the conquest in the Americas. The opera quickly turns from a spiritual to an aggressive tone, enveloped with mysticism. The opera was performed on special occasions, celebrations or religious holidays, and the Feast of St. Ignatius, the yearly remembrance of his death, July 31, 1556.

Illari labeled the opera as "mission style," meaning that it reflected the close relationship between the Jesuits, who composed, and the indigenous peoples, who performed the music, by singing, acting, playing instruments, creating stage sets and costumes, and constituted the audiences. It illustrates the cross-cultural endeavor of performances such as *San Ignacio*. Mission style became common in the reducciones through efforts of other Jesuits. Martin Schmidt (1694–1772), for example, a Swiss Jesuit, arrived around 1734 to work among the Chiquitos and promoted both music and theater in the missions. He probably brought the Zipili's opera and other music from

Cordoba to the missions. In order to make music possible, he learned to fabricate instruments; he made organs, violins, flutes, lyres, and trumpets. He taught the skill to mission residents. It has been concluded that this enabled indigenous peoples to master a variety of instruments that included bass, double bass, bugle, guitar, harp, harpsichord, lyre, organ, spinet, trumpet, violin, zither, and several types of mandolins. He also copied a great number of musical manuscripts and trained Indians to do the same.

A second opera, likely written by an indigenous composer, *Despedida*, features the career of Saint Francisco Javier (or Xavier), the cofounder of the Society of Jesus, with the libretto in chiquitano. One reduccion in present-day Uruguay was named for him. A few musicologists have identified this opera as a second part of Zipoli's life of Loyola, *San Ignacio*, but more recently it has been attributed to an anonymous indigenous composer around 1740 who wrote it for the Chiquitanos people.[15] Described as one of the evangelizing dramas in indigenous languages that characterized life in the reducciones, the opera follows San Francisco from his birth in northern Spain in 1491, through his career as a soldier in 1517, and eventually to his 1541 journey to the Indies as a missionary, with the focus on his decision to dedicate his life to the spiritual conversion of indigenous peoples. The account includes features shared with *San Ignacio* that describes Francisco as a holy warrior who combines aggressive, spiritual, and mystical characteristics. The libretto contains stage directions and cast instructions that it be sung exclusively by indigenous actors accompanied by indigenous musicians. The libretto, although written in Spanish, has a corresponding text in the Chiquitos language to explain the opera to an indigenous audience. This makes the musical composition the first-known opera performed completely by indigenous people. Fragments also survive of the opera *El Justo y el Pastor*, also in Chiquitano.

Both Zipoli's opera and the anonymous opera are distinctive in terms of brevity and difficulty. The technically demanding pieces require a trained soloist, suggesting the Jesuits had educated indigenous singers to this level of competence. The missionaries marveled at the indigenous aptitude for singing, dancing, and playing instruments. Their reports and letters led to popular stories circulated throughout Europe that describe the talent of indigenous musicians and singers said to be as good as, or better than, their European counterparts. Travelers reported that each of the missions had thirty to forty musicians. In some cases, the Jesuits also allowed Indians to occupy the post of chapel master in several churches and had trained them as copyists of musical works.

In another development, starting in 1972 Swiss architect Hans Roth worked for fourteen years in the Diocese of Concepción de Chiquitos renovating the San Rafael Church. Among other things, he assembled a catalog of thought-to-be-lost musical works and instruments from the former Jesuit reductions in Paraguay. He tried to convince musicologists for several years to visit the church and examine the manuscripts, but few bothered. In desperation, he went to Montevideo for a meeting with Francisco Curt Lange, a specialist on the composer Zipoli, to show him microfilm of the Chiquitos collection. Lange immediately recognized its significance as he identified several of Zipoli's works, including an additional fifty masses and several keyboard pieces that he may have written. Coincidentally, Roth noticed that Lange had a copy of Ertl's photograph of Indian men looking at sheet music and playing Western-style instruments in church. Roth remarked that the photograph was one of only five or six known to exist, because the negative had been lost. Lange did not know the church, but Roth immediately identified San Rafael, where he had been working and where some of the manuscripts had been found.

Inspired by Lange's identification of several scores, a few musicologists visited Chiquitos to review the collection. Roth affirms that they found many music booklets still being used by the Indian choirs. They used them for show, as these singers and musicians had learned by rote because they could not read the compositions. Although the written opera was lost for centuries, the indigenous tradition of musical memorization kept the work alive. Illari reports that the opera continued to be performed until recent years: in 1991, the aged native musician José Sátiba remembered the work presented perfectly as part of the annual celebration for the feast of the patron saint in San Ignacio de Moxos. This report encouraged interest in the musical conversion process used by the Jesuits. That these operas were produced in the seemingly unlikely location of the missions—and their survival—suggests that others may await discovery, especially since other musicians and composers made up the Jesuit contingents in South America.

The general lack of operatic works from the sixteenth through early eighteenth centuries in Spain and its colonies can be explained by keeping in mind the slow development of opera's content and structure, the enormous cost required to stage opera spectacles, as well as the general discontent of regular audiences not accustomed to the genre. Each of these obstacles led to only a few works being produced in the Spanish colonies during the period.[16]

Nevertheless, in Brazil, performances occurred during the eighteenth century, apparently developing from puppet theater (called *presépio*), at times using life-size puppets, dating from 1719. The programs had enough success that an opera house was built in Rio de Janeiro in 1763, and other theaters were constructed, also called *casas de opera*, but this may have been nothing more than a generic name. Theaters were also built in Minas Gerais and the Northeast region. Brazilian composers and actor-singers during this era were African or mulatto men and women. Opera productions received a strong push forward when the Portuguese king and court, fleeing from Napoleon's French invaders, arrived in Brazil in 1808. Opera became an integral part of life at the court of the monarch, and after independence it continued at the court of the emperor.[17]

In the 1820s, opera was conceived as a civilizing instrument for the newly independent Latin American nations. Opera performances functioned as a kind of club for social elites who shared in what they considered a cosmopolitan experience combined with European court pageantry. Moreover, it captured the pretentions of local, aspiring middle classes. In the first half of the nineteenth century, Italian companies, with their stars, traveled with great success to British Canada, United States, and Latin America. Mexican aristocrats had developed a strong interest in opera by the beginning of the 1800s. Cenobio Paniagua Vázquez wrote *Catalina de Guisa*, the first national opera after Independence, and he founded the Mexican Opera Company.[18] Until 1827, the operas were translated into Spanish but afterward they were performed in Italian—often with a printed program that included the libretto in Spanish. Over the course of the nineteenth century, eighty-six companies performed in Mexico. Some were Mexican, of course, but the majority of them were Italian, and there were also groups from France, Spain, and even the United States. This resulted in the circulation of European opera sheet music, librettos, and musical instruments.

Between late 1826 and January 1829, one of the most celebrated opera singers in the world, Manuel García (Manuel del Pópulo Vicente Rodríguez), lived in Mexico. Beside his singing performances, he was also famous for his compositions, especially his aria "Yo que soy contrabandista" (I am a smuggler)—from the opera-monologue "El poeta calculista." Romantics across all of Europe adopted the aria as their hymn of liberty and rebellion against all social conventions, including the law (see YouTube for Maria Cecilia Bartoli singing the song and http://www.prestoclassical.co.uk/w/112432 for recordings). García's performances became the focus of Mexican public opinion, which endowed the singer with great symbolic and political importance. He was responsible for introducing several European operas, none more successful than his leading role in the debut of Mozart's *Don Giovanni*. Newspaper articles and reviews during the tenor's stay in Mexico City reflect conflicts that divided public and star performers with varying opinions about politics and opera (e.g., should it be performed in Spanish or Italian) because of the conviction that the theater, especially opera, provided a civilizing force that would eventually bring Mexico into the mythic cosmopolitan universe called the "civilized world."

García became a part of Mexican literary history and memory when he decided to return to Spain. Just before completing the stage coach journey from the capital city to his ship at the port of Veracruz, bandits attacked the party on the plain of Tepeyahualco, robbed the travelers of their jewels and valuables, and then forced García to sing for them. The impromptu performance pleased the bandits to the point they returned some of the party's most valued possessions. The only source for these events came from García's accounts after he returned to Spain and later a recollection of his daughter, who was seven years old at the time of the robbery. After several decades, the collective memory of it served as the basis for a chapter in Manuel Payno's famous novel *Los Bandidos of Río Frio*. Many believe it was simply an event imagined by the composer of "Yo que soy contrabandista," and it contributed to the image of Mexico among Europe's romantic generation as a "beautiful, savage, fantastic, and dangerous land."[19]

Other opera companies continued sporadically to perform. The Italian Lauro Rossi spent the year 1836 in Mexico directing *La Sonnambula*, *Cenerentola*, *Il Pirata*, *Guillaume Tell*, and other operas the following year. Among Mexicans, Cenobio Paniagua Vázques remained active, both composing and directing performances. Visiting European opera companies inspired both European and Latin American composers. Rossi maintained an interest in Latin America during the time he directed the Milan Conservatory, 1850 to

1871. He inspired both Brazilian Carlos Gomes and the Mexican Melesio Morales.[20] No one in the century exceeded the career of Angel Peralta. This Mexican diva arrived in Italy and soon starred in all the great Italian venues. She sang in the opera houses of Rome, Florence, Bologna, Genoa, Naples, Lisbon, Madrid, Barcelona, St. Petersburg, Alexandria, and Cairo. Later she returned to Mexico, composed and trained a company. She performed with her own and visiting performers.[21]

The French invasion of Mexico resulted in the famous battle of Puebla, May 5, 1862, with a victory for the Mexican Liberal Army. In the capital Benito Juárez's wife organized musical, especially operatic, events to raise money for the Liberal War effort. Paniagua Váquez performed and also wrote an opera, *Pietro d'Abano* (the Italian philosopher who compiled a book of ritual magic), to commemorate the Cinco de Mayo victory (May 5, 1862), which premiered the year after the battle. Nevertheless, after about a year, the French regrouped and swept through Puebla and went on to occupy the national capital for the next four years.[22] Melesio Morales wrote his masterpiece *Ildegonda* in 1864 and it premiered in 1866 (without, legends notwithstanding, the diva Ángela Peralta) and three years later in Florence. Another premier, over a century later, occurred in Mexico City in 1994 and later the same year it was performed at the National University and recorded live. The recording received the French Orphéon d'or for recording achievement.

During fighting between the French troops and the Liberal resistance, battle and political songs became more important than opera. The French troops and their Mexican supporters adopted "La Paloma" because, among other things, it was a favorite of Emperor Maximilian. This song written by the Spaniard Sebastián Iradier is regarded by many as one of the two most famous songs in world history; the other, also composed by Iradier, is the *Habanera* that Georges Bizet adopted for his opera *Carmen*. Iradier left Spain for France, where he became the music teacher for Empress Eugenie, Napoleon III's wife. Sometime between 1850 and 1860, he apparently went on tour through the Americas with the star singers Marietta Alboni and the young Adelina Patti. It is supposed that he composed "La Paloma" during this voyage. This song, according to Universidad Nacional Autónoma de México Radio, has more than one thousand versions recorded, making it, along with the Beatles's "Yesterday," one of the two most recorded songs in the history of music. It is also one of the most played songs in the world: "In Zanzibar they play it at the end of weddings, in Romania at the end of funerals, in Mexico it is the hymn of demonstrators against newly elected presidents, in Germany it is known as a sailor's song from the North Sea," according to the Paloma Project, which includes a documentary about the song, famous versions, and additional information on its website.[23]

The Liberals used an old song from the War of the Reform (1858–1861), mocking the conservatives as crabs because of their red colors ("Los Cangrejos"), but then changed their song, keeping their tune to "Adiós Mamá Carlota" with the new lyrics adapted to the old music. The Liberal General, writer, and poet Vicente Riva Palacio wrote the words to what became the sarcastic song about the empress.

Even without full productions during the war against French intervention, the influence, especially of Italian, opera became inscribed in everyday culture. The Italian word *Alzati* refers to the popularization of Italian opera dramatizations, especially by Verdi, of masked dances. The word was adopted to indicate celebrations in Mexico involving masks, that were adapted from the operatic tradition and traditional fiesta or indigenous masked dances. This demonstrates in particular that the elite attendance at operas had been assimilated by the middle classes and popular sectors. This resulted in some measure to introduce what intellectuals regarded as cultivated cultural elements into popular fiestas. The idea was to combine pre-Hispanic and colonial masks with the cosmopolitan masked balls. In this way, Italian opera contributed to cultural pollination in Mexico and other parts of Latin America.[24]

Other composers in the last decades of the century continued to write operas. By the 1870s Carlos Gomes, inspired by Rossi, was writing operas in Brazil that looked at Portuguese-Tupiguarni relations and also Brazilian-slave relationships, all situated in the beauty of the Brazilian landscape. Gomes's masterpiece, *Il Guarany*, premiered during the Christmas holidays in 1883 in Mexico's National Theater with the Italian company Napoleón Siena. Morales wrote a critical review that said, among other sarcastic remarks, it was an opera better suited for New York audiences, in part because the composer had failed to examine the relationships between the Portuguese and the Guarani. Morales also composed a piano piece based on the themes of the opera to show the Brazilian what was possible. Gomes continued composing and his opera to celebrate the 400th anniversary of Colombus's voyage to the Americas, called *Colombo*, premiered in Rio, was presented in Genoa and then at the World's Fair in Chicago—where it was regarded as a particular failure.

In the last decades of the century, visiting European companies, most often from Italy, toured Latin American cities. The popularity of these performances, Verdi's *La Traviata* and *Aida* and Leoncavallo's *Pagliacci*, for example, encouraged aspiring social elites to move beyond the multipurpose colonial theaters to the construction of opera houses as one measure, along with public lighting, private electricity, and often street cars, of the sophistication of their cities and societies. Late in the nineteenth and early in the twentieth century, municipal authorities built elegant opera houses in Buenos Aires (famously with the new Colón Theater inaugurated in 1908), Mexico City, Lima, Bogotá, and San José. Local musicians soon traveled to Europe to study and seek positions.

Mexico City regularly had concerts on Sundays and other holidays in the *Alameda* (the city park), where programs included themes from operas. The *Zócalo* (the central plaza), which today is simply a paved plaza, in the last decades of the nineteenth century had a large garden and bandstand, where military bands usually played marches and polkas.[25] Other cities in Mexico and throughout Latin America also provided outdoor concerts.

In the 1880s a start to redefining nationalism had begun with the rise of *Costumbrismo* (local, especially folkloric, traditions) in literature and music. This culturalism echoed in many ways the popularity of both literary folklore and folkloric music in Europe. Honoré de Balzac, to give one example, with his *Comedia humana* (1842) and Béla Bartók, for another, famous for his incorporation of Hungarian folk themes in compositions both expressed the essence of this developing interest. This cultural current received enhanced intellectual development in the wake of the creation of republican Brazil, with the abolition of slavery (1888), and the overthrow of the emperor (1889), and the end of Spanish rule in Cuba with the Spanish-American War in 1898.

Costumbrista's influence on popular music focused on local customs and lifestyles of rural peoples and promoted the collection of their music. This inspired the decision of the Mexican government of Porfirio Díaz to initiate a program preserving the music of rural, indigenous communities. Díaz placed Manuel M. Ponce in charge of the effort, although today the materials appear lost, and it is not clear whether the collection included notes on the music or recordings with the newly invented Edison machines.

The intense collection and study of South American rural and indigenous music was initiated by Robert Lehmann Nitsche (1872–1938), a German linguist deeply interested in the folk music of Argentina. Near La Plata, he recorded fifty-one wax cylinders of the Tehuelche people, and before traveling to the St. Louis World's Fair in 1904, he sent the cylinders to be transcribed and analyzed in Berlin at the Institute of Comparative Musicology. Later he collected recordings of all of the indigenous groups of the Gran Chaco and others in Bolivia. Moreover, he recorded the songs of *payadores*, the gaucho singers of the pampas. The Institute in Berlin received these and other cylinders from anthropologists in Tierra del Fuego, Brazil, Chile, and the Andes and sent its ethnographer Manius Schneider to make recordings in Matto Grosso. The Institute made transcriptions of the recordings and published analyses of them before World War I in its professional journal, *Anthropos*.

Beyond the Germans associated with the Berlin Institute during these years, many French anthropologists worked in Latin America. Best known among them appeared the outstanding ethnomusicologist (although no one used this title at the time) working in Peru, Bolivia, and Ecuador, Margarita D'Harcourt, who collected and published significant studies with her archeologist husband, Raoul. The D'Harcourts also made recordings in Central America, where Frans Termer, working for the Völkerkunde Museum in Hamburg, made recordings in Huehuetenago, Guatemala.

Costumbrismo also had an effect on opera before World War I. The genres served as an expression in Latin America of the sophisticated culture attributed to the cosmopolitanism associated especially with Europe. Beginning during the last three decades of the nineteenth century, in addition to the construction of opera houses, high society was bolstered by composers who were inspired by traditional literature and musical developments that expressed local pride. These historical and nationalistic themes appeared in the writing of operas that celebrated local distinctiveness. Operas as examples included Antonio Carlos Gomes, *Il Guarany* (Brazil, 1870), Aniceto Ortega, *Guatimotzin* (Mexico, 1871), Ricardo Castro, *Atzimba* (Mexico, 1896), along with several others. Melesio Morales's last opera, *Anita*, portrayed life in Puebla under siege by the French in 1862. But only the songs without the staging were performed until 2002. This popular attitude resulted in the creation of Columbia's Academia Nacional de Música in 1882. Even when the influence of national pride, especially through what was called Costumbrismo, had resulted in operas with local themes or pre-Colombian legends, the performances remained the entertainment of the society who lived what was known as the high life.

More opera—both from Europe and modeled on Europe in Latin America—served to create the imaginaries of elite society and political control. It soon changed.

The European apocalypse occurred in the second decade of the twentieth century, caused by social revolution and World War I; it destroyed kingdoms, empires, and countries throughout the world with a tremendous loss of life. It eventually birthed nations in the 1920s based largely on culture, geography, and historic combinations of people identified by language and heritage. Inspiration for this new nationalism also came from the Mexican (1910) and the Russian (1917) revolutions that established new regimes committed to engendering inclusive societies with a shared national identity. The Allies who had defeated Germany in World War I assembled in Paris to make peace and remake Europe by restoring old and instituting new nations, especially republics. These representatives at Versailles used standard, uniform, and coherent culture as the definition of a European nation and to identify nationalities that, with exceptions, served for the re-creation of nations and the creation of new republics.[26] Culture meant common language, shared traditions apparent in literature, music, dance, folklore, costume, and cuisine, and coherent ethnicity. The latter, in writings and then policies of some European madmen, became a demand for racial purity (today's euphemism is *ethnic cleansing* for *mass murder*). The definitions of shared culture used by the diplomats to identify nationalities also influenced nationalistic programs in Asia, especially China, and the Americas.

Latin American observers took seriously these efforts at the peace talks and moved toward a cultural definition for their own nations. Seven Latin American nations had delegations at the peace conference. Probably Brazil and perhaps Guatemala acted independently, but the influence of the United States deeply marked the delegations from Cuba, Haiti, Honduras, Nicaragua, and Panama, where US marines and soldiers either occupied their territory or were prepared to do so.

As the peace process moved forward to the creation of the League of

Nations, Argentina, Bolivia, Brazil, Chile, Colombia, Cuba, El Salvador, Guatemala, Haiti, Honduras, Nicaragua, Panama, Paraguay, Peru, Uruguay, and Venezuela became original members. League organizers did not initially invite Mexico because it had not declared war against Germany. Moreover, when an invitation did come, Mexico refused until 1931 because the League had recognized the US policy of the Monroe Doctrine. When Mexico joined, it did so with a formal objection to the US policy.[27]

The Mexican and Russian revolutions added to the hemisphere-wide intellectual and political enthusiasm for the integration of all social and racial groups into national societies. In particular, Latin American intellectuals and reformers gave a good deal of attention to both Anatoly Lunacharsky, the first Soviet Commissar for Enlightenment in charge of culture and education, and José Vasconcelos, Mexico's Minister of Public Education. These Latin Americans shared the enthusiasm for new definitions of nationalism and nation identity that resulted from these revolutionary movements, local costumbrismo, and their participation in the Paris peace talks that led to the subsequent creation of the League of Nations. The young representatives of the Mexican revolution, for example, had closely followed the Paris negotiations and the creation of the League, and had connected the idea of cultural nationalism to both the peace treaty and the revolutionary programs of the Soviets, despite their commitment to class identification defining the union's republics.

Yet Latin American leaders, despite these influences, encountered intellectual problems as they considered the nations conceived in the Paris peace conference defined by common features of geography, language, culture, and ethnicity. In most Latin American nations, geography was the least of the issues, even where conflicting claims did exist (e.g., in Bolivia, for territory occupied by the Chileans and territorial conflicts between Ecuador and Peru), but in several countries, two or three substantial ethnic groups with distinctive languages and cultures existed within the population at a time when a uniform ethnicity defined national identity. As a result, programs called for incorporation of these populations into a standardized nationality.

The most famous solution to this difficulty came with the popularization of mestizaje and the publication of José Vasconcelos's *The Cosmic Race* (1927). Vasconcelos, with great fanfare, turned the hemisphere's seeming problem of racial and ethnic diversity into its major strength, arguing that the merger of European, American, African, and Asian peoples through both cultural and biological intermingling created a superior ethnicity. Mostly discussed in terms of the blending of European and American indigenous peoples and cultures, known as mestizaje, the creation of the mestizo people, the argument brilliantly turned what had been considered a weakness of American societies into its greatest strength (in the United States, the echo of this argument came in the heralded idea of the melting-pot society, although it applied almost exclusively to European peoples). In Mexico, Vasconcelos discussed the merger of Spanish and indigenous cultures. Rather than biological blending, cultural mestizaje had a greater urgency.

As the Minister of Public Education, Vasconcelos took the recognition of cultural differences, the realities of ethnic diversity, and the heritage of indigenous achievements that formed part of costumbrismo and merged them with the legacies of Spain in his call for new nationalities that distinguished the Western Hemisphere, especially Latin America. His educational program with its visions, goals, and guidelines resulted in a commitment to create a national culture and to recognize its hybrid population, resulting from ethnic mixture, as a positive development. It was soon called the Raza Cósmica (The Cosmic Race), which included capabilities beyond the characteristics of any single racial group.

The idea of creating a national aesthetic as part of a nation's culture, as Vasconcelos and others envisioned it, was not the exclusive goal of just one Latin American country,[28] but became a common objective throughout the hemisphere after World War I. This movement had a dramatic effect in music, and it built on the hemisphere-wide collection of folkloric and rural music that had begun at the turn of the century. In the 1920s such major works as *La musique des Incas et ses survivances* (1925), by Raoúl and Margarita D'Harcourt; *La música en el Ecuador* (1930), by Segundo Luis Moreno, and "La musique des Araucans," by Carlos Lavin and published in *La Revue Musicale* of Paris discussed these developments.

This attention to national populations by domestic and foreign musical collectors provide another key to the nationalism that emerged in the 1920s as new music appeared that contributed to the emerging cultural nationalism. It was made possible only through the fusion of the traditions of the learned music of Europe with the collected folkloric patrimony of the Americas.[29] Singers interpreted folksongs in forms of melodies for listeners interested in both art and popular music. Newly composed operas such as Pascual de Rogatis's *Huémac* (Argentina, 1916) and José María Valle Riestra's *Ollanta y Atahualpa* (Peru, 1921), along with symphonies, and popular song genres, contributed a significant dimension to official and unofficial designs for the definition of national identity. This movement influenced composers in Latin America and artists in other fields, resulting, in the early twentieth century, in naturalistic novels focused on indigenous peoples. Some became national classics, such as Alcides Arguedas, *Raza de bronce* (1919) in Bolivia; Enrique López Albújar, *Los Cuentos Andinos* (1920) in Peru; and Jorge Icaza, *Huasipungo* (1934) in Ecuador. The indigenista, that is the costumbrista, interest reached to other arts, such as the plastic works of Peruvians José Sabogal and Julia Codesido and the murals of Mexicans Diego Rivera, José Clemente Orozco, and Dávid Siqueiros. It developed between Brazilian literature and music in the relationship between Mario de Andrade (1893–1945), novelist from São Paulo, and Heitor Villa-Lobos that become apparent during la Semana de Arte Moderno (Modern Art Week), in three sessions in the Municipal Theater of São Paulo, February 13–15, 1922. The goals of the week included an emphasis on the indelible right of aesthetic investigations, the modernization of artistic intelligence, and the stabilization of a national creative conscience. "Modernism," in this case meant using advanced harmonies and breaking with the European clichés, while incorporating elements of popular music traditions.[30] Andrade's influence reached as well to the work of Camargo Guarneri, dedicated to the creation of music representing Brazilian national character.[31]

Composers across the hemisphere wrote music designed to express their national culture and they apparently worked with little or no knowledge, at least initially, of each other's undertakings. Leaders included Heitor Villa-Lobos in Brazil, Alberto Williams and Julián Aguirre in Argentina, Miguel Ponce in Mexico, Daniel Alomía Robles in Andean Peru, and Amadeo Roldán and Alejandro García Caturla in Cuba, who identified "lo negro" as essential in la cubanidad, similar to what Luciano Gallet identified for Brazil. The publication of reports on this musical development made composers aware of each other. The best known of these works on music in the hemisphere was the work by Panamanian composer Roque Cordero, who wrote the article "Vigencia del músico culto" (published in 1957, but discussed earlier). He identified a connection between the work of Villa-Lobos, the Nicaraguan

Luis A. Delgadillo, the Chilean Pedro Humberto Allende, the Colombian Guillermo Uribe Holguín, the Uruguayan Eduardo Fabini, and the Mexican Manuel M. Ponce. He concluded that the nationalist aspect of the work of these composers, although inherently limited with the use of folklore material, demonstrated great development beyond that of earlier generations whose nationalism resided most clearly in picturesque titles rather than in the contents of their music. Composers expressed nationalism in music through the romantic aesthetic using key, coloring, impressionism, polytonality, neomodalism, and even atonality—that is to say of modernity in music in the widest application of the word that developed first in Argentina, Brazil, Cuba, and México.[32] This hemispheric interest resulted in el Festival Panamericano de Música, sponsored by the Coolidge Foundation and held in Mexico City in 1937.[33]

By the 1930s, for the expression of national identity, music had become a major medium through radio, records, jukeboxes, and live performances. Not only did music play a role in everyday politics, social reforms, and national identity, but it also became an expression of playful commentary on and sarcastic criticism of national leaders. In Cuba, for example, Félix B. Caignet Salomón, author of radio scripts, novels, and songs, composed the popular children's song, "El ratoncito Miguel" (Mickey Mouse). It soon was played during fundraising meetings in the campaign against President Gerardo Machado. After several performances of it at the Teatro Rialto in Santiago de Cuba in 1932, Machado government officials banned it and had Caignet arrested. Imprisoned for three days, he was released when his fans, including children, demonstrated outside the Moncada barracks. Songs, with changed lyrics, appeared in presidential campaigns, satirical reviews of politicians, and simple comical reactions to life in general that could only be understood as part of the national culture.

The Revolution of 1930 in Brazil brought to power Getulio Vargas amid the world economic crisis. The new coalition focused on economic stabilization, labor reform, and government interventions in literacy, nutrition, and health; nevertheless, it crafted a regime using cultural forms to mold a unified national identity over fractious regional cultures and unassimilated ethnic enclaves through government authority and popular culture. New alliances of government officials and cultural representatives particularly shaped the culture of Carnival in Rio and in sports. The Vargas regime created a new federal minister of education and public health, and its first secretary Francisco Campos promoted an interventionist federal role in formal education, sanitation, and healthcare. He was soon followed by Gustavo Capanema, who served from 1934 to 1945, and was committed to remaking the ministry as the agency of national culture with a sustained "federal role in the patronage, regulation, advocacy, and censorship of the arts, mass media, cultural heritage, and civic culture." The office funded a modest output of original motion pictures and produced a nightly radio program, *Hora da Brasil* (The Brazil hour) that mixed scripted current-events reporting, cultural programming, and musical performance. The goal remained to create one Brazilian identity out of the regional identifications that existed.

Music became an essential aspect of national identity. In Colombia, efforts began to define a national music. In 1936, the first congress of music committed the organization to advancing musical culture as an integral part of nationhood within the master narrative of mestizaje.[34] This included the construction of myths associated with the nation's musical instruments and styles—"the flutes (*guitas*) are usually explained as Amerindian and the percussion as African, while the lyrics, and at times the choreography, are said to be Spanish"—that represented the three ethnic components of the population. The generalized poor were associated with cumbia (typically labeled música tropical or música costeña).[35] These Colombian efforts expressed the attempt to standardize national identities across Latin America.

Revolutionary programs, World War I re-creation of nations, and costumbrista-influenced discussions of mestizaje and nationalism all contributed to new programs in Latin America beginning in the 1920s. With its cultural programs for national integration, the Vasconcelos campaign in Mexico was a step ahead, but only a step, of similar campaigns in other Latin American nations with large unassimilated indigenous or immigrant populations. During the 1920s and 1930s, this resulted in programs that used the ideology of mestizaje, often mixed with the "anti-materialist and pan-Latin American school of thought spearheaded by the Cuban José Martí, Uruguayan José E. Rodó, and Mexicans José Vasconcelos and Antonio Caso."[36] In this latter development, mestizaje rejected European theories of racial degeneration and positivism and US economic and political policies. Often, they called for the institution of newly forged national identities that included inclusive national populations through ideas of mestizaje. Music, including opera, played a major role in these new national definitions. Moreover, mestizaje managed most of the time to balance the competing views of both hispanismo and indigenismo as the main source of national character. These inclusive definitions of national identity and assimilation programs, especially promoting education and folklore, often described as populist movements, dominated until the 1980s. It was around this time that the idea of mestizaje was undercut by ethnic politics, and also by intellectual deconstruction by Angel Rama, Guillermo Bonfil Batalla, and Roger Barta, who changed national cultural definitions.[37]

The chapters in this book give emphasis to the role of music, often operas, in the creation of both national and ethnic identities. The authors describe these campaigns and analyze the music from a variety of historical and ethnomusicological perspectives. The first chapter, "Music and National Identity in Mexico, 1919–1940," looks at the role of Vasconcelos and musical campaigns during the revolutionary era and examines his influence in the hemisphere. Chapter 2, "*La Hora Industrial* vs. *La Hora Intima*: Mexican Music and Broadcast Media Before 1934," also considers Mexico by focusing on the impact of radio—one of the new technologies of the 1920s—in the distribution of music and the formation of national identity. Chapter 3, "Guatemalan National Identity and Popular Music," discusses events in Guatemala that provide another dimension to this theme with particular attention to the incorporation of indigenous traditions into a fusion that some leaders hoped would became the new national cultural identity and preserve indigenous legacies through performances of the past. Chapters 4 and 5 provide an introduction to the fascinating music of Cuba with two selections. The first comes from the heralded Cuban author Alejo Carpentier. His book *Music in Cuba* was one of the first studies of music in that country and includes important discussions of the Afro-Cuban influence. A chapter from his book, "Cuban Music: Afro-Cubanism," is reprinted here. Cuba's influence on music in the hemisphere is, perhaps, no better illustrated than through the recordings and performances of Silvio Rodríguez. Jan Fairley interviewed him for *The Guardian* in 2006, reprinted here with the title "An Accidental Hero [Cuban Singer in the Special Period]," and provides an introduction to Rodríguez's influence throughout Latin America. Chapter 6, "Cuzcatlán (El Salvador) and Maria de Baratta's *Nahualismo*," offers a careful analysis of music and nationalism in

El Salvador with composers and performers drawing on traditions of indigenous groups that otherwise might be completely ignored in the discussions of nationality. The seventh chapter turns to Ecuador with a discussion of "Cumandá: A Leitmotiv in Ecuadorian Operas? Musical Nationalism and Representation of Indigenous People," a genre that captured an identity selected as representative of the nation. "Dueling Bandoneones: Tango and Folk Music in Argentina's Musical Nationalism," chapter 8, explores the conflict in nation building between substantial immigrant, rather than indigenous, communities and the neighborhoods of urban migrants arriving in Buenos Aires. Competing views of music, celebration, and nationalism, in chapter 9, "Carnival as Brazil's 'Tropical Opera': Resistance to Rio's Samba in the Carnivals of Recife and Salvador, 1960s–1970s," examines the music of carnival in these two northeastern communities and the local resistance to the nationally supported holiday musical campaigns from Rio de Janeiro. Chapter 10 provides an intriguing look at the use of music to establish ethnic identity. "The Opera *Manchay Puytu*: A Cautionary Tale Regarding Mestizos in Twentieth-Century Highland Bolivia" expresses Aymara identity at a time after 1980 when national cultural identity had broken down in much of Latin America. Ethnic politics had come to provide a different and often successful challenge to the meaning of nation—so much so that some analysts proclaimed the end of the nation-state. In a return to Mexico, the center of film production in Latin America, chapter 11, "Sounding Modern Identity in Mexican Film," discusses how music often has served as a bridge between popular media and national identity, expanding, popularizing, and giving voice to the heritage and particular legacies of the nation's culture. This pattern occurred as well in cinema in Spain, expressing the similar contradictory attitudes of local and global, folkloric and cosmopolitan, and, in particular, regional and national.[38] Movie directors, as this essay on Mexico demonstrates, work images and sounds together to reinforce national identity.

Notes

1. Associated Press, "Seductive Nahuatl opera to premiere in Mexico City," *DailyMail*.com, September 5, 2014, http://www.dailymail.co.uk/wires/ap/article-2745673/Seductive-Nahuatl-opera-premiere-Mexico-City.html#ixzz3XnAfV6Cl.

2. Louise K. Stein, "Auto," in *The New Grove Dictionary of Music*, ed. Stanley Sadie, 2nd ed. (London & New York: Macmillan, 2001), 433.
3. Louise K. Stein and José Máximo Leza, "Opera, Genre, and Context in Spain and its American Colonies," in *The Cambridge Companion to Eighteenth-Century Opera*, eds. Antony R. DelDonna and Pierpaolo Polzonetti (New York: Cambridge University Press, 2009), 244–45.
4. Fernando de Alva Ixtlilzochitl, *Obras Completos*, ed. by Edmundo O'Gorman (Mexico City: UNAM, 1875), 1:527.
5. Stein, 433.
6. Stein and Leza, 245–48.
7. "La purpura de la rosa: The First Opera in the New World," booklet in *La purpura de la Rosa: The Book of the Rose*, The Harp Consort, Deutsche harmonia mundi, 1999, compact disc, 4.
8. Louise K. Stein, "'La música de dos orbes': A Context for the First Opera of the Americas," *Opera Quarterly* 22, no. 3–4 (2008), 433–58, accessed January 18, 2016, https://doi.org/10.1093/oq/kbn004.
9. Stein and Leza, 268.
10. Chad M. Gasta, "Transatlantic Opera in Spain and the New World in the 17th and Early 18th Centuries," *Oxford Research Encyclopedia for Latin America*.
11. Chad M. Gasta, "Opera and Spanish Jesuit Evangelization in the New World," *World Languages and Cultures Publications* 22, no.1 (November 2007), 85–106, http://lib.dr.iastate.edu/language_pubs/9.
12. El Inca Garcilaso, in his *Comentarios Reales*, said the Jesuits, in order to create interest in Christian practices among the indigenous Peruvians, composed plays for them to sing and perform. He wrote that the missionaries knew the people had given musical performances in the times of Inca kings and that they possessed the ability to learn them. The leader of the order composed a performance in praise of the Virgin Mary in Aymará, one of the languages of peoples in modern day Bolivia, not of the Incas.
13. Ertl's daughter, Monika, fought alongside Che Guevara in his fatal effort to launch a revolution in eastern Bolivia.
14. Chad Gasta, "Imperial Stagings: Empire and Ideology in Transatlantic Theater of Early Modern Spain and the New World," p. 44.
15. Mission San Francisco Xavier, *Ópera y Misa de los Indios*, Reconstrucción y

Transcripción: Piotr Nawrot, SVD. K617. May 20, 2011, https://www.youtube.com/watch?v=YHFlgFcsAUA. The liner notes of this recording.

16. Chad Gasta, *Imperial Stagings: Empire and Ideology in Transatlantic Theater of Early Modern Spain and the New World* (Chapel Hill: University of North Carolina Press, 2013).

17. Manuel Carlos de Brito, "Portugal and Brazil," in *The Cambridge Companion to Eighteenth-Century Opera*, eds. Antony R. DelDonna and Pierpaolo Polzonetti (New York: Cambridge University Press, 2009), 242–43.

18. Angel Vargas, "Dos musicólogos ordenaron el catálogo de Cenobio Paniagua," *La Jornada* (May 27, 2002).

19. Luis de Pablo Hammeken, "Don Giovanni en el Palenque. El Tenor Manuel García y la Prensa de la Ciudad de México, 1827–1828," *Historia Mexicana* 61, no. 1 (July–September 2011), 231–73; quotation, 271.

20. Verónica Zárate Toscano and Serge Gruzinski, "Ópera, imaginación y sociedad. México y Brasil, siglo xix. Historias conectadas: Ildegonda de Melesio Morales e Il Guarany de Carlos Gomes," *Historia Mexicana* 58, no. 2 (October–November 2008), 803–60, accessed October 26, 2015, http://www.jstor.org/stable/25139868.

21. Ibid.

22. Vargas.

23. http://www.lapalomaproject.com/index.php?page_id=3&lang=en.

24. Carman Nava Nava to the author, November 15, 2015.

25. Cristina Barros and Marco Buenrostro, *Vida Cotidiana Ciudad de Mexico, 1850–1910* (México: Consejo Nacional para la Cultura y Las Artes, 1996), 163–64.

26. The diplomats did worry about creating small republics that could become the prey of larger nations, so they made exceptions to their cultural definition, such as Czechoslovakia and submerged populations of Germans in Austria and Poland. Hitler and the Nazis took advantage of this situation in the 1930s.

27. Fabián Herrera León, "Latin America and the League of Nations," *Oxford Research Encyclopedia for Latin America* (August 2016), doi: 10.1093/acrefore/9780199366439.013.39.

28. Roque Cordero, "Vigencia del músico culto," in *América Latina en su música*, rapporteur Isabel Aretz, 2nd ed. (México: Siglo XXI, 1980), 154–73.

29. Juan Orrego Salas, "Técnica y estética," in *América Latina en su música*,

rapporteur Isabel Aretz, *Historia de la etnomusicología en América Latina* 2nd ed. (México: Siglo XXI, 1980), 175–76.

30. Vasco Mariz, *Historia de la música en el Brasil* (Lima, Centro de Estudios Brasileiros, 1985), 105–106.

31. Mariz, 105; Luis Heitor Correa de Azevedo, "La música de América Latina," in *América Latina en su música*, rapporteur Isabel Aretz, 2nd ed. (México, Siglo XXI, 1980), 54.

32. Aurelio Tello, "Aires nacionales en la música de América Latina como respuesta a la búqueda de identidad," 1, 3, http://www.comunidadandina.org/bda/hh44/20AIRES%20NACIONALES%20EN%20LA%20MÚSICA.pdf.

33. Aretz, "Sintesis," in *América Latina en su música*, rapporteur Isabel Aretz, 2nd ed. (México: Siglo XXI, 1980), 34; Tello, 5–6, fn. 14.

34. Peter Wade, *Music, Race and Nation: Música Tropical in Colombia* (Chicago: University of Chicago Press, 2000).

35. Christopher Dennis, *Afro-Colombian Hip-Hop: Globalization, Transcultural Music, and Ethnic Identities* (Lanham, MD: Lexington Books, 2012), 132–33; 152, fn. 7.

36. Oscar Chamosa, *The Argentine Folklore Movement: Sugar Elites, Criollo Workers, and the Politics of Cultural Nationalism, 1900–1955* (Tucson: University of Arizona Press, 2010).

37. Marilyn Grace Miller, *Rise and Fall of the Cosmic Race: The Cult of Mestizaje in Latin America* (Austin: University of Texas Press, 2004).

38. Teresa Fraile, "Fragmentos de identidad nacional en la música del cine español contemporáneo," in *Creación musical, cultura popular y construcción nacional en la España contemporánea*, ed. Celsa Alonso (Madrid: Instituto Complutense de Ciencias Musicales, 2010), 1–24.

CHAPTER 1

Music and National Identity in Mexico, 1919–1940

William H. Beezley

Mexico's revolution against President José de la Cruz Porfirio Díaz began in 1910 and brought a new commitment to popular nationalism expressed through culture. Although insurgent politicians and social activists focused on immediate political and economic programs, especially land reform, worker benefits, and family rights, artists and intellectuals in Mexico City took a leading role in shaping the outlines of an inclusive national cultural identity. This occurred in classical and popular music, painting, dance, handicrafts, literature, and education. The thrust in classical music resulted from the leadership of Manuel M. Ponce, Carlos Chávez, and Silvestre Revueltas; popular music was inspired by Joaquin Beristáin and Tata Nacho; and education was led by José Vasconcelos and the rural teacher missions. Ponce, Chávez, and Revueltas played a critical role in musical activity in the early 1920s through consolidation of musical nationalism and symphonic organizations. Ponce and others began to publish music during the first decade (1910–1920) of the revolution that reflected the desire to create a national repertoire for the entire population. They held a paternalistic view of their duty to the people that continued through the efforts of Secretary of Public Education José Vasconcelos in the 1920s. A statement in the Department of Public Education teachers' magazine *Maestro* said that everyone should now share the music that previously had been limited to the elite.[1]

The revolutionaries did not start with nothing. They recognized the international reliance on culture as a defining factor in national identity. Standard, uniform, and coherent culture became the definition of a nation at Versailles when the Allies, who had defeated Germany in World War I, assembled to make peace, remake Europe, and establish new republics. Culture meant common language, shared traditions apparent in literature, music, dance, folklore, costume, and cuisine, and coherent ethnicity.

The revolutionaries had inherited a legacy from the previous Porfirian regime that they never mentioned, but nevertheless used. They turned to the heritage of the Porfirian era of local community traditions, manifested especially in the prevailing music and literature since 1880 called the costumbrista movement, that contributed to the rise of cultural nationalism throughout the Western Hemisphere. Beyond opera in the 1880s and 1890s, other music had a national flavor, such as Melesio Morales's *La Tamalera* (The tamale maker), and had become popular. Such music and songs grew in number in the early twentieth century in the compositions of Manuel Ponce and José Rolón. The earliest recordings, on wax cylinders, were made by the Norwegian anthropologist Carl Lumholtz in the 1890s in the northern Sierra Madre, along the tropical coast, and in Michoacán.[2] Soon US companies Edison, Columbia, and Victor also dispatched recording teams throughout the world and sent technicians to Mexico to capture the music of local communities on wax cylinders or discs. These companies and the smaller Mexican enterprises Zonophone and Odeon actively recorded beginning in 1902. These technicians sought sound reproductions of what was deemed authentically Mexican.[3] In short, these companies, before the revolution, bolstered Díaz's goal to promote his nation's reputation abroad, expressed by the regimental band in New Orleans and in Madrid at commercial and commemorative exhibitions,[4] and with recorded songs such "Aires Nacionales" (Edison Gold Moulded Record 18755 in 1905); "Besos y Pesos," by the Banda de Artilleria (Edison Blue Amberol 22038, 1909); and "Jarabe Tapatio," by R. H. Robinson (Edison Gold Moulded Record 18508, 1904).[5] A number of composers and musicians, following Ponce and Rolón, also began taking an interest in their nation's folk music, especially those who had spent time in Paris. They adopted the romantics' search for the "national soul" in music. While abroad they likely encountered, among others, the influence of Bartók, including his investigative trips to the countryside with Zoltán Kodály,[6] and Modest Mussorgsky, who displayed his interest in the history and folklore of his native Russia in his opera *Boris Godunov* and piano suite "Pictures at an Exhibition." This early phase ended with the outbreak of the revolution in 1910.

Recording and music programs resumed when the revolutionary regime initiated new cultural programs. Beginning in 1920, these composers and other artists and intellectuals serving as bureaucrats began to determine what was *lo popular, lo nacional, y lo mexicano* (the popular, the national, and

Postage stamp of José Vasconcelos, Minister of Public Education and author of *The Cosmic Race*, 1925.

the Mexican). This focus had the significant effect of the revolution's redefinition of the rural, poor, and indigenous peoples not as problems for both economic development and political administration but identifying them as part of the national society.

José Vasconcelos, as Minister of Public Education and an honored public intellectual at the time, attempted to increase the merging of cultures and simultaneously preserve a record of the indigenous practices and mores that would disappear with the extension of the new mestizo society. His program, succinctly stated by Leonora Saavedra, "was aimed at incorporating the . . . people—including the indigenous communities—into a unified, literate, Spanish-speaking nation, with a modern, secular, standardized education based on Western civilization at large, and Hispanic culture in particular"[7] through the three-part administration of schools, libraries, and fine arts (the Department of Bellas Artes—DBA). The latter had responsibility for the instruction of drawing, physical fitness, and singing in all schools, and supervision of existing institutions such as the Academy of Fine Arts, the National Museum, and the Conservatories of Music. The Department of Bellas Artes had the responsibility of bringing high culture to the majority of the people, and collecting everyday traditions, clothing styles, music, and dances from the rural communities (in 1946, the Department of Bellas Artes became the National Institute of Bellas Artes).[8]

Vasconcelos had no plans for an equal joining of Spanish heritage and indigenous legacy; rather he proposed an identity based on the patrimony from Spain that incorporated language, religion, and culture of art, literature, music, folklore, and education. This culture could be inflected, influenced, perhaps better served, with indigenous traits including cuisine and other local traditions. He recognized biological blending as well, but cultural development provided the focus of what he called the Cosmic Race.

Vasconcelos held staunch nationalist views that can be seen clearly in his promotion of music as part of his educational campaign. The secretary relied on a group that could be called pedagogical intellectuals, especially several from the Ateneo de Juventud (Athenaeum of youth) of which Vasconcelos had been a member, and they controlled official cultural programs to a large extent until the 1940s.[9] Vasconcelos's intellectual associates included Antonio Caso, Gerardo Murillo (Dr. Atl), Adolfo Best Maugard, and Roberto Montenegro, all of whom attempted to give value to the indigenous past by promoting events that would illustrate this base of national identity. Ponce was a member of this cultural circle that developed the campaign labeled *Salon Indigenism*[10] in favor of rural Indian peoples who had no role in its formulation. These intellectuals singled out indigenous art and music as the base for the new nationalist aesthetic. For example, professional dancers, notably Anne Sokolov, gave folkloric ballets such as *Fantasía Mexicana*, and composers Ponce and Carlos Chávez wrote classical music inspired by popular examples.[11] This resulted in a popular music conference held in 1922 that included film of the festival in Chalma. Participants discussed the need for an archive containing all or samples of all national traditions, fiestas, and music. The result came in 1926 with creation of the Archivo Nacional de Música (National Archive of Music), which soon started providing mimeographed copies of scores collected by folklorists Concepción "Concha" Michel and Alfonso Esparza Oteo.[12] Exhibitions of typical handicrafts were celebrated as expressions of the authentic national heritage, but neither Vasconcelos nor intellectuals such as Francisco Zamora, who used the authorial name Gerónimo Coignard, saw much in these items beyond stimulation for academy-trained artists.[13] The inspiration that he envisioned would enable "painters, musicians, poets, and later filmmakers" to draw on "indigenous colors, design motifs, musical scales, linguistic tropes, and panoramic landscapes."[14]

Vanconcelos's major campaign resulted in the posting of school teachers that he called "Missionaries of Indigenous Culture and Public Education" in rural communities to teach literature, hygiene, and national values. The first group consisted of "50 Maestros Misioneros Ambulantes," and by April 1922 there were seventy-seven mobile and one hundred residential teachers.[15] Rafael Ramírez, holding various titles including the Director of Rural Education, put this plan into operation: sending out teachers, supervising their daily activities, dispatching instructions and warnings about village life.[16] As part of the educational campaign, Ramírez developed a plan to send teams of specialists into the countryside for three- to six-week community visits, in some cases ahead of more permanent teachers for the community. The three-person teams were experts in "agricultural science, social work, health education and recreation, domestic sciences . . . and small industries (crafts and trades such as soap-making and tanning), and music."[17] Music was viewed as especially important because it could be used to overcome community resistance to government representatives. Investigators generally had ignored this aspect of the rural educational program.

Ramírez directed the first mission in 1923 that made a three-week visit to Zacualtipán, Hidalgo. Alfredo Tamayo Marín served as the musical specialist in this group and reported that he taught both adults and children to sing the national anthem as well as other patriotic songs, such as "La Cucaracha."

Tamayo had a major part in shaping the music that formed part of cultural nationalism. Born in Mérida in 1888, he apparently composed the popular "Soñó mi mente loca" when he was fourteen or fifteen. At nineteen, he went to México to study at the conservatory on a scholarship provided by the governor of Yucatán, Francisco Cantón, where he likely met Manuel M. Ponce. In the capital, he performed in *Aïda* and other operas and zarzuelas, at times using the pseudonyms Julio Rosales, Julio Borghetti, and Ricardo Gutiérrez. His passion for singing resulted in obtaining a position with theater owner and musical entrepreneur Esperanza Iris. He worked as musical director with Iris from 1910 to 1918, a time when, because of the revolution, the company left Mexico and traveled throughout South America. He also spent time in Río de Janeiro and São Paulo. Iris's manager was the father of the photographer Luis Marqués, who was left as a child with the family in Havana. Tamayo returned to Mexico at the beginning of the 1920s. He likely was well aware of developments in the Ministry of Public Education, where Luis Marqués had been hired by Vasconcelos as a photographer to record life in rural communities. With Vasconcelos, Tamayo organized the first Workers' Cultural Center and then became a member of the educational team. Later, during the regime of President Lázaro Cárdenas, he served in the Tamaulipas state government of Emilio Portes Gil and the Coahuila state government as Director of Aesthetic Culture. In 1950, he was named to the same position for the state of Yucatán.[18]

The education ministry judged Ramírez's first expert mission a success, sent him to other locations as well as creating new teams. By the end of Vasconcelos's term as minister, eight missions of specialists were operating, and by 1945 there were eighteen active groups.

In these groups, music teachers soon introduced other songs that also served as campaign songs for revolutionary armies, including "La Adelita," which was used as the refrain of the troops that marched with Emiliano Zapata. Others turned to "La Valentina" that had served as the expression of support for Venustiano Carrana.[19] Nevertheless, it was "La Cucaracha" and "La Adelita" that became the most popular. Besides teaching singing to both children and adults and organizing music groups, the music instructor also had the responsibility of collecting folk music in the community. The program, as it developed after 1924 into the 1940s, received praise from educational reformer John Dewey in the United States.

Collecting folk music was part of Minister Vasconcelos's design to preserve a record of the countryside. He instructed musicologist Joaquín Beristáin, working through the Ministry of Public Education's Dirección de Cultura Estética (Directorate of Aesthetic Culture), to record the music and sounds of the "popular soul," following a project initiated by Ponce during the Porfirian years.[20] Both the Departamento de Cultura Indígena (Department of Indigenous Culture), created by Vasconcelos, and the cultural missions (teachers) also collaborated in the rescue of artistic manifestations of the national folklore.

Beristáin was deeply involved in Minister Vasconcelos's musical preservation projects, especially the rescue effort that worked to preserve regional music was at the point of disappearing. Among this group, Ignacio Fernández Esperón became the best known as a performer, using the professional name Tata Nacho, especially with the song "La Borrachita." This is one of the songs he recovered and it became popular enough that Plutarco Calles adopted it as his presidential campaign song in 1924. In the Sotavento region of Veracruz (overlapping slightly into Oaxaca and Tabasco), José Acosta and the Spanish musicologist Vicente Ruiz Maza, in 1925, began to collect regional music, in particular the Son Jarocho. The effort, following Vasconcelos's general plan, resulted in scores adapted to classical music. José Pablo Moncayo, for example, wrote "Huapango" from the songs "El Siquisirí," "El Balajú," and "El Gavilancito."[21] Carlos Chávez drew on Yanquí music from the Northwest, collected by Francisco Domínguez, as he composed his classic *Sinfonía india*. Associated with this effort was the creation of local groups interested in folklore and traditional customs.

In 1926, the members of the Department of Bellas Artes began to focus on música típica (representative music). The researchers followed the Vasconcelos plan, which included the collection of lifestyle information, taking photographs to document the rural, especially indigenous, cultures, and musical staff annotation of village music—all deposited in the National Archive of Music under the direction of the Department of Bellas Artes. In 1930, Higinio Vázquez Santa Ana, then in charge of the DBA, held a meeting with the governors of some states, from Puebla the Presidentes Municipales and the Directors of Federal Education, and the Regional Normal School of Matamoros Azúcar to discuss the collection of folklore materials. The Archivo Nacional de Música soon held transcriptions of hundreds of music scores and descriptions of dances, fiestas, clothing, and activities from rural communities. Working for the Department of Bellas Artes in 1926, Concepción Michel published the first collection of the music from this archive. The documents were also used in composition workshops as inspiration for composers and in various other activities of the DBA.

Efforts expanded when Ramírez became the director of Cultural Missions in 1927, and beyond basic education, he reemphasized sport, art, dance, and popular music. Later, in the 1930s, as Director of Rural Education he developed extended literacy programs to teach soldiers how to read and give them a cultural education.[22] He called on the school teachers to provide cultural information, especially music, from the communities where they taught. The years of the teachers' greatest activity, based on the volume of reports, came from 1931 to 1934 and from 1937 to 1945, when they seem to have stopped their collecting efforts.

During the 1930s, significant investigations of rural music increased through the work of Francisco Domínguez, Luis Sandi, Blas Galindo, and Roberto Téllez Girón. Outstanding among other performers and collectors of folksongs were Concepción Michel and Carmen Herrera de Mendizábal. At this time Francisco Domínguez published *Sones, Canciones y Corridos Michoacanos* and *Música Popular de Oaxaca*.[23] Chabela Villaseñor, the heroine of Sergei Eisenstein's film *Thunder Over Mexico*, collected songs from Jalisco and recorded them—they are available now on a CD of Mexican love songs. Roberto Téllez Girón Olace went to the Sierra Norte of Puebla and the west of Veracruz and collected music there.[24] During the 1940s, Raúl G. Guerrero took a leading role in the IBA, compiling a great deal of music, including the recordings—the first done in 1942 for the department—made by Henrietta Yurchenco on an expedition to Lake Pátzcuaro; the small town of Paracho de Verduzco; Zamora, Spain; and Uruapán.[25]

Many of the pieces of music collected involved canción—or Mexican song—that Ponce had promoted through arrangements and compositions as early as 1913. Both Vasconcelos and Ponce in the early 1920s thought canción could be used in creating a national identity, but they differed on how canción should be used. Vasconcelos intended to create a mass culture and called on Beristáin to achieve this through what has been called "collective Neo-Platonist flights of the national soul."[26]

The Vasconcelos project for music, whether devised in practice by the Minister Ramírez or inspired by the collections of Beristáin, used developments in urban popular culture, popular music, and teatro de género chico (short plays with music), and accepted the importance of canción advocated by Ponce. The campaign promoted Mexican (Hispanic, really, as in from Spanish-speaking countries) songs to thwart, as Vasconcelos said, "the increasing popularity through movies and recordings of foreign popular genres." Vasconcelos's campaign relied not just on music but also on physical education in his effort to eliminate foreign influence in the new revolutionary society. He wanted to prevent the popularity of foreign music, especially tango and foxtrot.[27]

Foxtrot could bring it all down, in his opinion. Played on the radio, the Victrola, or the bandstand, it threatened cultural nationalism not just in Mexico but also across Latin America—politicians and intellectuals knew that for certain. Vasconcelos and other critics meant both US jazz and actual foxtrot music and dance bringing many listeners into close contact as couples. This rhythmic intimacy that dancers shared or listeners imagined had no legacy, no tradition, no roots among any of the Latin American peoples; it came from abroad and endangered the newly endowed standard national cultures. The radio broadcast what the minister saw as disgraceful: foreign music such as the foxtrot, rumba, tango, and jazz.

Manuel Puig Casauranc, the new secretary following Vasconcelos in 1924, placed writer and musician Rubén M. Campos in charge of the preparation of texts that guided folklore and musical investigations through the decade. He published, among others, three of great value: *El folklore y la música mexicana* (1928), *El folklore literario de México* (1929), and *El folklore musical de las ciudades* (1930). Other essays about music and instruments appeared in the National Conservatory of Music's periodical *Music* and in the annuals of the national museum.

Later in the 1920s, Campos worked with individuals such as Ponce, Guty Cárdenas, Ricardo Palmerín, and Ermilo Padrón López in promoting national music. Along with Ramón López Velarde, Gerardo Murillo, Diego Rivera, Roberto Montenegro, the brothers Enrique and Gabriel Fernández Ledesma, and others, Ponce promoted the sounds and dances of the Bajío (Central North Mexico) in defining this regional music as the idiom of national culture.

The push toward nationalistic classical music continued after Vasconcelos, especially through the efforts of Carlos Chavez. In 1928, Chavez, who had been in and out of the country during the previous decade, returned permanently to conduct the National Symphony Orchestra and direct the National Conservatory of Music. He devoted his efforts to the promotion of works that included both nationalism and abstract music. Then came Silvestre Revueltas, who also spent much of the revolution outside Mexico. He returned around 1929 to become the sub-director of the symphony orchestra. He quickly joined composers Candelario Huízar, José Pomar, and Eduardo Hernández Moncada, who consolidated national academic music. Revueltas was an unparalleled composer, who sensed popular flavor and recognized nationalistic themes. These can be sampled in his *Ensemble Works*, most recently published in 2015.

He provided a music analysis of the revolution in his unfinished composition *La coronela* for the ballet of the same name written by Waldeen that premiered in 1940. Painter Gabriel Ledesma designed the sets following José Guadalupe Posada's broadsheets, based on national folklore. One reviewer praised the music as a "witty and scornful portrayal of Los Privilegiados," that is, the Porfirian aristocrats. The composer compared the plutocrats with the general population, whom he presented in "a pitiful picture of Los Desheredados" (The disinherited). As a result, the revolution brought the "relentless disintegration of the former social order" that the composer named "Don Ferruco's Nightmare." The movement called "The Last Judgement" included a middle piece entitled "The Fallen." One reviewer described it as "too sad and wistful to make the final piece 'The Liberated' any kind of positive apotheosis." Revueltas's musical portrait of the revolution shows more pessimistic rage than any feeling of the inevitability of victory. It is a sad, but still musically satisfying, ending for a great composer's much too short life.[28] In the ballet Waldeen portrayed women participants in the revolution. As an early feminist, her ballet *Coronela* was the first of many works based on women's history in Latin America, their trials as well as their triumphs, and oddly has been ignored by historians and musicologists examining the revolution.

Not all composers of classic music during these years responded to the thrust of nationalistic and revolutionary campaigns. One distinctive example was Julián Carrillo (1875–1965) and his so-called *Sonido 13*.[29] Both he and this music are shrouded in mystery and have become part of cultural trivia. He developed an early microtonal system in the 1920s that achieved some attention in international avant-garde musical circles toward the middle of the century. Nevertheless, the nationalist focus that characterized musical life after the revolution and the composer's egomaniacal rhetoric concerning his microtonal compositions created misunderstanding of his compositions, alienated most of the mainstream music community, and resulted in neglect of his musical contributions. After Carrillo's death, something of a small cult devoted to *Sonido 13* appeared. Nevertheless, commercial recordings remain largely unavailable and those that exist—such as SONY-Mexico's two CD collection of symphonic and chamber works—contribute misinformation.

Much needed information comes from Jimena Giménez Cacho's recording of Carrillo's complete works for solo cello. The collection shows clearly a major set of works for the cello and provides the history of microtonality in Western society.

Nevertheless, for the 1920s and 1930s, the ballet *La Coronela* provided a much better capstone and captured the more popular formal, classical essence and the widespread efforts to give musical expression to the emerging national identity. During this time, others turned to popular music and countless regional representations soon emerged, which the cinema as well as radio and press promoted. Much in the fashion recently achieved by Nick Gold and World Circuit Records, especially through the success of the Buena Vista Social Club (the Grammy Award–winning Cuban group that since 1997 has sold eight million copies worldwide), films featured not only *charros* and mariachis but also additional regional examples, and cultural versatility appeared in such movies as *La Zandunga* (1937) by Fernando de Fuentes and *Huapango* (1937) by Juan Bustillo Oro. Other typical examples, like the *tehuanas* of the Oaxacan isthmus or the *jarochos* from Veracruz, also appeared. A wash of national music in romantic songs, such as the bolero, that soon made them part of the nationalistic identity also emerged.

As for popular music, the mestizo revolutionary leaders, who received Vasconcelos's praise and who made up the Obregón government, brought with them mariachi music, the rural sounds of both the western (Jalisco and Michoacán) and northeastern (Tamaulipas) regions, that quickly were popularized as unique national music. Contemporaneously, in Peru, rural mestizo music, especially with the charango, was labeled as neo-Indianist, while mariachi in Mexico became mestizo music representing wistful feelings for a rural life that had never existed. In both nations, the countryside, especially the pastoral landscape, provided inspiration for compositions, and this coincided with the campaigns of Vasconcelos to have youth learn the music and dance of this non-existent rural heritage through the folklorization of nostalgic attitudes. This popularization of rural life reveals Vasconcelos as the romantic intellectual that he was.

This emphasis on rural life served as the groundwork for later sentimental ranchero movies, which represent a legacy of the folklore programs of Vasconcelos. Nevertheless, the dynamic movie industry contemporary to Vasconcelos's ministry was in the hands of Best Maugard and others attempting experimental films. This relationship needs exploration and the connection of several filmmakers and their links to the romantic ideals of Vasconcelos merits attention.

This romanticism, especially as it has been ignored, must serve as a major theme in any discussion of Vasconcelos, but as David A. Brading noted twenty-five years ago, no biography and little careful analysis of him exists. Vasconcelos repeated time and again his romantic views. President Obregón sent him to Rio de Janeiro as Mexico's representative to the centennial celebration of Brazilian independence. He took with him a statue of Cuauhtémoc, based on the monument in the traffic circle at Reforma and Insurgentes Avenues. He made clear in statements that he did not support Indianism that rejected the Spanish culture, but at the same time that he saw in the image of Cuauhtémoc a call for a cosmic race that would represent a second era of independence in the hemisphere—an expression of his romantic notions.[30]

These romantic ideas, especially of the mestizo, allowed Vasconcelos and other revolutionary officials, in the words of Guillermo Palacios, to "kidnap history and convert it into [their] history, a narrative used to solve the problems of . . . legitimacy. . . . History became an instrument of consolidation and an ideological guarantee of authenticity." [31] In this way, it served in the construction of the popular imaginary of the revolutionary political administration, its society and its culture. The goals of mestizaje made hostages of the indigenous peoples, who escaped this status only through the ethnic politics that followed the First National Congress of Indigenous Peoples in 1975, leading to the 1992 amendment to the national constitution that Mexico is a pluricultural nation with an indigenous base.[32]

The mestizo, Vasconcelos's savior of the nation and avatar of the Cosmic Race, represented the human expression of the solution that national intellectuals proposed to solve persistent national problems. The lines of romantic thought leading to Vasconcelos can be traced to the positivism beginning with Gabino Barrera, in his *Oración Cívica* (1867), through conclusions of Andrés Molina Enríquez in *Grandes Problems Nacionales* (1906), continuing to Antonio Caso and Vasconcelos. The Minister of Education's programs reflected both this intense romanticism and revolutionary fervor, joined, in the case of the minister himself, to an elitist predilection for high culture and artistic endeavor. Moreover, Vasconcelos should be credited in many ways as the father of mass culture that shortly, with the rise of the popular media, resulted in the new culture of comic books, movies, records, and radio. This has remained imbedded in both Mexican and Latin American cultural practices, despite the rise of ethnic politics. This is especially the case in music, as made evident in the exhibit *A tres bandas: mestizaje, sincretismo e hibridacion en el espacio sonoro iberoamericano* in 2010 at the Museo de Antioquia, Medellin, Colombia.[33]

The integrity of the country's identity defined both its peoples and politics and, its promoters such as Vasconcelos proclaimed, it lifted semi-colonial and marginal regimes into modern governments with productive populations. Reaching this status required identifying the authentic cultural heritage, previously ignored as simply rural folklore or dismissed as atavistic Indian practices, merging it with modern European traditions and disseminating it through education and entertainment to the nation's peoples, so they would speak the same language, sing the same song, and share the same story.

Notes

1. Jessica Gottfried Hesketh, "Tras los Pasos de Roberto T llez Girón Olace," in *Tras los pasos de Roberto Téllez Girón Olace*, eds. Jessica Gottfried Hesketh and Ricardo Téllez Girón López. (Puebla: CONACULTA, Secretaría de Cultura de Puebla, 2010), 35.

2. Benjamín Muratalla, "Carl Lumholtz, Primeras grabaciones etnográficas en México," in . . . *y la música se volvió mexicana*. Testimonio Musical de México núm. 51 (México: Instituto Nacional de Antropología e Historia, 2010), 157–72; Isabel Aretz, *Sintesis*, in *América Latina en su música*, rapporteur Isabel Aretz, 2nd ed. (México: Siglo XXI, 1980), 33–36.

3. Alejandro L. Madrid, "Sound Recordings," *Transnational Encounters: Music and Performance at the U.S.-Mexico Border* (New York: Oxford University Press, 2011), 96.

4. See the work of Charles V. Heath, such as *The Inevitable Bandstand: The State Band of Oaxaca and the Politics of Sound* (Lincoln: University of Nebraska Press, 2015) on this topic.

5. These wax cylinder recordings are all available at the University of California–Santa Barbara Library, "Mexican Cylinder Collection." See http://cylinders-stage.library.ucsb.edu/mexico.php.

6. See Liliana Toledo, "El programa de música de las Misiones Culturales: su inscripción en las políticas integracionistas posrevolucionarias y en la

construcción del nacionalismo musical mexicano (1921–1932)," (M.A. thesis, CIESAS-Tlalpán, 2016), 18; and Béla Bartók, *El folklore y la música popular*, that by 1997 was published in its 5th ed., Siglo XXI ed., in Mexico.

7. Leonora Saavedra, "Manuel M. Ponce's Chapultepec and the Conflicted Representations of a Contested Space," *The Musical Quarterly* 92, nos. 3–4 (Fall–Winter 2009), 289–90.

8. Jessica Gottfried Hesketh, "Music and Folklore Research in the Departamento de Bellas Artes. 1926–1946," in *Oxford Research Encyclopedia for Latin America*, ed. William H. Beezley, online publication. Jessica Gottfried Hesketh, "Tras los Pasos de Roberto Téllez Girón Olace," in *Tras los pasos de Roberto Téllez Girón Olace*, eds. Jessica Gottfried Hesketh and Ricardo Téllez Girón López. (Puebla: CONACULTA, Secretaría de Cultura de Puebla, 2010), 35.

9. Guillermo Palacios, "The Social Sciences, Revolutionary Nationalism, and Inter-academic Relations: Mexico and the United States, 1930–1940," in *Populism in Twentieth Century Mexico: The Presidencies of Lázaro Cárdenas and Luis Echeverría*, eds. Amelia Kiddle and Maria Muñoz (Tucson: University of Arizona Press, 2010), 59–60; D. A. Brading, "Social Darwinism and Romantic Idealism: Andrés Molina Enríquez and José Vasconcelos in the Mexican Revolution," in *Prophecy and Myth in Mexican History* (Cambridge: Centre of Latin American Studies, 1984), 71–72.

10. Stephen E. Lewis, "The Nation, Education, and the 'Indian Problem' in Mexico, 1920–1940," in *The Eagle and The Virgin: Nation and Cultural Revolution in Mexico, 1920–1940*, eds. Mary Kay Vaughan and Stephen E. Lewis (Durham, NC: Duke University Press, 2006), 178.

11. Rick A. López, "The Noche Mexicana and the Exhibition of Popular Arts: Two Ways of Exalting Indianness," in *The Eagle and the Serpent*, 24–42; Julia del Palacio Langer, "The Construction of a Presidential Figure: Lázaro Cárdenas and His Use of Music as a Political Tool" (M.A. thesis, Columbia University, May 2008); Ricardo Pérez Monfort, *Expresiones populares y estereotipos culturales en México. Siglos XIX y XX. Diez ensayos* (México, CIESAS/Publicaciones de la Casa Chata, 2007).

12. Gottfried Hesketh, "Music and Folklore Research."

13. López, "The Noche Mexicana and the Exhibition of Popular Arts," in *The Eagle and the Serpent*, 24–25.

14. Brenda J. Bright and Liza Bakewell, eds., *Looking High and Low: Art and Cultural Identity* (Tucson: University of Arizona Press, 1995), 24.

15. Toledo, " El programa de música de las Misiones Culturales," 35.

16. Lewis, 179–180; Elsie Rockwell, *Hacer escuela hacer estado: La educación posrevolucionaria vista desde Tlaxcala* (Zamora, Michoacán: El Colegio de Michoacán, 2007).

17. Toledo, "El programa de música de las Misiones Culturales," 35.

18. David G. Tovey, "The Role of the Music Educator in Mexico's Cultural Missions," *Bulletin of the Council for Research in Music Education*, no. 139 (Winter, 1999), 1–11; Carlos A. Echanóve Trujillo (ed.), *Enciclopedia Yucatanense*, vol. 4 (Gobierno de Yucatán, México, 1944), 805; Gerónimo Baqueiro Foster, *La canción popular de Yucatán (1850–1950)* (Editorial del Magisterio, México, 1970), 234–38; "Entre el 'nacionalismo' 'el regionalismo' y la 'universalidad.'Aproximaciones a una controversia entre Manuel M. Ponce y Alfredo Tamayo Marin en 1920–1921," *Diccionario Histórico y Biográfico de la Revolución Mexicana*, vol. 7 (México: Instituto Nacional de los Estudios Históricos de la Revolución, 1992), 791.

19. George C. Booth, *Mexico's School-Made Society* (Stanford, CT: Stanford University Press, 1941), 115.

20. Carlos Monsiváis, "Bolero: A History," in *Mexican Postcards*, ed. and trans. by John Kraniauskas (New York: Verso, 1997), 173.

21. Rafael Figueroa Hernández, *Guía histórico-musical* (Xalapa: CONACULTA FONCA, 2006), 85–86.

22. "Alfabetizacion," *Excelsior*, December 5, 1929.

23. Ernest Gruening, *Mexico and its Heritage* (New York: Century, 1928), 653; Carlos Monsiváis, "Yo soy un humilde cancionero (De la música popular en México)," in *La música en México: Panorama del siglo xx*, coor. Aurelio Tello (México: Consejo Nacional para la Cultura y las Artes, 2010), 211.

24. Review of Jessica Gottfried Hesketh y Ricardo Téllez Girón López, *Tras los pasos de Roberto Téllez Girón Olace* (CONACULTA: Secretaría de Cultura de Puebla, 2010), available at http://ohbeltran.blogspot.com/2013/03/tras-los-pasos-de-roberto-tellez-giron.html.

25. Henrietta Yurchenco, *Around the World in 80 Years: A Memoir* (Point Richmond, CA: Musical Research Institute, 2002), 184.

26. Leonora Saavedra, personal communication to author, June 13, 2010.

27. Vasconcelos, *A Mexican Ulysses: An Autobiography*, trans. and abridged by W. Rex Crawford (Bloomington: Indiana University Press, 1963), 180; Leonora Saavedra, personal communication to author.

28. Liner notes from *La Coronela Itinerarios Colorines Ben-Dor*; Santa Barbara Symphony Orchestra; English Chamber Orchestra (Performer), Revueltas Silvestre (Composer) Format: Audio CD; review by Dean Frey published September 27, 2010, accessed at https://www.amazon.com/Coronela-Itinerarios-Colorines-SILVESTRE-REVUELTAS/product-reviews/B0037TTQCE; César Delgado Martínez, *Waldeen: La coronela de la danza Mexicana* (Mexico City: Escenología, 2000), 86–87.

29. Alejandro L. Madrid, *Latin American Music Review* 30, no. 1 (Spring–Summer 2009), 103–5, doi: 10.1353/lat.0.0029. Madrid praises the recordings by Jimena Giménez Cacho, the first four of which range from baroque music to Spanish twentieth-century repertoire and her playing of the Sonido 13, her skill and commitment to the music, as he says, "helps us listen to these passages with new ears and renovated interest," 104.

30. Vasconcelos, *Mexican Ulysses*, 172; D. A. Brading, "Social Darwinism and Romantic Idealism: Andrés Molina Enríquez and José Vasconcelos in the Mexican Revolution," in *Prophecy and Myth in Mexican History* (Cambridge, MA: Center of Latin American Studies, 1984), 72–73.

31. Palacios, "The Social Sciences, Revolutionary Nationalism, and Inter-Academic Relations," 69.

32. Carrie C. Chorba, *Mexico, From Mestizo to Multicultural: National Identity and Recent Representations of the Conquest* (Nashville, TN: Vanderbilt University Press, 2007).

33. Joshua Lund, *The Impure Imagination: Toward a Critical Hybridity in Latin American Writing* (Minneapolis: University of Minnesota Press, 2006), 80–82; *A tres bandas: Mestizaje, sincretismo e hibridación en el espacio sonora iberoamericano* (Catalogo de la exhibición, el Museo de Antioquia, 2010).

CHAPTER 2

La Hora Industrial vs. *La Hora Intima*

Mexican Music and Broadcast Media Before 1934

Sonia Robles

Mexico's Golden Age of radio began with the inauguration of XEW *La voz de América Latina desde México* (The voice of Latin America from Mexico) on September 18, 1930. In the hands of elite businessmen like the Azcárraga family, who were behind XEW, radio became an excellent instructor, training listeners how to love, laugh, sing, forget, dream, cry, and become first-rate consumers for the next two decades. But to the government, radio's purpose was multidimensional: the medium was used as a tool to unify the population and indoctrinate them with patriotic ideas via music and cultural programming. State-sponsored radio stations competed with commercial stations for the attention of the public, who was eager to absorb the music of their past, the sounds of the future, and programs that relieved and distracted them from daily life. Musical programming quickly became an easy target for critics, who used the pages of the daily press to express concern and sometimes ridicule about the effectiveness of mass media in the hands of the government.

In 1935, the *El Caballero Pálido* (The pale gentleman) used his weekly column in *El Universal Ilustrado* to admonish XEFO *Radio Nacional* (national radio), the radio station of Mexico's *Partido Nacional Revolucionario* (National Revolutionary Party, or PNR), for providing "hundreds of peasants" dull music. "How much fun do the working and laboring masses have listening to operas, rhapsodies, sonatas, etc., all the time?" he asked. "What about the *Huapangos, corridos, sones*, and Revolution tales, and all of that music and popular literature, which is of real importance to the people, when will that be broadcast? In the year 2000?"[1]

"The Pale Gentleman" posed a legitimate question. During a time when it was promoting, subsidizing, and even sponsoring mural projects, outdoor art schools, and public education, why did the government not insist on different genres of music for radio listeners who had limited knowledge of the sounds heard in other parts of Mexico? It appeared illogical for the government, who had co-opted popular forms of expression and converted what was "popular" into being "Mexican," to use classical music in their daily broadcasts.[2] This chapter uses the medium of radio to understand why, before 1934, the government believed that only programs of a high cultural standard should be presented to the population through its own channels. Broadcast media demonstrated the transformation of music—from "popular" to "Mexican"—and how, during a time of government-sponsored modernization, music over the radio lagged behind other cultural forms in promoting unity among the population.

A number of composers, pianists, and musicians who had been living in Europe returned to Mexico in the 1920s and made a commitment to create national art and music. Led by José Vasconcelos and the Ministry of Public Education, or SEP, folklorists and composers like Manuel M. Ponce traveled the countryside to collect and document the musical traditions of the people. Artistically, at this time, the *corrido*, or narrative ballad, was widely popular. After 1920, corridos appealed to the public because of their direct correlation with the years of upheaval. The Revolution of 1910 had been a time when people from different regions of the country were forced to interact with one other, and this clash led to a wide range of musical styles. Thus, because the corrido invited listeners to hear stories about heroes, battles, and notable fighters, it became the portable poetry of the people.[3] The other genre of music reflecting the people during the 1920s was the *canción mexicana*, which is synonymous with the *canción popular*. This music was described as "the genuine product of the *pueblo*, born in the modest dwelling places of the poor. It is simple, painful like the life of a laborer, filled with hope like the dawn."[4] Like the corrido, the canción mexicana also turned into a portable and succinct expression of cultural nationalism.

Not until Lázaro Cardenas toured with the Mariachi Marmolejo in 1933 was popular music considered patriotic and worthy of commercial attention by media. The government's narrow view of broadcast media, it appears, limited the number of popular—that is, rural and patriotic—tunes that entered the airwaves in the 1920s and early 1930s. For the most part, before 1934, this was not considered "national" music. It was during Cardenas's term (1934–1940) and the parallel rise of Golden Age cinema, that on-air music began to project the government's revolutionary objectives and include patriotic exaltations of the countryside and its people. In large part, this genre was the *ranchera*. Derivative of the canción mexicana, the *canción ranchera* had existed in the nineteenth century, but began to be called *ranchera* (literally, "of the ranch") when, songs, in order to be truly Mexican, "had to invoke the rural world."[5] After 1930, rancheras became standardized forms of popular music designed to attract audiences on a national and international level. Hit songs like "Allá en el Rancho Grande," introduced a new musical trend, which coincided with the growing national film industry. This genre became also influential because it was integrated with the *Mariachi*, the interpreter of the canción ranchera who traveled the world as a symbol of Mexico.[6]

Rancheras moved people. In keeping with the "sentimental mythology" of both literature and music, men cried and wailed and women, like the legendary Lucha Reyes, moved audiences to tears. Despite the many songs that mention loss of love, betrayal, and loneliness, Carlos Monsiváis argues that their distress came from work because, in reality, most of the time their personal relationships were going well. This genre prevailed because it validated passionate feelings and because the possibility of pain was more appealing than thoughts of happiness.[7] In fact, other musical genres, like the *bolero*, favored sadness and gloomy tales of loss over passionate love songs. Of all boleros 80 percent contained a negative association with love—disdain, rejection, insecurity—while the remaining 20 percent describe love in a happy way.[8]

The 1920s included widespread violence, repression, illicit money making, and looting. Until 1934, the nation experienced "an open struggle for power."[9] Scholars who study the post–1920 period have noted that the project of the state was not a program passed down from the government to the people, but one in which a significant amount of negotiation took place between these two forces. Indeed, historians have identified multiple sites of struggle on the local, regional, and national level.[10]

After the revolution, sociopolitical strains, in the opinion of some political leaders, would be eased by reforming the education sector and funneling attention to culture, specifically to art and music. Beginning in 1921, nationwide efforts toward creating a culturally cohesive population with a shared identity and some level of solidarity were implemented. The purpose was to indoctrinate the people through programs focused on education, public health, agrarianism, and anticlericalism. Professors and educators delivered political messages preached by revolutionary leaders.

After 1920 a new culture was being constructed, but this plan was not effective throughout the nation, nor did it succeed in consolidating power and authority in the capital city.[11] Those who study the revolutionary cultural project specifically, explain its wide range of manifestations across the country, highlighting three areas: the artistic movement that emerged with art, muralist paintings, and the efforts of the Ministry of Public Education, US–Mexico relations, and the post–1940 period.[12] With the exception of a handful of books, music studies do not consider the rise of broadcast media and the cultural project of the revolution, which happened simultaneously.[13] Moreover, the scholarship on broadcast media focuses primarily on the birth and role of the radio and includes topics ranging from studies of influential stations, to the way the medium reflected the government's discourse during the first half of the twentieth century.[14] The seminal work on radio convincingly argues that political leaders were fortunate that radio was part of a new mass media technology that was perfected at the moment that the government and commercial interests were looking for an efficient means of reaching the people, yet it omits the music that created a "Radio Nation."[15] By focusing on broadcast music and listeners, this study illustrates the role that radio played in creating national music during the 1920s and early 1930s.

Media historians and theorists claim that the mechanical reproduction of cultural forms such as music during the twentieth century reconfigured the understanding of space and time.[16] The transmission of voices, especially, contributed to fundamental changes in gender roles, the public's view of the environment, and even the private sphere in Mexico. Before 1921, the only way to bring music inside the home was through records for phonographs or Victrolas. Radio surpassed these methods and offered not only classical music to families but, later, also popular and folkloric music, radio-dramas, national and international news, and annual government celebrations and rituals. Many women responded to the arrival of radio either by staying at home glued to their receivers as they listened to the voice of the crooner "make love" to them through soft romantic music, or by finding ways to travel to the cities and begin a career in the budding industry.[17]

Inside a Mexican home during the 1920s, "the radio was placed in the center of the living room, like a magic box that had the power to gather the family with truly stellar auditions."[18] Radio was "a phenomenon of unprecedented penetration," one historian notes. "It surrounds public and private spaces, enters living rooms in homes, in the same way that it wanders through the shop windows of the central avenues, it penetrates the dining room, the bedrooms, the parks, the corners."[19] Broadcasts had the ability to travel from radio studios to the kitchen, living room, or bedroom, other intimate secret places, and, in the public realm, they moved from studios to street corners, central meeting salons, dance halls, and auditoriums.

Broadcast media, additionally, played a role in migration patterns during the first half of the twentieth century. The inauguration of XEW, for instance, contributed both to the legitimacy of the industry and to the rural-to-urban migration. After 1930, "musicians and singers from every region . . . began to arrive in the DF [federal district]."[20] Some, like *Los Gavilanes del Sur,* left the tranquility of their village in Guerrero, picked up their guitars and "came to the city, to get drunk on lights, noise and the longings of success."[21] Music and the possibilities of performing on the radio drew people to Mexico City. During the 1930s, Pedro Vargas left his home in San Miguel de Allende, Guanajuato, after finishing grade school at the age of thirteen because he did not want to be a *campesino* (farmer) like his father "I had a fervent desire to be somebody in life. That was my obsession," he recalled.[22] These developments took place, mostly, because the radio industry created new possibilities for employment and because transmissions were providing listeners with a wide range of music.

"Free Music to the World"

In the 1920s, radio broadcasting transformed daily life. Its arrival coincided with important national events; most notably the cultural project of the government that utilized art, music, folklore, and other objects as part of the official discourse. The government used film, radio, and, later, television to instill principles of nationalism and bring the people together under the ideology of the ruling political party. Broadcasting was eagerly embraced by national officials because it simplified existing forms of communication and for its potential to reach the most dispersed *pueblos* in the interior. In 1922, General Plutarco Elías Calles stated, "Never before has there been an opportunity for the teacher, the artist, the businessman to be in intimate and direct contact with millions of people, through one effort."[23]

From the outset, programming over the radio varied. The majority of stations initiated their daily programs at 7:00 a.m. with news, sometimes followed by stories for children or women, but always with a potpourri of live or recorded music, usually foxtrots and waltzes, which alternated between announcements from local and foreign businesses. These "performances" or "concerts," did not resemble the broadcasts of amateur stations that invited professional or novice singers to stand in front of a microphone and sing several songs. Beginning in 1930, the new radio programming borrowed its model from the *Teatro de Revista*, or musical revue, with short one-act burlesques containing music and comedy pieces.

For decades, theater imitated Spanish styles, with its predominant form, the *Zarzuela*, or Spanish operetta. In the first decades of the twentieth century, Zarzuela was being challenged by the Teatro de Revista as the prominent source of entertainment in cities. Teatro de Revista opened new spaces for the urban population, who preferred attending a public event in a crowded room over sitting at home listening to the piano or the Victrola. Quickly, this low-brow activity became the most important source of music and entertainment.[24]

Radio stations duplicated the format of Revista—live audiences, recognizable characters, satire, parody, drama, and music—that instantly gave programs credibility with the public. At times, the programs also drew artistic talent from musical theater companies. In the early 1920s, when a large portion of the radio transmissions were symphonic and orchestra concerts, radio stations in Mexico looked to the Teatro de Revista for their *cancioneras* (singers) and *tiples cómicas* (comical sopranos), contracting them to sing on stages and in radio studios. It was common for a man or a woman to make the jump from tent or traveling theater company to the radio in their artistic career, especially at the end of a tour. These singers were said to "give themselves to the art out of pure love for it."[25]

The broadcasting activities of Mexico City's first commercial radio stations and its most vibrant official station demonstrate how radio drew from preexisting cultural institutions and why patriotic music did not comprise the bulk of programming before 1934. The first two commercial stations to go on the air in Mexico City, CYB and CYL, were unique enterprises affiliated with national and international companies unrelated to broadcasting. CYB-*El Buen Tono* boasted being the first commercial station to go on the air in Mexico City on the night of September 15, 1923.[26] From the outset, the public held the station in high regard for transmitting quality radio concerts and for aiming to reach the entire North American continent.[27] "When in Mexico the *nueva maravilla* (new marvel) began," noted *El Universal*, El Buen Tono had the first transmitting station.[28]

The other commercial station, CYL, funded by the local newspaper *El Universal*, initiated its programming in 1923. This resulted from the efforts of Raúl Azcárraga. As early as 1921, he saw the arrival of radio broadcasting as an opportunity to make money selling transmitting equipment to amateurs and radio "tinkerers" and opened a shop, *La Casa del Radio* (The house of radio), in downtown Mexico City. This store specialized in selling wires, antennas, and light bulbs, necessary instruments to assemble properly a radio receiver. In the spring of 1923, Azcárraga asked *El Universal* to partner with him and launch a commercial radio station in the capital city. He agreed to provide the equipment, an RCA transmitter he had purchased in the United States, if the newspaper company would handle the details and content of the broadcasts. *El Universal* designated its weekly cultural magazine, *El Universal Ilustrado*, to join forces with him. The result was the birth of CYL or *El Universal Ilustrado–La Casa del Radio*, as the station was officially known.[29]

At first, both stations played foreign and national music. Evening programs included "a recorded US fox-trot" followed by "a piano solo of Mexican music." On November 30, 1923, CYB broadcast Eduardo Gómez, who sang the Spanish tango "Mi Querida" (My loved one), which he "interpreted with deep emotion."[30] Stations occasionally chose to stage concerts, which they advertised days in advance in the newspapers. The concerts allowed performances by small musical groups, such as the jazz band Lone Star, on loan to CYB from the owners of the movie theater *Cine Majestic* for their radio transmissions.[31] By 1928, folklorist Ruben Campos declared that Mexico lived in "a splendid era, in which the Ministry [of Public Education] and two other newspaper companies offer free music to the world."[32]

Campos referred to the two private stations and to CZE (later XFX), which was the station under the auspices of the SEP.[33] A handful of government institutions managed radio stations in the 1920s and 1930s, including the Ministry of Industry, Commerce, and Labor, the Ministry of War and Navy, and the Ministry of Foreign Relations. Their instructions were to contact the people, indoctrinate them with ideas of nationalism through radio programming, and, overall, carry out work that was pro-Patria, that is, "for the betterment of the motherland." Above the others, it was the Ministry of Public Education's station that gained national and international prestige. As head of the ministry in the 1920s, José Vasconcelos eagerly supported efforts to acquire the technology necessary to build a modern radio station. He thought the station could serve as a tool for education of the illiterate and dispersed population. In addition, this station broadcast a live transmission of the presidential inauguration of Plutarco Elías Calles on December 1, 1924, during its first official transmission.[34]

The station devoted most of its time on the air to broadcasting government bulletins, weather reports, recipes, home remedies, and national events featuring a speech or a parade, such as the September 16 Independence Day festivities or the commemoration of the Revolution on November 20. The SEP imagined radio to be a medium for educating audiences, both culturally—through classical music—and pedagogically—through lectures, seminars, or instructional presentations. XFX disseminated knowledge by teaching technical and agricultural skills to the rural people in the ranches and haciendas. One of the projects born under XFX specifically targeting the female audience was a broadcast titled "La Hora del Hogar" (The hour of the home). The first of its kind in Mexico, this show offered women advice on how to manage their home, learn about domestic hygiene, daily food prices, fashion, and even some world news. To the station, the goal of broadcasting specifically to women went beyond education; it consisted in creating a moral, cultured family life.[35] This genre of programming began in 1927 and continued through to the next decade. Immediately, women became avid listeners of programming that was intended to suit their needs. The ministry reported in 1929 that housewives owned the largest number of radio receivers.[36]

In its second mission, the station promoted arts and culture by live transmissions of concerts, operas, and conferences. As the other commercial stations, CYL and CYB, XFX broadcast foreign and national music and news programming. Two examples illustrate the variety of music on the air. In the spring of 1930, the Ugarte and Loyola families of Teotihuacán, just outside of Mexico City, sent a letter to XFX's offices. As avid nightly listeners of the station, they requested "No te engañes, corazon" (Don't fool yourself, heart), "El Tísico" (The consumptive), and "El Pagano" (The pagan), clearly not "popular" music.[37] Two years later, as the station prepared its annual report, the radio office announced that it had included great concerts by "Bach, Beethoven, Wagner, Lisz," and Mexico's classical music composers, "Revueltas, Pomar and Chávez."[38] During the 1920s and early 1930s, the station was mostly preoccupied with education and used its airwaves to transmit cooking classes, children's programs, live congressional sessions, Public Health Bulletins, and other news. Music was almost an afterthought; a strange occurrence for a station associated with the SEP, who, under Vasconcelos, had a project to collect the people's musical traditions.

By 1930, despite its stronghold in society, and the ways it was augmenting other cultural forms, Revista began to decline. In many urban centers, the theater industry suffered, and musical theater, which projected the popular base of the emerging national culture during the 1920s, was replaced by the cinema, radio, and eventually television. As this transformation occurred, sentimentality began to permeate the radio, film, and theater industries, and music abandoned "collective causes," installing itself "completely in the heart."[39] Revista's demise coincided with the rise in commercial radio, in particular the arrival of XEW. Revista was also overshadowed by live radio programs, which, along with Golden Age cinema, began to be avidly visited by the urban popular masses as the decade progressed. In many ways, the cinema and live radio logically substituted for Revista, since both mediums catered to the general population and reflected the strengths and the ills of society.

As radio listeners and movie goers increased, musical theater adopted more romantic themes and was transformed into *Teatro de Variedades*, a genre similar to Revista in that it was a play centered on a script with several musical selections. But the competition between theater and radio was futile. The theaters provided training for those who were aiming for a career on the radio.[40] After the disappearance of Revista, radio maintained the most salient part of popular entertainment, the ability to serve as a mirror and reflect society in its programming. The radio industry, which relied on live radio programs more and more during the 1930s, transformed into a place for the display of new artists and, in particular, urban melodies.

"Tu Ya No Soplas"

Live radio coincided with the arrival of a unique genre of music, the metropolitan, melancholic sound of the bolero. While the canción mexicana had an ability to interpret the feelings of the people, this genre of music was more "romantic" and different from popular music because it abandoned the adoration of the past and its heroes and focused on individual feelings, *sentimientos*, through song lyrics. In the early 1930s, when distinguishable urban sounds appeared, a new style of music labeled *cursi* (genteel or tacky) emerged in the cities. Music that emerged from the urban environment caused apprehension in Mexico. "From the city are the songs of the scoundrel: in them there is mention of jail, of vices, of the mother who kneels before her son while begging for forgiveness," wrote a critic.[41]

Since the early twentieth century, composers such as Miguel Lerdo de Tejada had incorporated romantic themes in music, yet the major difference between this and trends in the late 1920s and early 1930 was the introduction of Cuban themes and melodies, most important through the bolero. Imported from Cuba in the late nineteenth century, the bolero circulated in the Yucatán Peninsula and the state of Veracruz before arriving in Mexico City. There, it was popularized by the emergence of the composer, poet, singer Agustín Lara after he made his first public appearance in 1928. Lara presented the bolero "in a very personal way," through song lyrics that gave reference to deep expressions of love, loss, regret, and passion.[42] Generally, boleros were straightforward, less individualistic, and patriotic than the canción mexicana and included feelings of loss, regret and desire.[43] For example, their lyrics were forthright, including phrases such as "Let me seduce her," as opposed to "Seduce her, sir."[44] Because they adopted this different method and their words provoked emotions that men and women were not supposed to feel, this genre, and its producers, was not included within the canon of popular music by the fathers of Mexican music, such as Manuel M. Ponce. In fact, in the late 1930s, Ponce considered the lyrics of boleros to come from "degenerates" since the rhythms and words followed those themes. He did note the songs were escape valves for many housewives.[45]

In general, song writers who were labeled cursi and wrote boleros had a "sentimental spirit" and took refuge in personal feelings. For much of the 1930s and 1940s, the emotions expressed in boleros came directly from the personal experiences of the composers. Lara, in particular, because he chose not to interpret an authentic, popular spirit, was labeled cursi and even antinationalist. Common themes in his songs were love, jealousy, and resentment. "In his good songs Lara responds to a deep sentimental spirit," wrote an observer. "His success emanates from that, because our *pueblo es todo sentimiento* (the Mexican people are nothing but feelings)."[46] At times, there were social ramifications for composing cursi music. Composers were often blamed for producing song lyrics that aroused people's feelings and made them behave in certain ways. In the spring of 1937, for instance, Ernesto Cortázar, who wrote the lyrics to "Tu ya no soplas" (You don't cut it anymore / You can't fulfill me), was publicly critiqued when the song reportedly caused suicides and duels between lovers.[47]

The emotions awakened by boleros clashed with the conservative values of society. Once labeled "the singer of vices," Lara composed a style of music based on sexuality.[48] His rapid rise to fame in the 1930s, according to some, was due to these sexual lyrics that had no edifying character to them.[49] Critics believed that Lara recognized the potential of the female market and made an effort to appeal to them. His songs, so some critics said, gave words to the "sinful vibrant desire of innocent virgins."[50] Lara's song lyrics provided a voice, according to others, for the modern urban woman and "helped . . . to liberate her body from the corset and confessional." Nevertheless, while Lara challenged women to think about their own sensuality and made pleasure a socially tolerable subject, his music followed misogynistic traditions.[51] These boleros and other cursi music easily found their way to the airwaves during the 1920s and early 1930s.

"Now Broadcasting: Live *Cursilería*"

With the success of radio, theaters became places featuring live theatrical performances, the screening of a film, performing of a comedy sketch, or broadcasting of a live radio program. During the 1930s and 1940s, the radio studios of stations XEW, XEB, or XEQ, among others, were spaces where the urban population visited to witness a live musical performance by their favorite singer, composer, or film star. Men and women from different social backgrounds could walk the streets of Mexico City, enter a radio studio, and come face to face with the people behind the voices they heard daily on their home receivers. One option was to visit XEW's legendary studio on *Avenida Ayuntamiento*.[52] To ensure studio seats were occupied, downtown Mexico City stations scheduled live programs "at the time that the '*muchachas*' would accompany the '*señoras*' to the San Juan market," for their daily shopping. (In this context, muchachas refers to maids or servants and señoras to their employers, the women of the household in which they worked).[53] For years, a fan would see and hear their favorite singer for the first time during a live broadcast.

Live radio programs created new opportunities for the public. This experience was new, exhilarating, and unforgettable. Even though radio programs could not rely on audience interaction like popular theater, as on many occasions audience members had to remain silent, they still transformed how people received and related to music. As soon as they stepped inside the studios, radio listeners became audience members. For some, it was disheartening to see that the voice of the "invisible artist" actually belonged to an ordinary person. Yet to others, young women especially, seeing a famous male artist in person or listening to his voice over the air sparked unprecedented and sometimes hysterical behavior.

This occurred, for instance, when Agustín Lara took the stage in the capital city during the 1930s. "Minutes before 10 p.m., there is not one romantic young woman . . . restless and adventurous young man, or a single lady . . . who does not tune in their radio to the hour of Agustín Lara," wrote a radio critic. At 10 p.m. every Tuesday, Thursday, and Saturday evenings during the 1930s, XEW transmitted "La Hora Íntima de Agustín Lara" (The intimate hour of Agustín Lara), a live radio program in which the legendary figure sat before his piano for several hours. Drawing from his vast repertoire of romantic and evocative songs, he dedicated special numbers to audience members and radio listeners, who often fainted when they heard the voice of Lara mention somebody's real name, often in the following way: "This song of mine, like a bouquet of roses, I place before the diminutive feet of the beautiful Josefina Garza of Monterrey!"[54] A live program such as Lara's, as one commentator observed, also served an important social function as it shifted family recreation to the family instead of the cinema or some other public center.[55]

At first, live radio programs were successful because they combined already known artistic talent with a new space where new entertainment styles and stars could be discovered. Additionally, the public did not have to purchase tickets, as with the theater; instead, they had to wait in line before programs for free passes. Commercial radio stations, during the 1930s and 1940s, thrived thanks to live radio programs. These stations created two listening audiences: one at home and the other in the studio. Yet forces outside of innovations in broadcasting contributed to the lack of patriotic tunes over the airwaves before the mid-1930s. Remarkably, these were associated directly with the way the government utilized radio.

Government Oversight

Between 1920 and 1934 the airwaves carried a limited amount of patriotic music because, at the time, the government was more interested in using popular music to project a positive image of the nation abroad. During the 1920s, once most of the violence associated with the Revolution subsided, revolutionary leaders began to focus attention to what was occurring outside of its borders, especially in the United States. A group of intellectuals and artists believed it was urgent to expose the factual and pure manifestations of art, culture, and music to US audiences, who were being shown a distorted view of the nation through the press, cinema, and the theater. These leaders turned to programing to provide a better view of their reforms abroad.[56] This effort specifically used music to change the opinions that US officials and citizens had about Mexicans and their culture.

At the time, Mexican music was recognizable across the globe. Since the 1910s composers exposed the world to Mexican music in orchestra halls and auditoriums in Europe and North America. The composer Manuel M. Ponce's song "Estrellita," for instance, was played in auditoriums in the United States while Alfonso Esparza Oteo's music "Un Viejo Amor" was translated into four languages. Juventino Rosas was another musician whose waltz "Sobre las olas" is one of the most famous Latin American pieces in the world. Archival records prove that this was, in fact, a familiar number. In the spring of 1931, from his home in Cincinnati, Ohio, Rudolph Kuré wrote a letter to Mexican radio station XFX declaring that he had used his short-wave receiver to tune in to a program where "a Spanish tenor sang the beautiful Mexican waltz entitled 'over the waves.'"[57]

Spreading positive images in the United States was necessary during the 1920s because negative images of its southern neighbor appeared in the US press. Noted painter and film director Adolfo Best Maugard, after visiting the United States in 1925, believed that Mexico urgently needed to publicize its traditions and art.[58] The mass and entertainment media in the United States continued to use stereotypes of Mexico.[59] As one listener wrote from New Jersey to Mexican radio station XFX in 1929, "Speak of Mexicans or Mexico and immediately people think of Indians or bandits."[60] Furthermore, the government could not always depend on performers to do their part in showcasing the best attributes of Mexico, as not all of them supported the government's project or wanted to showcase Mexico in a positive way. Abroad, some Mexican actors and singers (including exiles) disregarded how their actions might tarnish the national image.

A practical way both the government and the cultural elite could influence public opinion was to send musical groups abroad, a practice that took place before the arrival of broadcast media. The first musical ensemble on record to cross Mexico's northern border on tour was a military band led by José Encarnación Payén, who traveled to an exposition in New Orleans in 1885.[61] In the early twentieth century, the government sponsored overseas trips of a number of theater actresses and concert singers, including Esperanza Iris, Mexico's foremost "cultural ambassador," and Fanny Anitua, a mezzo-soprano who was regarded as "Mexico's spiritual ambassador." Through the Ministry of Public Education, the government funded the tours of artists in the 1920s.[62] On some occasions, the cost for the tours of trios, orchestras, and classical music performers came out of the pockets of government officials. In 1925, when he served as governor of the state of Tamaulipas before becoming president, Emilio Portes Gil extended economic and moral support to the musical ensemble Los Trovadores Tamaultipecos. With the financial help of Portes Gil, Los Trovadores traveled to New York City where they performed on Broadway and in other area theaters before returning in 1928.[63]

By the following decade, even when these trips included performers deemed "unpatriotic" by some, they were considered important ways to boost nationalism. This was the case in 1932, when Agustin Lara and his company toured the state of Texas. In their stopover in San Antonio, the Mexican Consul, Eduardo Hernández Cházaro, noted that he was pleased to have Lara and his troupe visiting; in particular, he was grateful that they had chosen to visit "this country on a cultural tour *hacienda labor Pro-patria*."[64]

Over the airwaves, Mexico could project a positive image through music. The territorial span covered by radio broadcasts and the endless possibility of transmissions persuaded the government to look to the industry as an agent that spread national culture and folklore abroad, and especially in the

United States. During the 1920s and 1930s, government ministries, such as the *Secretaría de Relaciones Exteriores* (Ministry of Foreign Relations), collaborated with consulate offices in cities throughout the United States to ensure folklore and music circulated abroad via radio. After attending a concert on December 5, 1935, by the Mexico City Police Band in Laredo, Texas, the migration delegate of Nuevo Laredo, Tamaulipas, Mexico, reported that musical performance was the best way to remember the nation.[65]

The Ministry of Public Education, through XFX, participated in this effort. The director of radio operations, Maria Luisa Ross, stated in the station's 1927 annual report, "Especially in the United States, listening to our music and conferences has awakened an interest to know us better. The radio department frequently receives requests for pamphlets, magazines, photographs, in general, all kinds of publications that can illustrate our way of life, our customs and the evolution of our national spirit."[66] Letters from listeners of XFX demonstrated the influence of the music and events, such as the nation's annual November 20 commemoration of the anniversary of the revolution with its parade, civic ceremonies, and a speech given by the president. In 1931, XFX, along with XEW and XET of Monterrey, transmitted the presidential address and the concert that followed throughout Mexico and the United States. That night, under the direction of Carlos Chavez, the National Symphony gave a concert at the Arbeu Theater in downtown Mexico City. The concert, and the radio broadcasts that accompanied it, were a huge success. Audience responses to this broadcast arrived in the radio office from New Orleans, Laredo, St. Louis, and even Chicago. "A true work of art," wrote one listener, "it gives great pleasure and satisfaction to us Mexicans living outside of the homeland that our country can count on such a great orchestra as the National Symphonic Orchestra. I can assure you . . . that neither the Philharmonic of New York nor the Philadelphia Symphony can supersede it and I have listened to them perform the same numbers."[67] Mr. A. C. de Laurel of Laredo, Texas, wrote, "The educational worth of this work is highly important for lovers of good music, and thanks to the wondrous power of radio it is possible for all of us who do not reside in the capital city to have the privilege of delighting ourselves with the concerts of the symphonic orchestra."[68]

Thus, during the 1920s and early 1930s, the Mexican government used its own radio stations to transmit music abroad. They failed to connect with people in Mexico through music because of their own shortcomings: the concern to use music to bolster Mexico's image abroad and the short-sighted radio project, which used broadcast media not as a weapon for national unity but mostly as an apparatus for instruction. The music that radio absorbed before 1934 was cursi, sometimes lewd, and never the reflection of the cultural project of the Revolution.

Conclusion

After receiving economic and political support from a more stable national government, Mexican canciones evolved and developed clearly and identifiably as nationalist.[69] Yet this music was not featured over the radio before the mid-1930s. While the canción mexicana became "a fundamental component of the feelings and imaginary nationalism that inhabited the official cultural discourse," it did not appear over the radio because at the time the government was preoccupied with other features and potentials of radio; namely, using the medium for education within Mexico and shaping public opinions about Mexico abroad.[70]

Media mogul Emilio Azcárraga once said, "The pueblo . . . will not become educated through radio, because they regard it only as entertainment."[71] Azcárraga, who embodied the quintessential example of the "cordial relationship" that the telecommunications industry enjoyed with the government, homed in on an important aspect of radio broadcasting history.[72] Despite receiving the direct support of the government, state-sponsored radio stations were unable to promote national unity through music. Years later, when XEW inaugurated their new studios on Avenida Juárez in Mexico City, neither the public nor prominent critics in the press complained that the national anthem was followed by Agustín Lara's highly provocative song, "Cada noche un amor" (Each night a new lover) in the studio's first broadcast.[73]

Notes

1. *El Universal Ilustrado*, November 14, 1935, 10.
2. Ricardo Pérez Montfort, *Expresiones Populares y Estereotipos Culturales en México. Siglos XIX y XX. Diez Ensayos* (México, DF: CIESAS y Casa Chata, 2007), 97–98.
3. Vicente T. Mendoza, *El Corrido Mexicano* (Mexico City: Fondo de Cultura

Económica, 1992); Rubén M. Campos, *El folklore y la música Mexicana. Investigación acerca de la cultura musical en México (1525–1925)* (Mexico City: Talleres Gráficos de la Nación, 1928); Yvette Jiménez de Báez, *Lenguajes de la tradición popular fiesta, canto, música y representación* (Mexico City: El Colegio de México, Centro de Estudios Lingüísticos y Literarios, Seminario de Tradiciones Populares, 2002).

4. Juan S. Garrido, *Historia De La Música Popular En México, 1896–1973* (México, DF: Editorial Extemporáneos, 1974), 189.

5. Ibid., 105.

6. For an overview, see Jesús Jáuregui, *El mariachi: símbolo musical de México* (México, DF: Instituto Nacional de Antropología e Historia, 2007).

7. Carlos Monsiváis, "Yo soy humilde cancionero (de la música popular en México)," in *La música en México Panorama del siglo XX*, ed. Aurelio Tello (México, DF: Fondo de Cultura Económica, Consejo Nacional para la Cultura y Las Artes, 2010), 234.

8. María del Carmen de la Peza Casares, *El bolero y la educación sentimental en México* (México, DF: Universidad Autónoma Metropolitana-Xochimilco, 2001), 69–70.

9. Nicolás García Cárdenas, *La reconstrucción del Estado Mexicano en los años sonorenses (1920–1935)* (Mexico City: Universidad Autónoma Metropolitana, 1992), 126.

10. Gilbert M. Joseph and Daniel Nugent, *Everyday Forms of State Formation: Revolution and the Negotiation of Rule in Modern Mexico* (Durham, NC: Duke University Press, 1997); William H. Beezley, Cheryl English Martin, and William E. French, eds., *Rituals of Rule, Rituals of Resistance: Public Celebrations and Popular Culture in Mexico* (Wilmington, DE: Scholarly Resources, 1994); Jeffrey W. Rubin, *Decentering the Regime: Ethnicity, Radicalism, and Democracy in Juchitán, Mexico* (Durham, NC: Duke University Press, 1997); Alan Knight, "Cardenismo: Juggernaut or Jalopy?" *Journal of Latin American Studies* 26, no. 1 (February 1994), 73–107; Mary Kay Vaughan, *Cultural Politics in Revolution: Teachers, Peasants, and Schools in Mexico, 1930–1940* (Tucson: University of Arizona Press, 1997).

11. Erik Velásquez García et al., *Nueva historia general de México* (Mexico City: Colegio de México, 2010), 592.

12. Mary Kay Vaughan and Steven E. Lewis, eds., *The Eagle and the Virgin: National and Cultural Revolution in Mexico, 1920–1940* (Durham, NC: Duke University Press, 2006); Gilbert M. Joseph, Catherine LeGrand, and Ricardo D. Salvatore, eds., *Close Encounters of Empire: Writing the Cultural History of U.S.–Latin American Relations* (Durham, NC: Duke University Press, 1998);

Helen Delpar, *The Enormous Vogue of Things Mexican: Cultural Relations Between the United States and Mexico, 1910–1935* (Tuscaloosa: University of Alabama Press, 1992); and Gilbert M. Joseph, Anne Rubenstein, and Eric Zolov, eds., *Fragments of a Golden Age: The Politics of Culture in Mexico Since 1940* (Durham, NC: Duke University Press, 2001); Rick Anthony López, *Crafting Mexico: Intellectuals, Artisans, and the State after the Revolution* (Durham, NC: Duke University Press, 2010); Mary K. Coffey, *How a Revolutionary Art Became Official Culture: Murals, Museums, and the Mexican State* (Durham, NC: Duke University Press, 2012).

13. Juan S. Garrido, *Historia de la música popular en México, 1896–1973* (México, DF: Editorial Extemporáneos, 1974); Ricardo Pérez Montfort, *Estampas de nacionalismo popular mexicano: ensayos sobre cultura popular y nacionalismo* (Mexico City: CIESAS, 1994); and *Expresiones populares y estereotipos culturales en México. Siglos XIX y XX. Diez Ensayos* (Mexico City: CIESAS y Casa Chata, 2007); Claes af Geijerstam, *Popular Music in Mexico* (Albuquerque: University of New Mexico Press, 1976); Yolanda Moreno Rivas, *Historia de la música popular mexicana* (Mexico City: Editorial Océano, 2008); Alejandro L. Madrid, *Music in Mexico: Experiencing Music, Expressing Culture* (New York: Oxford University Press, 2013).

14. Jorge Mejía Prieto, *Historia de la radio y la televisión en México* (Mexico City: Colección México vivo, O. Colmenares, 1972); Fernando Mejía Barquera, *La industria de la radio y la televisión y la política del estado mexicano* (Mexico City: Fundación Manuel Buendía, 1989); Gabriel Sosa Plata, *Las mil y una radios: una historia, un análisis actual de la radiodifusión Mexicana* (Mexico City: McGraw-Hill, 1997); Ángel Miquel, *Disolvencias: literatura, cine y radio en México (1900–1950)* (Mexico City: Fondo de Cultura Económica, 2005); Fátima Fernández Christlieb, *La radio mexicana: centro y regiones* (Mexico City: J. Pablos Editor, 1991); Juan Leyva, *Política educativa y comunicación social: la radio en México, 1940–1946* (Mexico City: Universidad Nacional Autónoma de México, 1992); Pavel Granados, *XEW: 70 anos en el aire* (Mexico City: Editorial Clío, 2000); Elizabeth Joy Hayes, *Radio Nation: Communication, Popular Culture, and Nationalism in Mexico, 1920–1950* (Tucson: University of Arizona Press, 2000); and "National Imaginings on the Air: Radio in Mexico, 1920–1950," in *The Eagle and the Virgin: Nation and Cultural Revolution in Mexico, 1920–1940*, eds. Mary Kay Vaughan and Stephen E. Lewis (Durham, NC: Duke University Press, 2006), 243–55.

15. Elizabeth Joy Hayes, *Radio Nation: Communication, Popular Culture, and Nationalism in Mexico, 1920–1950* (Tucson: University of Arizona Press, 2000), xi.

16. See Walter Benjamin, Michael William Jennings, Brigid Doherty, Thomas Y. Levin, and E. F. N. Jephcott, *The Work of Art in the Age of Its Technological*

Reproducibility, and Other Writings on Media (Cambridge, MA: Belknap Press of Harvard University Press, 2008).

17. Elizabeth Joy Hayes, *Radio Nation: Communication, Popular Culture, and Nationalism in Mexico, 1920–1950* (Tucson: University of Arizona Press, 2000), 23.

18. Jorge Mejía Prieto, *Historia de la radio y la televisión en México*, 49.

19. Roberto Ornelas Herrera, "Radio y Cotidianidad en México (1900–1930)," in *Historia de la vida cotidiana en México*. Tomo V. Volumen 1. Siglo XX. Campo y Ciudad, ed. Aurelio de los Reyes (México, DF: Fondo de Cultura Económica, 2005), 154.

20. Yolanda Moreno Rivas, *Historia de la música popular Mexicana* (México, DF: Editorial Océano, 2008), 71.

21. *El Universal Ilustrado*, February 18, 1937.

22. Years later, Vargas became one of the most popular singers in Mexico, having had a personal relationship with every president in Mexico since the 1920s and traveling the world, singing over the radio and recording boleros, rancheras, and other popular music. José Ramón Garmabella, *Pedro Vargas: Una vez nada más* (México, DF: Ediciones de Comunicación, 1985), 28. For example, he performed during the Colombian national civic holidays in July 1940 in Bogotá's Teatro Colombina.

23. Fideicomiso Archivo de Plutarco Elías Calles y Fernando Torreblanca. Ex. 18 Inv. 63.

24. *El País de las Tandas. Teatro de Revista 1900–1940* (México DF: Consejo Nacional para la Cultura y las Artes, Dirección General de Culturas Populares é Indígenas, 1984), 93.

25. *El Universal Ilustrado*, August 16, 1924.

26. CYB later became XEB, "La B Grande de México," which is still in operation today. *El Universal Ilustrado* (Mexico City), May 24, 1923.

27. *El Universal Ilustrado*, May 24, 1923.

28. *El Universal Ilustrado*, June 1924.

29. Mejía Prieto, *Historia de la radio y la televisión en México*, 26.

30. *El Demócrata*, November 30, 1923, 5.

31. Archivo Histórico de la Secretaría de Educación Pública (Hereafter AHSEP), Expediente A-4/235.3(73).

32. Rubén M. Campos, *El folklore y la música Mexicana*, 154.

33. In compliance with the National Radio Congress taking place in Washington, DC, in 1927, in September 1928 the station was assigned the signals XFX. By 1936 the station broadcast as XEXM, long wave, and XEXA, short wave.

34. Fernando Curiel, *La telaraña magnética y otros estudios radiofónicos* (México, DF: Ediciones Coyoacán S. A. de C.V.), 306.

35. *El Universal Ilustrado*, March 6, 1927, 10.

36. Archivo General de la Nación, Fondo Secretaría de Comunicaciones y Obras Públicas (Hereafter AGN, SCOP), Expediente 22/131.6 (725.1)149. For more on women and SEP radio, see Ageeth Sluis, "Revolution and the Rhetoric of Representation: Gender Construction in Mexican Radio and Cinema, 1920–1940," (Master's Thesis, University of Wyoming, 1997).

37. AHSEP, Expediente A-4/235.3(73), Carta, 23 de marzo de 1930.

38. AHSEP, Expediente 135.2/146, Informe Presidencial Memoria Anual. Informe de las labores desarrolladas en esta Ofna. Radiocultural del 1/o de agosto de 1931 al 31 de julio de 1932.

39. *El País de las Tandas. Teatro de Revista 1900–1940* (Coyoacán, México: Museo Nacional de Culturas Populares, Dirección General de Culturas Populares, 1986), 112.

40. Ibid., 111.

41. *El Universal Ilustrado*, March 12, 1925.

42. Juan S. Garrido, *Historia De La Música Popular En México, 1896–1973*, 65.

43. Songs followed the model of Mexican popular music, but the lyrics were more direct. Because they adopted this different method and their music spoke of emotions that men and women were not supposed to feel, at first this genre, and its producers, was not included within the canon of "popular" music by the fathers of Mexican music, such as Manuel M. Ponce. *La Prensa*, March 15, 1936, 3, 8.

44. *El Universal Ilustrado*, July 7, 1932, 30, 41.

45. *La Prensa* (San Antonio), March 15, 1936, 3, 8.

46. *El Universal Ilustrado*, June 15, 1932.

47. *La Prensa*, July 4, 1937, 2.

48. *El Universal Ilustrado*, June 15, 1932.

49. *La Prensa*, July 4, 1937, 2.

50. *El Universal Ilustrado*, June 9, 1932.

51. Mary Kay Vaughan and Marco Velázquez, "*Mestizaje* and Musical Nationalism in Mexico," in *The Eagle and the Virgin: Nation and Cultural Revolution in Mexico, 1920–1940*, eds. Mary Kay Vaughan and Stephen E. Lewis (Durham, NC: Duke University Press, 2006), 109.

52. *Avenida San Juan de Letrán* (today Eje Lázaro Cárdenas) was the principle thoroughfare for cultural and artistic activity in Mexico City during the 1930s and 1940s. Until 1937, when the Ministry of Communications and Public Works ordered radio stations to leave the city center, all radio activity was concentrated along the avenues surrounding the *Centro Historico*, the historic downtown district.

53. Bertha Zacatecas, *Vidas en el aire. Pioneros de la radio en México* (Mexico City: Editorial Diana, 1996), 29.

54. *El Universal Ilustrado*, February 22, 1934.

55. *El Universal Ilustrado*, June 15, 1932.

56. *El Universal Ilustrado*, November 5, 1925.

57. AHSEP, Expediente A-4/235.3(73).

58. *El Universal Ilustrado*, April 23, 1925.

59. Helen Delpar, *The Enormous Vogue of Things Mexican: Cultural Relations Between the United States and Mexico, 1910–1935* (Tuscaloosa: University of Alabama Press, 1992), 165.

60. AHSEP, Expediente A-4/235.3(73).

61. Rubén M. Campos, *El folklore y la música Mexicana*, 202.

62. *El Universal Ilustrado*, June 7, 1923. In late March 1922, for example, Isabel Zenteno sent a letter to President Alvaro Obregón, hoping that her life as an artist would be funded by the government. Archivo General de la Nación (AGN), Ramo Gobernación, Fondo Dirección General de Gobierno (DGG), Expediente 805-Z-13.

63. *El Universal Ilustrado*, December 26, 1929; Juan S. Garrido, *Historia de la música popular en México*, 63.

64. AHGE, SRE, IV-376–48.

65. Archivo General de la Nación (AGN), Ramo Presidentes, Fondo Lázaro Cárdenas del Rio (LCR), Expediente 135.2/146, Caja 102.

66. *Boletín de la SEP* 6, no. 12 (1927), 308.

67. AHSEP, Caja 8, Exp. A-4/253.3 (73).

68. Ibid.

69. Erik Velásquez García et al., *Nueva historia general de México* (Mexico City: Colegio de México, 2010), 590.

70. Pérez Montfort, *Expresiones populares y estereotipos culturales en México*, 97–98.

71. *La Prensa*, May 1, 1938, 8.

72. Hayes, *Radio Nation*, 78–79.

73. *Radiolandia*, June 22, 1942.

CHAPTER 3

Guatemalan National Identity and Popular Music

William H. Beezley

Guatemala's musical cultural identity developed through three dimensions in the nineteenth and, especially, early in the twentieth centuries. The themes included the rise and promotion of the music of the marimba, which was recognized as the national instrument; classical, including religious, music; and operas and dramas influenced by indigenous traditions.

The marimba was introduced perhaps as early as the 1550s by West Africans brought as slaves by the Spaniards. Mention of the instrument appears in colonial accounts for Antigua, and later it received distinctive development in 1894 in the community of Xelaju, or Quetzaltenago, as it is now formally known. Previously restricted to the diatonic scale, composer Julián Paniagua Martínez and marimba builder Sebastián Hurtado developed it as a chromatic instrument, capable of playing melodies. To the diatonic row of sound bars, comparable to the white keys of the piano, the two men added a second-row equivalent to the black keys. Marimba players quickly adopted much of the fashionable repertoire of salon and poplar music. As a result, this light music—with catchy melodies, sentimental harmonies, and dance rhythms—became the signature of the instrument, disseminated at home and abroad by the countless marimba bands formed at the beginning of the twentieth century. For festive occasions or casual listening, the marimba captured popular sentiments like no other music. Much of this early music remains alive in the memorized repertoire of present-day groups. Composers such as Domingo Bethancourt (1906–1982) and others wrote dance pieces, and singer Paco Pérez (1917–1951) achieved fame with his waltz "Luna de Xelajú," one of best-known marimba pieces that quickly became regarded by many Guatemalans as a sort of unofficial national anthem. It expressed the nation's identity because, it was said, it drew on the African, indigenous, and Ladino (creole) roots of the nation's colonial past.[1]

Album cover for *Guatemalan Marimbas!*

Other trends also developed in the nineteenth century other than the chromatic marimba and its music. These included the introduction of opera, the training abroad of pianist-composers and in country with the influence of military band music, and a growing interest in indigenous-influenced music. Piano music received promotion by scholarships for talented musicians to study in Italy and France. In Europe young scholarship pianist-composers, such as Luis Felipe Arias (1876–1908), and Herculano Alvarado (1879–1921), among others, studied and then returned to introduce Beethoven, Chopin, and Liszt, composers never heard before in Guatemala. The European-trained pianists also had considerable influence on younger composers such as Rafael Vásquez (1885–1941), Alfredo Wyld (1883–1947), and Jesús Castillo (1877–1946), who flourished during the first decades of the twentieth century.

Within the country, other composers received instruction from the Prussian conductor and bandmaster Emil Dressner. Individuals such as Germán Alcántara (1856–1911), Rafael Álvarez Ovalle (1855–1946), Manuel Moraga (1833–1896), Julián Paniagua Martínez (1856–1946), and Fabián Rodríguez (1862–1929) contributed salon pieces, military music, and opera fantasies.

Opera had come to Guatemala through the efforts of composer Benedicto Sáenz and his brother Anselmo, who presented Italian operas in 1843. Following initial failures, they achieved enough success that they took the lead in the construction of the National Theater, later called the Teatro Colón. The promoters continued to offer performances of Italian or European style programs before the 1920s as opera and religious music took prominence.

The opera *Quiché Vinak*, written by Jesús Castillo, changed that. At the end of the nineteenth century and in the first part of the twentieth century, the development of cultural nationalism received a dramatic dimension, especially through music; several composers turned to Maya legends and folk music, on which they based their compositions. Their efforts formed part of the movement in Latin America to write operas expressing historical and nationalistic themes to celebrate cultural identity. Other such operas included Antonio Carlos Gomes, *Il Guarany* (Brazil, 1870), Aniceto Ortega, *el Guatimotzin* (Mexico, 1871), Ricardo Castro, *Atzimba* (Mexico, 1896), Pascual de Rogatis, *Huémac* (Argentina, 1916), and José María Valle Riestra, *Ollanta y Atahualpa* (Peru, 1921). The folk music that formed part of Guatemala's cultural nationality drew on the musical experience of the indigenous people and the Spanish effort to convert them, especially through the use of music, to Christianity. The missionaries organized *autos sacramentales* or *misterios*, the popular religious dramatic performances popular during the medieval period in Spain,[2] that included music and dancing to teach conversion, explain the sacraments, and to demonstrate Christian life. Of the dances, the jota especially was presented throughout the colonial era and it was incorporated into these performances. Despite local names, the music and dances recalled their Spanish origin, for example, the jota from Extremadura.[3]

Quiché Vinak had its origin in 1917, when Virgilio Rodríguez Beteta wrote the text that served as the libretto based on Mayan folklore and suggested that Jesús Castillo, drawing on his indigenous musical research, write the first national opera. Castillo accepted. He noted later in his autobiography that the Maya-Quiché music he had collected was not totally indigenous music, because it had been influenced by Spanish-Moorish melodies introduced by the conquistadors. His effort received encouragement when the members of La sociedad de geografía é historia de Guatemala (The Geographic and Historical Society of Guatemala) requested that Rodríguez arrange a performance of vernacular music as part of an evening entertainment during the society's annual meeting.

Quiché Vinak, the nation's first opera, premiered for residents of Guatemala City, as part of the four hundredth anniversary of the founding of their city, on July 25, 1924. Performed at the Teatro Abril, *Quiché Vinak* or The Quiche People, portrayed indigenous life on the eve of the Spanish invasion, using indigenous legends, music, and scenes. The Geographic and History Society sponsored the opera that brought together outstanding musicians. Jesús Castillo composed the music, using melodies and rhythms taken from Quiché and Mam music he had collected during his investigations in the department of Quetzaltenango, and composer Fabián Rodríguez arranged the orchestration for sixty musicians. Leading singers took the roles of folkloric indigenous characters. Clara Andreu portrayed Alitza; Augusto Monterroso played Amalchi; and Francisco Brewer played the role of the Brujo coyote. Manuel Pinto directed a chorus that included ten principal priests. Choreographer Elisa Padilla and Franciso Cordón supervised dozens of dances. The opera was not completely finished before its first performance; nevertheless, it was proclaimed a success.

The opera, in three acts, performed a prophetic legend of Quiché-Maya life on the eve of the arrival of the Spanish conquistadors in 1524. It opens as Quiché high priests prepare to sacrifice the Kaqchikel princess Alitza to stop the gods from destroying the world through famine, disease, and earthquakes. At the last possible moment, the Quiché Prince, Amalchi, who possesses powers of magic, flies down, frees her, and they fly away to safety in the mountains. The priests, fearing even more the wrath of the gods, select one of their number to find the couple and recapture the princess. The appointed priest, after transforming himself into a coyote, goes into the forest and finds the two, who had by this time fallen in love. The coyote priest, using potent incense, places them into a deep sleep and strips the prince of his magical powers. He returns the couple to the central plaza to be burned at the stake as a sacrifice to the gods. As the flames consume them, the two swear eternal love to each other. The agony caused by the flames gives them the power of divination and they predict the destruction of the Quiché by the Sons of the Sun. At that moment, fulfilling the prophecy of Armageddon, Spaniards, with the sun reflecting in their armor and helmets arrive on horses to conquer the Maya.

As recognition of Castillo's work on the opera, the French consul-general arranged for his government to honor the composer with the Palmas Académicas at the opera's premier. The performance at the society's meeting so impressed the Mexican Minister Juan de Díos Bojórquez that he arranged an invitation for Castillo to visit Mexico City, where he could make an analysis of the structural differences between the music of the Maya-Quiché and of the Aztecs. Unfortunately for Castillo when he arrived in December 1923, the De la Huerta Rebellion had broken out and he could not complete his study.[4]

Once the opera was fully completed in 1925, Castillo almost immediately received requests from the Pan American Union for sheet music selections that could be played by the US Army Band in Washington, DC. The band, according to Castillo, played his compositions both going and coming on the voyage of the US delegation to the 1930 World's Fair in Seville, Spain. The Pan American Union published several of his pieces in its bulletin, and this resulted in further requests to publish pieces elsewhere in Mexico, Guatemala, and in the United States for the Pan American Union series American Capitals. He also received inquiries from several organizations for his music, including the Institute for Intellectual Cooperation of the League of Nations, headed by Gabriela Mistral. The Fleisher Collection of Orchestral Music in the Free Library of Philadelphia also asked for his music. It now preserves conductor scores and instrumental parts for two excerpts from this opera (the library possesses neither an audio recording of the complete opera nor any portion of it).[5]

Castillo's success with *Quiché Vinak* showed the possibilities of collecting and using numerous folk tunes in new compositions. He further incorporated them in other overtures and symphonic poems. His half-brother Ricardo Castillo (1891–1966), one of the musicians who studied in Paris and acquired impressionist and neoclassical techniques, also drew on indigenous folk melodies. Fusing contemporary art with Mayan mythology in both piano and orchestral music, he drew heavily from the legends and myths from the *Popol Vuh*. A later example, José Castañeda (1898–1983), adapted the Mayan past in his productions such as the ballet *La serpiente emplumada* (The feathered snake) that premiered in 1958.

The decade of the 1930s resulted in even greater attention to the cultural dimensions of Guatemala national identity, especially through music. Miguel Angel Asturias, who won the 1967 Nobel Prize for Literature, wrote his college thesis at the Universidad de San Carlos about the "Indian problem" (published in 1923); in 1925 he began a forty-year project to translate the Mayan sacred text, the *Popol Vuh*, into Spanish and moved to France where he studied ethnography at the Sorbonne. He also began writing and in 1930 published his first novel, *Leyendas de Guatemala*—a collection that explores Mayan myths from before the Spanish conquest and themes related to the development of national identity—shortly before returning to Guatemala. During the 1930s, in his political and cultural activities, he advocated *mestizaje*, as Vasconcelos was doing in Mexico, as the solution to national identity. His interest in the indigenous people resulted in what many consider his masterpiece, *Hombres de maíz* (Men of maize) (1949), an explication built on his extensive knowledge of Mayan beliefs with his political convictions. This work and his writings in general are identified with the social and moral aspirations of the people.

Of more immediate influence, in 1930, TGW, the Voice of Guatemala, the nation's first long wave radio station, began broadcasting as the nation's radio. The military dictatorship of Jorge Ubico used it in an effort to promote Guatemalan national identity, with programs such as "Chapinlandia" that featured marimba music and continued to so for several decades. The effort mirrored programs in several other Latin American countries.[6] The station provided for a major event in the efforts to recognize the indigenous features of national culture. From September 16 to 19, 1931, officials from the General Office of Electronic Communications and the Ministry of Development arranged to broadcast concerts of indigenous music, with the intention they would be heard in the United States and Mexico, considered a sister nation with an indigenous culture. More than 160 músicos vernáculos (musicians) came to perform the concerts. They stayed at the Capital City's Hipodromo del Norte for twenty days.

Ethnomusicologist and composer Jesús Castillo and the poet and composer Rogelio Galvez Valle used the opportunity to collect melodies, some of which they did not know. They obtained pieces from Purulha, Culan, Cuhulco, and other communities even though these areas did not meet their criteria to be considered completely indigenous. Nevertheless, Castillo believed they represented national music of what he called the era of interpolations—indigenous and Spanish-Moorish inflected music. The two men collected what they considered authentic examples of indigenous music from the Quiché area of Totonicapan (the department capital), the villages of Momostenango, Santa Maria Chiquimula, and San Andres Xecul; in the department of Quiché, its capital Santa Cruz, the town of Chichicastenango, and the community of Sacapulas; in the department of Quezaltenango, the settlements of Cantel and Almolonga; and in the department of Baja Verapaz, the village of Rabinal, the center of what they considered vernacular music. They also collected Man (an indigenous group) cultural music from the villages of Hitan, Cabrican, and other points that Castillo considered uncivilized from the Costa Cuca in the department of Quetzaltenango; from the department of Huehetenango, the zone of Santa Cruz Barillas and the meadows of Chancol. They also identified and collected two Lacandon songs. The radio broadcasts created extraordinary interest not only in Mexico and the United States but also in other Hispanic American nations, especially Cuba and Colombia.[7]

These radio broadcasts, World Fair's exhibits in New York in the 1930s, and additional popular displays of textiles created a good deal of interest in Guatemalan culture and handicrafts in the United States. Several enterprising US citizens, with some artistic skills, attempted to copy the textile designs. Macy's Department Store became involved, arranging for blatantly plagiarized cloth and selling the chic reproductions of the textile designs. Guatemalan government officials became so enraged they embarked on the effort, bizarre and ultimately misguided, to obtain a US patent for their indigenous textile designs in order to halt their reproduction.[8]

During the same period in the United States, the Works Progress Administration Music Copying Project was established at the Free Library (1934–1943) in Philadelphia. The collection's founder, Edwin Fleisher, sought unpublished manuscripts of orchestral works from contemporaneous composers from across the Americas in order to produce full performance sets (conductor's score with a complete set of parts). In 1938, Fleisher began concentrating efforts on Latin American works. In May 1940, Fleisher acquired a copy of "Preludio e Himno al Sol" through William Manger and the Pan American Union. In 1941, Fleisher pulled $10,000 out of pocket to sponsor personally Nicolas Slonimsky's trip to Latin America to acquire more scores. Slonimsky produced his book, *Music of Latin America*,[9] as a direct result of this trip. In April 1942, Jesús Castillo's brother, Ricardo, sent the score for "Una Danza" (A dance) to the Fleisher,[10] but he did not provide a complete score for *Quiché Vinak*.

These events did little to discuss ethnic issues in the country. Considered the national radio, TGW was a government broadcasting medium. During the October Revolution (1944–1954), the station achieved popularity and recognition for its live performances. TGW created imaginative national radio novellas, or soap operas. After the 1954 counter-revolution, the quality of the programing, focused on national life, declined as the station became the voice of the repressive government. This continued without change until the end of the 1970s. One effort to make the radio station the voice of the people rather than the government failed, and in the recent era of Alvaro Colom it reverted to control of the government, in this case as the president's ministry of communication, where it followed guidelines for the promotion of governmental image.[11]

Composers from this next generation, some of them Ricardo Castillo's and José Castañeda's students, profited from the teachings of Austrian composer Franz Ippisch, as they continued to focus on the autochthonous indigenous cultures. These composers would expand their stage, vocal, and instrumental works from Maya projects, and some developed an interest in Garifuna culture and music. Among these composers, Joaquín Orellana (b. 1930) has developed instruments derived from the marimba and other folk instruments that he uses in some of his compositions that deal with the social strife of present-day ethnic groups.

Among other former students, the Gandarias brothers recently have focused on electronic folk music and bird calls recorded on-site.[12] At the beginning of the twenty-first century, two multimedia works by contemporary composer Dieter Lehnhoff, *Memorias de un día remoto* (Memories of a distant day) and *Rituales nocturnos* (Night rituals), evoked the Mayan past, but in a contemporary style as the soundtrack to an imaginary film. The journey of the Garifuna to Central American shores is the subject of *Satuyé*, his opera in progress. Among the younger composers, several have written works in a variety of styles, often using traditional or free tonality in their compositions.

Guatemala's most famous performance remains the *Rabinal Achí*, the Maya theatrical play performed in Rabinal, Baja Verapaz. Under its original name,

Xajooj tun (Drum dance), this dynastic Maya drama has been performed by the Rabinal community since the fifteenth century, although some sources date it as early as the twelfth century. It remains a rare example of pre-Hispanic traditions. The performance comprises myths of origin and addresses popular and political subjects concerning the inhabitants of the Rabinal region, as it combines masked dancing, melodramatic theater, and indigenous music. The musicians play the tun, a wooden slit-drum of great antiquity, and two trumpet-like instruments or *shawms*. The tun player normally serves as both the stage and the music director, in charge of the production.

The drama continued, partly under Christian wraps and partly in private, until the middle of the nineteenth century. Since 1856, the drama has been publically known through the efforts of the brilliant Belgian cleric and ardent Indianist, Abbot Charles Etienne Brasseur de Bourbourg (1814–1874), who arrived in 1855. Brasseur had already developed a passion for pre-Colombian cultures, especially the Aztecs and the Maya. In 1848, he had gone to Mexico City and served as the chaplin of the French legation there for three years before returning to Paris to prepare for a trip to Nicaragua, San Salvador, and Guatemala. In 1857, he returned to France, then in the years 1859 and 1860, he visited the Isthmus of Tehuantepec, Chiapas, and also parts of Guatemala. In 1864, he became attached to the French scientific mission to Mexico, occupied by French troops, but political events there drove him briefly back to Guatemala in 1865 before he returned to Europe. Brasseur was, above all, an indefatigable student of indigenous cultures. During his journeys in Mexico and Central America he stayed with various Indian groups, and his frequent visits to Europe were made usually for the purpose of delving into archives for ethnographic, linguistic, and historic materials. He collected a large number of manuscripts and prints dating from both pre-Hispanic and colonial times in Central America, and he practiced his apostolic duties among the Indians for ethnographic purposes. His publications embrace the years from 1857 to 1871, and the value of these publications, if not unimpeachable, remains significant. His works suffer from the defects of too great an enthusiasm and too vivid a fancy, and his correspondence with the historian of the conquest, William H. Prescott, whom he personally knew, did not lessen these failings. Later on, he attempted to trace relationships between American peoples and Eastern civilizations and, as he advanced in years, the connection between the ancient Middle Eastern World and the Americas in pre-Columbian times. While not impossible, the connection he developed was, in his mind, absolutely certainty. His main works are *Histoire des nations civilisees du Mexique et de l'Amérique centrale* (Paris, 1857–1959, 4 vols.); *Voyage sur l'Isthme de Tehuantepec dans l'état de Chiapas et la République de Guatémala, 1859 et 1860* (Paris, 1861); *Popol Vuh, le Livre sacré des Quichés, &c.* (Paris, 1861); *Grammaire Quichée et le dramede Rabinal Achí* (Paris, 1862); *Quatre lettres sur le Mexique* (Paris, 1868); *Cartas para servir de introducción á la historia primitiva de las naciones civilizadas de la América setentrional* (Mexico, 1851); and *Relation des choses du Yucatán* (Paris, 1864). The latter work contains a translation of the manuscript by Bishop Landa that includes the so-called Maya characters. The significance of the following have not been established: *Monuments anciens du Mexique* (Palenque, etc., Paris, 1866); *Manuscrit Troano* (Paris, 1869–1870); and *Bibliothèque mexico-guatémalienne* (Paris, 1871).[13]

Brasseur learned in Rabinal from a servant that a friend, Bartolo Ziz, a member of a *cofradía* (religious brotherhood), could recite the lines of the long ancient story *Rabinal Achi* from beginning to end. The account aroused Brasseur's curiosity and he talked with Ziz, who told him he had learned the epic story from his father and that it had been preserved by word of mouth for untold generations. The Abbe prevailed upon Ziz and his friends to assist him in writing it down. According to his account, he and the informants met for twelve days, and he wrote down exactly what they dictated in Quiche. Then he immediately translated the drama into Spanish and French.

This drama narrates the rivalry of two Maya princes. It opens with the capture of the Quiche prince by the Rabinal prince after a bitter battle. The drama includes a group of characters representing Maya villages, especially Kajyub', the regional capital of the Rabinaleb', the people of Rabinal, in the fourteenth century, who appear on stage and perform the narrative. The four-act drama deals with conflict between two major political groups in the region, the Rabinaleb' and the K'iche' and their princes, the Rabinal Achí and the K'iche Achí. The other characters are the king of the Rabinaleb', Job'Toj, and his servant, Achij Mun; Ixoq Mun, who has both male and female traits; the green-feathered mother Uchuch Q'uq', Uchuch Raxon; and thirteen eagles and thirteen jaguars who represent the warriors of the fortress of Kajyub'. The Rabinaleb' capture K'iche' Achí and place him on trial, charging he had attempted to steal the Rabinal children, a grave violation of Maya law. They trade mutual recriminations and the drama finally ends with the sacrifice of the Quiche prince. Typical of pre-Hispanic civilizations, while in a year-long detention, the royal prisoner was showered with luxury and privileges. Only his request for the Rabinal's wife was turned down. The drama consists of long speeches (probably chanted) by the major characters, enhanced by mime, song, dance, and music.

Not content with the *Rabinal Achi* as narrative, Brasseur wanted an actual performance, but leaders of the community hesitated because they worried about performing a non-Christian work that had been largely hidden so long from authorities. Brasseur devised a plan to bring his project to fruition: he quickly memorized part of the text, called the elders together, and recited the lines to them. Completely astonished by this feat, the elders gave in. Brasseur paid all the expenses for the performance, including costumes, music, and masks. The Abbe also had a Christian purpose in mind. The day before the performance, he called the community together to hear his benediction. According to his own recollections, as he made his entrance the war cry reverberated through the nave of the church; the sound of drums and trumpets filled the air, and the dancers executed the initial dance with great dignity. As the performers passed before him, bowing in the ancient manner, Brasseur made the sign of the cross over them. This was to remind them that they were Christians and that the Maya past was over. Although the *Rabinal Achi* has nothing to do with Christianity, Brasseur did what Catholic priests have done since their arrival in the America; he used a pre-Hispanic ceremony to honor a Christian saint.

The next day St. Paul's Day (San Pablo), the members of the cofradia and the community performed the drama in its entirety. The Abbe, seated on a raised platform, presided above the crowd. There were twenty-six performers, men and women, with substitute actors, directors, and musicians. Brasseur directed his chapel music master to notate the music during the performance. This was the last time it was given as a local affair in what was believed to be ancient manner. Ethnomusicologist Henrietta Yurchenco later compared the notation of the music she recorded with Bourbourg's music master and found there was no resemblance. She comments, "And no wonder, it was a devilishly difficult music to commit to our Western staff."[14]

The *Rabinal Achí* dance performances have become the staple of Saint Paul's day on January 25, coordinated by members of cofradías, local brotherhoods responsible for running the community. The rediscovery had enormous importance as the only theatrical work of high Maya pre-Hispanic civilization preserved to modern times. The work is now available in Spanish translation by Luis Cardoza y Aragón, a Guatemalan writer. According to Yurchenco, barely hidden in the rhetoric is evidence of Rabinal hierarchal society, warlike mentality, barbaric cruelty, intolerance toward neighboring tribes—yet love of the arts and treatment of their women as booty in war. By taking part in the dance drama, the living establish "contact" with the dead, their ancestors represented by masks. For the Achis of modern-day Rabinal, recalling their ancestors is not just about perpetuating the heritage of the past, it also provides a vision of the future, for one day the living will join their ancestors. In 2005, UNESCO named the Rabinal dance drama one of the Masterpieces of the Oral and Intangible Heritage of Humanity.

As this significant dance drama continues and the people of Guatemala attempt to recover from the catastrophic effects of the military and paramilitary death squads, other forms of music have emerged to provide solace, promote joy, and celebrate indigenous cultures. These music expressions include *Chapino* (i.e., Guatemalan) rock that began in the mid-1960s with one of its first successful performers, Luis Galich, with his band Santa Fé and the creation in 1973–1974 of the rock opera *Corazón del sol naciente* (Heart of the sunrise), by *Sol Naciente*, a large youth group formed by dancers, solo vocalists, an extended chorus, as well as a band that included Guatemalan percussion instruments along with acoustical guitars, violin, and piano. A unique case is the band *Sobrevivencia* (Survival) from Huehuetenango that sings its lyrics in Mam, the Mayan language of the region. A recent development has been the creation, in 2011, of El Ritmo de La Paz, a contest for amateur rock bands. It has become an annual festival with the message calling for national peace that every Guatemalan desires.[15]

Hip-hop has also emerged. Trasciende, a hip-hop academy founded by five break dancers (or B-boys) in 2009, offers art workshops as a means to draw the youth away from violence and into a peaceful environment. The head of the academy insists that the Trasciende workshops promote four values—peace, love, unity, and enjoyment.[16] A hip-hop group, Balam Ajpu, which means Jaguar Warrior or Warrior of Light, rap in the Tz'utujil Mayan language with the goal of teaching young people their ancestors' stories and customs. The release date of their debut album, *Tribute to the 20 Nawuales*, or spirits, coincided with the March 20, 2015, spring equinox. The musicians rapped in both Tz'utujil and Spanish, blending their hip-hop beat with marimba and natural sounds like bird songs and running water. Group member Tz'utu Baktun Kan, with the stage name of Rene Dionisio, said the album's songs pay tribute to the region where the Mayan civilization achieved its apex around, A.D. 250 to 950; it includes each of Guatemala's twenty-two provinces, plus Mexico's Chiapas and Yucatan. A young Mayan priest, Venancio Morales, provided the lyrics after entering trance states as dictated in Tz'utujil. The album explores the concept of spirits represented by animal glyphs in Mayan mythology and it offers a guide for listeners to find their own *nawuales* based on birthdate. Balam Ajpu members said Tz'utujil lends itself to hip-hop rhythms, and their music remains faithful to the percussive tradition of their ancestors. The group, with face paint, traditional dress, and incense-burners, plays ceremonial flutes and rattles to contrast with the occasional improvised beatboxing. It performs in communities like Quetzaltenango, San Marcos, San Pedro la Laguna, and Solola, in the highlands west of Guatemala City. Balam Ajpu is working on a second record, which will explore the thirteen "energies" associated with the nawuales, as established by the Mayan calendar. In a country plagued by gang activity and high homicide rates, Balam Ajpu sees its music as an instrument to teach young people to live in harmony with each other and nature by returning to the principles of the Mayan calendar. As one group member said, "This is our cultural registry of the past for future generations."[17]

Notes

1. Smithsonian Folkways: Chapinlandia—Marimba Music of Guatemala, SFW40542.
2. M. Latorre y Badillo, "Representación de los autos sacramentales en el periodo de su mayor florecimiento (1620–81)," *Revista de archivos, bibliotecas y museos* 25 (1911), 189–211; xxvi (1912), 235–62.
3. Rafael Paraíso to author, November 26, 2011.
4. Jesús Castillo, *La música maya quiche* (Guatemala: Editorial Piedra Santa, 1977), 34–35.
5. Stuart Serio, Assistant Curator, Fleisher Collection of Orchestral Music,

Free Library of Philadelphia (Pennsylvania), May 3, 2016, to the author. Other efforts to find a recording of the opera have proven unsuccessful.

6. E-mail Eduardo Gularte, gulartecos@gmail.com, April 27, 2016.

7. Jesús Castillo, *La musica maya quiche: region de Guatemala* (edición homenaje a Jesús Castillo, año del centenario de su Nacimiento; Guatemala: Editorial Piedra Santa, 1977), 50–51.

8. Lisa Munro, "Inventing Indigeneity: A Cultural History of 1930s Guatemala" (PhD dissertation, University of Arizona, 2014).

9. Nicolas Slonimsky, *Music of Latin America* (New York: Thomas Y. Crowell Company, 1945).

10. Gary Galván, Musicologist/Archival Consultant, Fleisher Collection of Orchestral Music, Free Library of Philadelphia, 19103–1116 to the author.

11. E-mail, Ramiro MacDonald, professor of the Universidad Rafael Landívar, April 27, 2016.

12. See IASPMLIST@liverpool.ac.uk for a long thread dealing with found sounds, especially including those from nature or reproduced to sound like nature, especially birds.

13. A. F. Bandelier, "Charles Etienne, Abbé Brasseur de Bourbourg," in *The Catholic Encyclopedia*. New York: Robert Appleton Co. Accessed March 22, 2016, from http://www.newadvent.org/cathen/02743a.htm.

14. Henrietta Yurchenco, *Around the World in 80 Years: A Memoir* (Point Richmond, CA: Musical Research Institute, 2002), 147, 150–51.

15. https://en.wikipedia.org/wiki/Guatemalan_rock.

16. Monse Sepulveda, "Guatemalan Youth Transcend Violence Through Hip-Hop," September 15, 2011, http://wagingnonviolence.org/feature/guatemalan-youth-transcend-violence-through-hip-hop/.

17. Fox News Entertainment, "Guatemalan Musicians Perform Hip-Hop in Mayan Language to Make It Cool for Youth," February 21, 2015, http://latino.foxnews.com/latino/entertainment/2015/02/21/guatemalan-musicians-perform-hip-hop-in-mayan-language-to-make-it-cool-for/.

CHAPTER 4

Cuban Music

Afro-Cubanism

Alejo Carpentier

[Eduardo] Sánches de Fuentes's repugnance in admitting the presence of black rhythms in Cuban music [can] be understood as a reflection of a general outlook during the first years of the republic. Years had transpired since blacks were no longer slaves. However, in a newly conceived country that aspired to bring itself up to date with the cultural currents of the day, the authentically black cultural experience—that is, those deeply rooted and surviving African elements that remained in a pure state—was looked upon with disgust, as a kind of barbaric holdover from the past, and could be tolerated as a necessary evil. In 1913, the traditional *comparsas* were prohibited. The religious festivities of blacks were prohibited. Undeniably, certain ritual crimes, committed by witch doctors, justified police persecution against the practices of the *babalawos* (Santeria priests). Some street fighting between enemy *ñáñigo* groups had also logically generated repressive measures. But it should not be believed that these deeds were so frequent or that they reached the magnitude of the common crimes committed. It had been a long time since knife-wielders like Manuel Cañamazo, Manita en el suelo, or the black Sucumento were the terror of neighborhoods outside the city limits. Furthermore, if so many blacks were loitering among hoodlums with a drum on their belly, much of the blame rested with whites, who always relegated

Reprinted from *Music in Cuba*, ed. and intro. Timothy Brennan, trans. Alan West-Durán (Minneapolis: University of Minnesota Press, 2001; originally published in 1947), 256–67. As complementary videos to Carpentier's essay, see the outstanding video on singers and dancers, https://www.youtube.com/watch?v=i-8dExdlPU8; the discussion of forgotten showgirls, vedettes en el olvido—La historia detrás del mito at https://www.youtube.com/watch?v=IGCo67MY6R4; and The World Music Guide to Cuban music, "Cuba: Son and Afro-Cuban Music," http://www.worldmusic.net/guide/music-of-cuba/.

them to a marginal existence, offering them the worst jobs, except when they wanted votes, in which case they appealed to their baser qualities. The kind of politicking that went on during the first years of the republic did nothing to improve the social or cultural condition of blacks; indeed, it fueled their vices as long as blacks were useful for political ends. All these factors contributed to the attitude held by well-heeled men of mistrusting all matters black, and since they were not inclined to ask difficult questions, they did notice that high on the scaffolds, in the heat of the foundries, under the sun of the rock quarries, or in the coachman's seat, an entire sea of humanity was on the move, a people who conserved their poetic and musical traditions, quite worthy of being studied.

Of course, these traditions offered a wide spectrum in their purity of preservation. As Ramos puts it so aptly:

> In the New World, the relationships between blacks and whites brought as a corollary the subordination of one to the other, segregation and separation, and all the subsequent racial and cultural conflict (at times, acute) this subordination implied. This segregation caused the utmost total disappearance, in some cases, of primitive institutions. When an individual is separated from his cultural group and placed in contact with other groups and cultures, he tends, in the second or third generation, to forget the primitive cultures and to assimilate the new cultures he has come in contact with.

This process of transculturation has happened several times in previous centuries. The "Son de la Ma'Teodora" constitutes the most typical sixteenth-century example of this. For an Ulpiano Estrada, a Brindis de Salas, black Creoles of several generations, little was left in the nineteenth century of the primitive cultures of their grandfathers. Only an instinct survived—in this case a rhythmic instinct—of these black musicians and composers who contributed to the evolution of Cuban music in its first phase, without changing the form or the existing melodic sources. Nothing differentiated "the black Malibrán woman," married to an officer of the Spanish army, from any other Cuban woman of her time, except the color of her skin. This explains why so many blacks made "white music" during the nineteenth century, refusing to play the roles of "black professors," while the whites—A. Bartolomé José Crespo, a Guerrero—were the ones who dressed up as blacks.

But it must not be forgotten that while the transculturation process had completed itself for certain generations, the slave ships arrived with a horrendous regularity, their cargo "ebony flesh." Thousands upon thousands of slaves kept swelling the workforces of Cuba's plantations, reinitiating a cycle of adaptation whose earlier phases were fixed in the Cuban vernacular: *bozales*, when they arrived from Africa and spoke only in their dialects; *ladinos* when they began to speak in Spanish; *criollos*, the offspring of the ladinos; and the *reyoyos*, the children of the criollos. With free slaves or those recently emancipated, the process of transculturation took place swiftly, since contact with the outside was immediate. But in the slave barracks it was infinitely slower, because knowledge of white culture was gleaned from what the slave could observe at a distance, as when there was a party in the master's house. The slave was told to dance his native dances, because it was considered important for the preservation of his health. The slave traders had learned this much earlier than the landowners. However, there were limitations. In 1839, a circular by General Ezpeleta established that "the slaves in the countryside should be allowed to dance their dances known as 'with drums,' on holidays under the vigilance of their overseers, without blacks from any other farm being present." That is, if the slaves from one farm were, in their majority, from one tribe or nation, they would not have the slightest opportunity to have contact with a neighboring workforce of different ethnic origins. The varying conservation or dilution of African traditions derives from this history and holds true even today among Cuban blacks. Certain old men, born in captivity, remember legends and songs from Africa with extraordinary precision. The black man Yamba, more than a hundred years old, whom I met at a farm in the remote countryside, spoke just like blacks in the work of Bartolomé José Crespo, without knowing any other type of dance than what he had seen in the slave barracks as a child. Those same dances are long gone, a tradition the black university student is unaware, equally true for the mulatto musician of a Havana swing orchestra. After severing the umbilical cord of the slave trade, Cuban blacks lost their contact with Africa, conserving an ever-hazier memory of their ancestral traditions. When the *comparsas* were allowed to function again, about ten years ago [1937], they no long had the same power; they had gained much as a moving spectacle, as luxurious theater, in abundance of instruments; but they had lost authenticity. There are not many performers today who are capable of making the array of *batá* drums speak. And yet, their musical awareness is incomparably vaster than that of their grandfathers.

This might explain why certain arcane aspects of black music have taken so long to interest more "serious" composers, more directly drawn to what they immediately heard: the rhythms and singing of the comparsas, incorporated into the *contradanzas* in the last phase of their evolution. There was more. Much more. Without mentioning groups from long ago, like Nuestra Señora de los Remedios, founded by free blacks in Havana in 1598, nor the petition for land to establish *cabildos*, which figure in the town records of the eighteenth-century Santiago, in 1796 there was already a Cabildo de Congos Reales, under the name of one of the Three Kings, Saint Melchior. The increasing black population together was a proportionately greater manumission of slaves, made these groups proliferate. Essentially, the cabildos were "mutual aid socieities," which prevented the ex-slave from being buried in a common grave. The following cabildos appeared: Arará, Apapá, Apapá Chiquito, Mandinga, oro, Lucumí, Carabalí Ungrí, Nación Mina Popó de la Costa de Oro, Arará tres oos, and so on. The blacks from calabar created secret *ñáñigo* societies, whose first activities date from around 1835, when the Acabatón society appeared in Regla. Although the cabilidos composed of offspring of the "nations"—blacks from different regions-ethnicities—endured to our times, ñañiguismo spread throughout Cuban society, because it had a more inclusive notion of membership. They admitted people of all races and walks of life into ranks, as long as they observed the established rules, (Chinese, Creoles, even Spaniards were affiliated with ñañiguismo), their initiation ceremonies, and the true brotherhood of those who belonged made ñañiguismoa true popular masonry. Around 1914, in Havana, Regla, Guanabacoa, and Matanzas, there were fifty-seven *jueogos* [groups] of ñáñigos. Currently, even though ñañiguismo has lost a lot of its strength because of the previously described transculturation process, various groups still remain, strict guardians of the language and the ritual.

If the black cabildos were mutual aid societies, they also specified, when legally registered, that they were created for "recreational and leisurely pursuits." This authorized them to hold dances and form comparsas for Three Kings Day (January 6) or, after the abolition of slavery, for carnival. In different periods the comparsas paraded through the streets of Havana, sporting vivid names: El gavilán (The hawk), Los congos libres (The free congos),

El alacrán chiquito (The small scorpion), La culebra (The snake), El pájaro lindo (The pretty bird), Mandinga Moro Riza (Mandinga curly Moor), Mandiza Moro Azul (Mandinga blue Moor), Los moros (The Moors), Los peludos (The hairy ones). The comparsas, more than just a marching rhythmic collective, were like an itinerant ballet. They had their "themes." A spider or a snake, represented by a huge figure held on high by an expert dancer, served as the focal point for dancing and singing. The comparsa members would "kill the spider" or "kill the snake."

Mamita, mamita,	
yen, yen, yen.	
Que me mata la culebra,	(The snake's gonna kill me)
yen, yen, yen.	
Mírele los ojo	(Look at its eyes
que parecen candela;	they seem like fire;
mírele lo diente,	look at its teeth,
que parece file (alfileres).	they seem like needles.
Mentira, mi negra,	It's a lie, my black woman,)
yen, yen, yen;	
son juego de mi tierra	(they are the game of my soil)

As Ramos observed, referring to similar dances seen in Brazil, those figures that used to (and still do) inspire the name of certain comparsas undoubtedly represent a totemic survival. In the snake dance, Fernanco Ortiz sees an offshoot of a Dahomey snake cult that still persists in Haiti, where a serpent of forged steel appears on all voodoo altars. As for the violent and bloody strife between ñáñigo groups in the nineteenth century, Vivó maintains that they reflect old intertribal rivalries from Africa. The initiation ceremony of the ñáñigos, which we have witnessed many times, is truly a collective spectacle, in which episodes of the same legend are mimed, danced, and sung with slight variations. Something of old funeral rites has stayed embedded in them. A government edict in 1792 prohibited that "blacks could conduct or allow others to conduct, to the cabildos the cadavers of blacks, in order to sing or cry as is customary in their native land." Yet later, the bishop Trespalacios insisted on the point. As for the festivities with magic—a different issue altogether—their main objective continues to be a believer's possession by a saint or divinity in the black pantheon is syncretically represented almost always by a Catholic image. This is currently referred to in Cuba as *bajar al santo* [to make the saint descend; used in possession rituals] or *subirse el santo* [to make the saint rise]. But let us not linger here on matters amply dealt with by specialists in the field.

Musically, the matter is very complex. Because to say "African music" is the same as saying "medieval knights." As Ortis has pointed out, "In studying Afro-Cuban music one has to distinguish between music descended from Dahomey, or the Yoruba, or the Carabalí and Conga." Unfortunately, a scientific work of notation, compilation, comparison, rhythmic and modal study, with its ensuing classifications, still has not been undertaken, because the task, admittedly so, is beyond the scope of one individual. In the first place, if one does have informants who are intelligent and trustworthy, it is impossible to find out when and where a religious ceremony or a profane drumming session will be held. In the second place, because the true ñáäigos—that is, the most interesting ones—ascertained on many occasions, are opposed to having their musical rituals notated or taped, since they view these acts as a profanation of their secrets. In the third place, a researcher's interest quickly awakens the greed among people who do not know any better, who then scheme up some kind of charade in exchange for a few coins. Fernando Ortiz, appealing to a heroic sense of patience, is the person who has most deeply researched these matters. But he is not a musician, nor does he claim to be, and for different reasons he has been bereft of the best collaborators that he could have had in his musical research.

Let us rely, then, on certain authoritative conclusions drawn by Ortiz:

> The river peoples of the Niger, particularly the Yorubas and the Nagós, in Cuba known as *lucumís*, brought, along with complex religious beliefs, drums, songs, and dances of their ancient rites that still resonate intact under the skies of the Americas imploring favors from their African divinities. Dhomeyan music, or of the *dajomés*, as in Cuba they have been referred to with true phonetic propriety, is almost identical to that of their neighbors, the *arará*, and both have been maintained, sheltered by *lucumí* rites. We know that the Yoruba pantheon spread among the bordering towns, especially toward the north, penetrating Dahomey and its coastal area, in the ancient Ardrá or Ará region, absorbed more than a

century earlier by that very powerful kingdom. For this reason, among blacks of this region one finds an advanced theological and liturgical syncretism, and the chants, drum beats, and instruments have intermingled, where similar deities are invoked under different names. This allows us to infer, if we know beforehand the religious nomenclature of these peoples, whether a chant is Dahomeyan or Yoruba, according to the language of the prayer or name of the god being propitiated. It is easy to deduce that a chant to Shangó (deity of lightning), is from the *lucumís*, and one for Ebioso (also an igneous god) is from Dahomey or the *dajomés*. *Ñañiguismo* has an unmistakable musical personality; its naked simplicity sustains *carabalí* music in Cuba.

And Ortiz adds in another work:

Here, at the core of our people, there is still much music of *bantú* or *Conga* origin in the dances of our peasants; we have *gangá* music, from which the primitive rumba is derived; some bits of *arará* or *dajormé* music, called voodoo in Haiti, which here tends to mix in with *lucumí* music; and, finally best-conserved and varied of Cuba's African music, the religious liturgy of the Yorba.

Lucumí and ñáñigo music generally has melodies that are ample, noble, slow in contrast, with the dynamism of the percussion. It is sung by the faithful, in unison or in octaves. In all the hymns, one observes an antiphonal form: a soloist and a chorus or two semichoruses, the second repeating the phrases of the first. "In Yorba religious chants the antiphonal soloist initiates or raises the chant to a pleasing level, and the chorus, called the *ankori*, responds in the same tone as the soloist." This liturgy comprises, among others, song to Elegguá, overseer of all roads; to Ogún, blacksmith and inventor of the anvil, represented by the image of Saint Peter; to Ochosi, god of hunting and warriors (Saint Norbert); to Babalú-Ayé (Saint Lazarus); to Yemayá, a goddess of the sea and cosmic mother; to Obatalá, Ochún, to Changó, to Oyá. It is extremely rare to find a theme of these chants that begins on the dominant note. The elimination of the leading note is so frequent that when a popular composer wants to impart an "African air" to a melody, by instinct he suppresses or alters the seventh note. Quite frequently the hymns are based on pentatonic scales without semitones. But the use of these ranges is capricious, without obeying the rules. We will not speak of modes or particular characteristics of one or another kind of music, since the scarcity of scientifically established documents makes any analysis pointless.

As for percussion, it is simply prodigious. The Afro-Cuban drums composed an entire arsenal: the ñáñigos, tensed with strings and wedges, one-sided, played with two hands, designed generically with the name of encomos, although the family includes, as Israel Castellanos points out, the *boncó enchemillá*; the *batá* drums, "bimembraned, played on both sides, with a wooden hourglass shape, closed, permanently taut with a rope-like skin," which are called, as we have seen, *okónkolo* (the smallest), *itótele* (the medium-sized one), and *iyá* (the largest), which is "the mother of the drums." In addition, one must mention the *tumba* and *tahona*, used for profane and sacred functions. To these are usually added, although not as a rule, the *cajón*, the *marímbula*, the *guiro*, the *econes*, or the little iron bells without tongues, and the *claves*. Also used are the two types of *marugas*: the one that consists of two tin cones, welded at the base and filled with little stones (what is called in other Antillean isles the *chá-chá*), and the one that consists of a cone made of laced fibers, filled with seeds or *mates*, which is shaken from top down, and held by a ring fixed at its vertex (one of the many kinds of basket rattled known by certain indigenous peoples of the Americas).

Notice that Afro-Cuban music dispenses with any melody-making instruments, pure singing over percussion. On the other, in the ceremonial rituals—the ñáñigo initiation, for example, or those of Santeria—one does not observe the slightest watering down of a way of singing that remains true to old African customs. Blacks who pride themselves on knowing ancestral hymns and traditions are unaware of hybrid genres, analogous to the windward *fulía*, for example, and that the *décima* derived from the *romance*—in Cuba part of the cultural patrimony of white peasants—alternated with sung and instrumental passages of purely African technique. There are cases where the batá drums, aided by their rich tuning and the virtuosity of their performers, play entire solo passages, eliminating the voices. Once, at a Santeria party in regla, we heard the drummers play a "march" and a "wail" of considerable duration, which were true pieces, complete, balanced, developed within the tempo, evolving from fundamental rhythmic cells. In many cases, this prime beat flowers into a *rhythmic mode.* Really, how can we properly speak of rhythm when faced with a true phrase, composed of notes and groups of notes, that outpaces all metrical limits before acquiring a rhythmic function through sheer repetition? When this happens—and it does so frequently—we are in the presence of a rhythmic mode, with its own accents that have nothing to do with accepted notions of a strong or weak beat. The player stresses this note or another, not for scansion reasons, but because the traditional expression of the rhythmic mode demands it. It is not mere happenstance that blacks say, "They make the drums speak!" Now consider the disconcerting effect of movement, of internal palpitations given off by the simultaneous pacing of various rhythmic modes, which end up establishing mysterious relationships among themselves, conserving, however, a certain independence, and you will have a remote idea of the kind of bewitching effect produced by certain expressions of the batá drums!

On the other hand, we must not forget that in certain kinds of ceremonies the chants respond to very diverse uses and emotions. If the practice of "making the saint descend" is accompanied by a monotonous chant whose purpose is to engender an obsession, a fixed idea conducive to an ecstatic state; conversely, in the ñáñigo celebrations, for example, there are so many different chants and phases that accompany an intricate initiation ceremony. A true mystery play, the juego includes, in this case, antiphonal hymns, dances by diablitos [little devils], prayers for the dead, marches, processionals, and an invocation to the sun, as well as recitations of formulas "in native tongue," measured out on the skin of the drum. It is pointless to go on about the rich sonorities fo these types of folkloric expression.

In 1925, Amadeo Roldán began to consciously exploit this wondrous wellspring of rhythms and melodies. However, a phenomenon prevalent in all Afro-Cuban symphonic output bears pointing out: bereft of scientific work where they can study the modal and rhythmic laws governing black music, the Cuban composer works with materials haphazardly chanced upon at a ceremony that he has personally witnessed, without really knowing the rich textures of this sonorous treasure. Although ñáñigo music is a branch of the *carabalí* tree, it is easy to note that, along with its basic percussion, it is unaware of the music's origins. This allows us to differentiate between what is ñáñigo and what is carabalí, an almost imperceptible difference if compared to the dissimilarities between certain expressions of Yoruba music from lucumí or conga music. Under apparent similarities, each one of these musics possesses its own sound environment, rules, ways of being. Without having to subscribe to the role of cultural composer as ethnographer when approaching the primitive soul and his music, we see how, in the work of Roldán, as well as in that of a García Caturla—when they compose girded by the document in hand—all of the elements of that vast sonority of the Afro-Cuban realm are all mixed together. And, thus, we find, side by side, the lucumí hymn, the tune of a bembé, the ñáñigo invocation, as well as an array of percussion—from the regular and symmetrical that accompanies the dance of the diablito or írime, to the complex percussion of the Yoruba drums.

The Afro-Cuban music movement initiated by some composers provoked a violent reaction from those opposed to anything black. Guajiro music pitted against Afro-Cuban music, the former purveyed as representative of white music, more noble, melodic, pure. However, those who claimed to utilize guajiro music in larger-scale works were surprised that after a first score nothing else was left to be done. And this for an unforeseen reason: the guajiro sings his décimas with the accompaniment of the *tiple* [treble guitar], but he does not invent anything new musically.

This unique fact is explainable: when he sings, the guajiro's poetic invention is fitted to a traditional melodic pattern, whose roots are steeped in the tradition of the Spanish romance [ballad], brought to the island by the first colonizers. When the Cuban guajiro sings, he sticks to the inherited melody with utmost fidelity. Throughout the Cuban nineteenth century, the popular printing presses flooded the towns and villages with reams and reams of décimas "to be sung accompanied by the tiple." But all of those volumes did not include a single bar of music. Why? The reason is simple: if it is true that the guajiro was included to renovate the lyrics to his songs, learning the words of others, or relying on his own inspiration, he made no pretense of introducing the slightest variety in terms of the tune. The décimas offered had to adjust to a model known by all. Quite the poet, the guajiro is no musician. He does not create melodies. Through the island, he sings his décimas over ten or twelve fixed patterns, all similar to one another, whose original sources can be found in any old anthology of ballads from Extremadura [Spain]. (The Venezuelan poet and folklorist Juan Lisbano made the same observation when studying certain popular expressions of his country, quite rich in poetic content, but always the same musically.) The same thing happens with the *zapateos* [footstomping]. There is only one, always the same, which returned after eighty years, like a classical quote, in the works of popular Cuban composers: Anckermann, Marín, Varona, and so on. (Formerly, there was another type of zapateo that has disappeared without a trace, and it is harmonized in published works of last century, in pure Haydnesque style.) At times, and what recently occurred with "La guantanamera," is an example, a guajiro singer seems to have invented a new melody. But let us not fall for the ploy. It is simply a reappearance of the ballad, whose song was conserved by those in the interior. And as for the much-heralded "total Cubanness" of the guajira melody, we should not have too many illusions. The guajira melody of Cuba is identical to that of the Venezuelan *galerón*. (The only difference between the two genres is in the type and number of verses employed.) The only thing that imbues any élan to this static folklore is the virtuosity of the performer or the inventive verse of the singer. But felicitous moments do not a tradition make. Furthermore, the song of the Cuban guajiro seems to have lost the luster of its grace, praised a hundred years ago by the Countess of Merlín. There is an evident impoverishment of material.

This explains why scores such as *Suite cubana* by Mario Valdés Costa (a prematurely deceased composer) or the *Capricho* for piano and orchestra by Hubert de Blanck, based on guajiro themes, exhausted the possibilities of a folklore after the first attempt. In mixed-blood and black music, on the other hand, if the interest in the lyrics seems scant, the sonic material is incredibly rich. This is why attempts to create a work of national expression always return, sooner or later, to Afro-Cuban and mestizo genres or rhythms.

CHAPTER 5

An Accidental Hero [Cuban Singer in the Special Period]

Jan Fairley

For Latin Americans, Silvio Rodríguez is the equivalent of the Beatles and Dylan rolled into one.

Silvio Rodríguez has just rerecorded [2006] a song he wrote nearly forty years ago. It's called "The Under-Development Epistle" and it's about young people who are more focused on the make of their jeans than heroism or revolution.

As ever, it marks him out as a musician who gives voice to the experience of everyday life and legitimate concerns of many young Cubans. The—if you like—anti-hero of the revolution, Rodríguez has always sung about everyday things, and in the process given voice to a generation of Latin-Americans. We meet in the office of his Havana recording studios Ojalá, named after one of his best-known songs. An Arabic-Spanish word meaning "let's hope so," "Ojalá" sums up the questioning attitude to life he's held since he began composing with his guitar while doing military service back in the 1960s. By writing songs that capture the doubts, dreams, and beliefs of people's inner lives, he has become one of the most influential political singers alive, the man who changed the face of twentieth-century song in Latin America and Spain, even if he is still largely unknown in the English-speaking world. His visit to Britain next week will be only the second in a forty-five-year career.

Rodríguez's fame owes less to his fifteen bestselling albums and more to his live performances and alternative distribution networks. Such was the popularity of his music among leftwingers, he was banned by various Latin

https://www.theguardian.com/music/2006/sep/15/popandrock.worldmusic, Friday, September 15, 2006. Last modified on Thursday, October 26, 2006. A discography of Rodríguez's recordings is available at https://www.discogs.com/artist/400811-Silvio-Rodr%C3%ADguez; also see http://www.allmusic.com/album/15-great-classic-cuban-songs-mw0000013115.

American military dictatorships so for many years his songs circulated clandestinely on cassettes. Several generations of Latin Americans know Rodríguez's "Unicornio" by heart, with its appeal to anyone who could recognize a lost blue unicorn to get in touch. Widely adopted as a metaphor for seeking utopia, it became the soundtrack for guerrilla struggle in Nicaragua and El Salvador, and a challenge to the military dictatorships in Argentina and Chile. It was Rodríguez who, along with fellow singer-songwriter Pablo Milanés, gave the first big concert in Argentina to mark the end of military dictatorship after the Falklands war. And when Pinochet fell, Rodríguez returned to the Chile he'd first visited during the Allende government of the early 1970s, to give a concert in memory of his friend, singer Victor Jara, murdered by Pinochet's henchmen.

If Rodríguez remains largely undiscovered by English speakers, this is because the poetry of his lyrics is an intrinsic part of his appeal. For Latins, Rodríguez is the equivalent of the Beatles and Dylan rolled into one, with Baez and Mitchell on the side. His beautifully crafted songs, sung in his high yet grainy voice to insinuating melodies and brilliant arrangements, so precisely captured people's experience that generations of Spanish speakers map key moments in their lives and the lives of their countries by them. Rodríguez has written hundreds of songs about everything from Che Guevara to prostitution, about dreams, hummingbirds, love, of course, and the business of living.

Wearing a checked shirt and jeans, he's in buoyant mood, talking of how, with his partner, the flautist Niurka González, and toddler daughter Malva, he's heading for Britain. Niurka is appearing as guest of honor at the 2006 international Flute Congress in Manchester; Rodríguez will give a keenly awaited concert in London. This is to raise funds for the restoration of a Havana theater for the Cuban music schools, which will be channeled to the island through a foundation set up in memory of the singer Kirsty MacColl. MacColl had a great love for Cuba, celebrated in her final disc, *Tropical Brainstorm*, and in a Radio 2 series on Cuban music made just before her untimely death in Mexico in 2000.[1]

The music schools are important to Rodríguez as they are to all Cuban musicians. Active support of music and the arts as professional careers, through education, infrastructure, and monthly salaries, is what keeps the Cuban music scene so fruitful. Now approaching sixty, Rodríguez recalls how complex the Cuban cultural scene was when he began his career.

At that time their songs, attitudes, looks, and lifestyle irritated bureaucrats with Stalinist tendencies and propagandist notions of culture. They, in sharp contrast, heralded the renaissance of medieval troubadour traditions chronicling lives and loves of their times. "It was the sixties and we were writing our songs. We liked the Beatles and experimental rock. I remember when we first heard 'Oyé Como Va,' Carlos Santana's version of a classic Cuban song, and said, 'Look what can be done with our music,' but it fell on deaf ears. There were a lot of conservative ideas around, prejudice against 'imperialist music,' but over the years with a lot of discussion and music-making, people have become more reasonable."

To avoid the hardliners, Rodríguez and other like-minded musicians found a home at the intellectual powerhouse Casa de las Américas and the Cuban Cinematographic Institute, ICAIC, where leading cultural figures gave them work and helped them fight their corner. Forming the Experimental Sound Group (GESI), they composed songs and music for films. "It was amazing because we listened and encouraged and helped each other and wrote lots of songs. We showed how you could create even a poetic rock-influenced disc like *Cuba Va!* and still be revolutionary."

Where does he think his generation found the knack to create such potent and popular material? "It's because we became adults when we were still adolescents during the revolution's infancy, when it was tackling urgent social problems. I was only fourteen when with about six thousand others I was involved in the literacy campaign, teaching volunteer militia men defending the island on beaches and charcoal makers in the mountains to read and write. We were privileged to be struggling for ideals in everyday life, which was an amazing way to acquire a revolutionary conscience. We saw contradictions and discrepancies and said so, accepting the revolution in all its complexity and expressing it in our songs."

By negotiating their way through Cuban cultural politics, Rodríguez's generation defined their politics in the process, proving Cuban culture to be diverse and inspiring, instead of monolithic. They kept pushing frontiers, joining together in what became known as the new trova movement, modern troubadours challenging propaganda clichés by creating the distinctive self-critical songs of the Cuban revolution.

In a country not blessed with newspapers, the words of songs matter: songs like the iconic "Ojalá," a song about impossible desire and dreams that seems to capture all life's uncertainties in one, became the soundtrack of everyday life across the Spanish-speaking world. Although he was no apologist for the revolution, Rodríguez's popularity at home became so great that people joked that he had gone from being "banned" to "obligatory."

By the 1980s, Rodríguez was meeting his counterparts from other parts of Latin America in festivals from Mexico to Berlin, and between them creating a hugely powerful movement of musicians speaking out for democracy and freedom.

Remembering all this now, he invokes the Russian revolutionary poet Vladimir Mayakovsky, "Ask me for poems and even if we're fucked, I'll do one!" When he recently received the Latino lifetime achievement award at the Madrid music academy, he quoted from his own much-anthologized *Story of the Chairs*, "He who has a song will have torment. But it is worth it to have the good song that torments."

He tells me, laughing, that people are always asking him, "What will happen when Fidel dies?" So, what does he tell them? "I think the transition has begun. Cuba has capable, experienced leaders running the country, many of them very young. The only danger is, as it's always been, invasion, which could cause chaos. We know the US congress has approved an additional $80 million to destroy the Cuban government. That's why we've spent half a century sleeping with one eye open!" His other eye is on his own life, Malva, and writing new songs as he continues to look forward as well as back.

Notes

1. See the homepage of the program with clips and links to the eight programs of the series, http://www.kirstymaccoll.com/media/kirsty-maccolls-cuba/ and http://news.bbc.co.uk/2/hi/entertainment/1147046.stm.

CHAPTER 6

Cuzcatlán (El Salvador) and Maria de Baratta's *Nahualismo*

Robin Sacolick

El Salvador's 1935 dance drama named *Nahualismo* and its composer María de Baratta are imbued with duality and contradiction that constitute a mystery. The title of the composition refers to Amerindian beliefs that include the doubling of an individual, from birth, by her *nahual* (animal or spirit guide). The composer María de Baratta doubled up herself, on roles and responsibilities. She played the traditional wife of the early twentieth century, raising three children with her upper-middle-class husband; at the same time, she plied a dynamic musical career that involved performing, promoting, groundbreaking ethnography, prize-winning composing, and extensive travel. These accomplishments were extraordinary enough for their time and place that they could inform an epic Merchant-Ivory film. Yet her exploits went further: while the composer's economic status provided her the comforts of El Salvador's aristocracy, she nevertheless protested against the

Salvadoran folk musicians. Courtesy of the author.

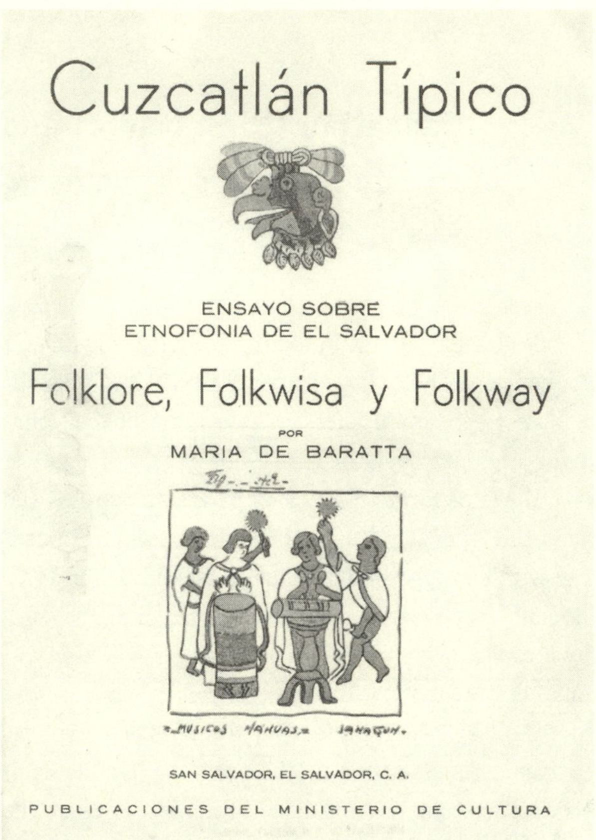

Classic source of folklore and music.

military dictatorship that carried out the tragic *Matanza*, a massacre of indigenous people. For her action, she was incarcerated. Cryptically, she publicly sided with authorities in certain political and cultural matters, while her private choices apparently remained contradictory.

Baratta chose *Nahualismo*, for example, as the subject of this composition that her grandson has deemed her "most beautiful"[1] that foregrounded beliefs and practices prohibited by church authorities. The composer's ambivalence toward cultural and political matters appeares in her monumental 740-page ethnography *Cuzcatlán Típico: Ensayo Sobre Etnofonía de El Salvador, Folklore, Folkwisa y Folkway*. She explains in the preface that she prefers the Nahuatl "Cuzcatlán" over "El Salvador." Yet, in the same volume, she dismisses *Nahualismo* beliefs as "absurd."[2]

Thus, the mystery: Why did de Baratta dismiss Nahualism if she was the descendant of the last Lenca chief of Cuzcatlán,[3] if she was attempting to "analyze the music of the Indian"[4]; and if she esteemed the cultural production of indigenous Salvadorans in all other categories? In a more tolerant regime, society, or age, would she have been as dismissive? How was it consistent for a woman whose actions often flouted convention to conform summarily to hegemonic strictures on this one point? Why the contradiction? Was it dissimulation or some form of doubling?

One answer to the mystery might draw on a Kantian prescription for middle-class behavior: acceding in public life to consensus values while nurturing individual views in private. Yet the mystery deserves closer attention. The issues involve treatment of ancient belief systems that have survived, to the limited extent they have, by the tactic of public acquiescence and dissimulation doubled up with continued practice in private of the traditions.

This mystery reveals repeated instances of duality and contradiction, especially within *Nahualismo*. Unravelling the mystery begins by setting the historical and cultural context of the composer's life and paradoxical approach to the nationalist muse. Then it delves into specifics of Nahualism and how she evoked them musically. Analysis of her compositional procedures, compared with indigenist techniques of her contemporaries, suggests that composition functioned for her as a crucible for uniting dualities, both in her cultural environment and in her identity. Finally, a dyad of theoretical constructs—postnationalism and Chicana feminism—provide a means with which to resolve the paradoxes through evaluation of de Baratta's output and sustain the proposition that she was a *bruja* feminist.

A Postnationalist Composer

"Postnationalism" accompanies "poststructuralism," "postmodernism," and "postcolonialism" in negating mainstream epistemologies in favor of greater tolerance of contradictions and dualities. De Baratta identified some of nationalism's critical weaknesses and transcended them musically. Moreover, she was a self-defined woman, at times of seemingly magical capabilities. Her modus operandi bore evidence of early versions of transgressive technologies. She shared professional methods with peers across borders, and pursued projects that at times conflicted with national priorities.

Yet the majority of her work transpired with fashionable nationalism. Her output, moreover, dealt with cultural matters within the nation, even when it was at odds with national policy. To the extent that the government took credit for, or featured, her work (e.g., in 1936 when *Nahualismo* premiered on national radio), she became publicly associated with nationalism.

Partly this resulted from her peers. Some of her closest colleagues and role models were nationalists. Jesús Castillo, Guatemalan composer and ethnomusicologist with whom she maintained correspondence, composed music on Mayan themes, at times by request of the Guatemalan government. In his ethnographic work among the Maya, he modeled many of the methods she came to apply. Their interests had much in common, as Guatemala and El Salvador were united during significant intervals until the late nineteenth century, and as several ethnic groups inhabit lands spanning the border between them. Both he and de Baratta acknowledged in print the importance of the other's work.[5]

Concurrently in Mexico, Carlos Chávez was a leading exponent of nationalistic music, along with other composers including José Moncayo, Silvestre Revueltas, Daniel Ayala, Luis Sandí, and Blas Galindo. Mexico's revolutionary project to promote a unified national identity had seized upon a symbolic Aztec imaginary.[6] Accordingly, Chávez wrote several pieces that re-imagined Aztec music. Other composers incorporated melodies from surviving indigenous groups of Northwest Mexico and the Yucatan. Thus *indigenismo* became interchangeable with *nationalismo* in their music.[7]

De Baratta's other contemporaries included Jesús Castillo's younger half-brother Ricardo, Luis Delgadillo of Nicaragua, Cuba's Amadeo Roldán, Ecuador's Luis Salgado, Brazil's Villa-Lobos, Panama's Roque Cordero, and more. Each of these composers invoked a unique approach to indigenismo or *costumbrismo* under the more or less overt guise of nationalism.[8]

At home in San Salvador, de Baratta enjoyed the company of leaders in the arts, such as the nationalist spiritualist and theosophist poet Salarrué (Salvador Salazar Arrué) who dubbed her "the last true princess of *Cuzcatlán*" as one of a "Laudatory Litany of Fourteen Names," which he wrote for her. Other names included "orchid of the virgin forest" and "mirror of lost time."[9] According to her grandson, José Olmedo Baratta, she "inhabited a magical bohemian world, and in her house the salons lasted until four a.m. with contests of versemaking between Arturo Ambrogi and Salarrué, my grandmother playing piano, and Vicente Rosales y Rosales reciting poetry."[10]

Despite the romantic imagery of such idylls, reality, at least for the less privileged, stood in stark contrast. Even in revolutionary Mexico, reforms that benefited many still excluded some of indigenous and those of African ancestry, while the same people's ethnic expressions were appropriated to construct the national identity. In El Salvador, the government also promoted homogenization of identity,[11] although it worried that it might fall to what they considered the communist revolution in Mexico. This dynamic, interwoven with milestones in de Baratta's life, holds clues to the mystery of her contradictions.

Maria's birth year in San Salvador varies, with 1890 as the most common. She was the daughter of Dr. José Angel Mendoza, head of the medical faculty at the national university, and Doña María García González de Mendoza, a pianist educated at the Colegio de Ursulinas in Guatemala. Her known ancestry included, at least, some Spanish and Amerindian Lenca. Her affinity for music emerged early and was nourished by study with her mother and leading local musicians. She continued her education with Vincente Arrillaga at the San Francisco Conservatory and with Agustin Roig, a student of Enrique Granados, in Italy. She became an accomplished pianist, performing concerts in New York, San Francisco, Rome, and Bologna. This set her apart from many young women of her era, for whom career aspirations were confined to domesticity. Her interests extended further still to composition, an ambition even more rarely admitted by women at that time. She won prizes for her efforts, including Doce Canciones Folkloricas (San Salvador, 1930); Ofrenda de la Elegida and Bacanal Indigena (Piedras Negras, Mexico, 1934 and City of David, Panama, 1947); and Historia de Moros y Cristianos (1949). Moreover, in 1939, she won a Salvadoran prize for her prose composition *Collar de Dientes* (Necklace of teeth, a translation of *Cuzcatlán*).[12] The extent to which these achievements exceeded the norm comes into better focus when juxtaposed against their landscape.

El Salvador, comprising just over eighteen hundred square miles, has borders with Guatemala and Honduras, and more than one hundred miles of tropical Pacific seaboard. Before conquest and colonialism, the land, known as *Cuzcatlán*, was inhabited by Olmecs, then Maya, and later Maya along with Toltec-descended Pipiles. A chain of high volcanoes (the necklace of teeth) descends through thick jungle to the sea. By the time of the conquest, the inhabitants were Mayan-related Lencas in the areas bordering Honduras,

Pokomam Maya in the areas bordering Guatemala, and Pipiles in the central and Pacific coastal areas. During the colonial era, Cuzcatlán endured events similar to those in other Latin American lands. Spain ruled it in conjunction with Guatemala. As elsewhere in Latin America, African slaves supplemented the harshly impressed indigenous labor force, which had been diminished by European diseases; their monoculture was indigo. The extreme topography, combined with high population density, created poorer economic conditions than elsewhere in Latin America. Additionally, government and church authorities exacted great concessions from the indigenous populations, eliminating even more of their cultures, and sending the remnants underground. Independence from colonial rule came in 1822, after which Guatemala and Mexico each made unsuccessful attempts to rule the region.

A thriving coffee monoculture emerged from the 1870s through the 1920s, a period known as the Coffee Republic.[13] In the first decade of the new century, conflicts with international neighbors led to establishment of a Central American Court of Justice to avoid violence. At home, the Meléndez-Quinónez dynasty of 1913–1927 provided relief from frequent coups. During de Baratta's early career, the country was somewhat stable.

Nevertheless, matters could not have differed more. Legislation enacted in 1881 had drastically disempowered subsistence farmers, the bulk of the population, in favor of coffee planters. It abolished *tierras comunales* (communally farmed lands or *comarcas*), enabling a coffee oligarchy that came to be known as "The Fourteen Families" to gain ownership of a huge share of the country's acreage while removing means of food production from the majority. Moreover, the government raised revenue by taxing not the corporate income of the coffee planters but imported goods needed by all. While the affluent sent their children to Europe to be educated, little to no education or health services existed at home. Rural people entered the commercial agricultural workforce. The apparent prosperity of the Coffee Republic came at the expense of an ever-widening gap between rich and poor. The life of many women, already accustomed to the rigors of the self-sustaining household, fell somewhere on a continuum of subjection, from patriarchal *machismo* to domestic abuse. This is the context in which Maria grew up. During her travels, she married Augusto Baratta, an Italian architect who relocated to San Salvador, where he designed several prominent buildings.

When the Mexican Revolution broke out in 1910, all levels of Salvadoran el desarrollo de los diferentes ráficos, el pito de caña y el tam- ajo tocan el mismo sonecito, sin elodía que está vaciada en ocho lamente, que siguen después de longado indefinidamente, lo mis- mo que la repetición de ocho la melodía.

Dato curioso: los dos músicc tocan el pito y el tamborcito, cansarse, a medida que tocan c dor y siguen con mayor entusi

LA YEGÜITA. SON INDIGENA.

Allegretto con motto

Pito.

Tamborcilo indio

ESTUDIO

Composer's sheet music.

The composer at about age twenty.
Courtesy of the author.

society watched. Maria was then about twenty years old. Soon afterward, childrearing and the Great War circumscribed her travels. Instead, the projects of her fellow artists fueled her curiosity about the foundational cultures within her own country. By the 1920s, the work of Jesús Castillo and Carlos Chávez was well under way.

The situation in El Salvador during the 1920s fomented the evolution of traditional artisan guilds into trade unions representing tens of thousands of workers with communist sympathies—the same workers that the monoculture had converted from subsistence farmers of communal lands. Sra. de Baratta must have witnessed this from a double perspective. While she belonged to a privileged social stratum under a regime that discouraged indigenous culture, as an artist she admired role models like Chávez, who represented a revolutionary regime that promulgated indigenous mythology. Moreover, she associated with a set of educated artists of San Salvador such as Salarrué, who had come to share a Durkheimian anomie of disaffection with class inequality, injustice, and suppression of indigenous cultures.[14] How she resolved this internally is only possible to surmise through analysis of her work.

De Baratta began substantial fieldwork in indigenous areas of El Salvador. *Cuzcatlán Típico*, which did not appear until 1951 (perhaps because it was not long before then that the military dictatorship was finally dismantled) contains many of her findings from the intervening decades. In it, she effuses about the significance of preserving the cultural heritage of the Pipile, Lenca, and Pokomam, which had been vanishing due not only to assimilation into a proletariat but also to church and state prohibitions such as those against Nahualism.[15] While her ethnography contains, among many precious artifacts, anecdotes about this system of beliefs and practices, it puzzlingly dismisses them as "absurd."

Was this a dissimulation based upon a need to conform to official policies banning the practice? Was the value judgment inserted so abruptly among the plethora of cultural riches in the volume to take the perfunctory reader's attention away from the description of Nahualism or to defuse any sense a critical reader might intuit that her sympathy for indigenous causes went beyond loyalty to the government? Or was it baldly and directly a statement of the author's belief, a knee-jerk, blinders-on, gloves-off *Credo in unum deum*, refusing to consider the possibility of residual value in millennia-old practices of peoples whose art she loved and esteemed?

Whichever answer inhered, de Baratta succeeded in preserving bits of Nahualist lore that have not been documented elsewhere—while also preserving her standing with the authorities. During the 1920s and 1930s, she dedicated significant time to field research in Pokomam, Lenca and Pipil villages. This mirrored the efforts of Jesús Castillo more than it did those of Chavéz, whose research was relatively casually structured. De Baratta collected lexicons of endangered languages for each of the ethnicities: samples of art, musical instruments, descriptions of festivals, lists of foodstuffs, transcriptions of melodies, interpretations of religious beliefs, rosters of deities, keys to ancient hieroglyphs, legends, tall tales, and more. She and her husband became particularly interested in collecting and preserving preconquest incense burners and *tepunahuaxtles*, *Cuzcatlán*'s name for the sacred slit drums that date back to ancient Mesoamerica. De Baratta recalled repeated visits to remote locations, knocking on strangers' doors, participating in fiestas and daily life, for such extended periods that she later often found herself in need of returning there when her research became drudgery.[16]

The Great Depression of 1929 dealt a drastic blow to the Coffee Republic, whose one export collapsed in the world market. The coup that followed, thus, came somewhat as a backlash against communist organizing and put conservative military officer Maximiliano Hernández Martínez into power in 1931. Whereas his idiosyncrasies ostensibly included belief in some version of theosophy, his actions belied any sense of moral or spiritual restraint. Almost immediately after assuming control, he oversaw the slaughter of perhaps thirty thousand indigenous, African, and poor civilians, in retaliation for a skirmish of perceived communist threat. The horror of *La Matanza* (The massacre) effected the entire nation, which even now numbers only about seven million.

De Baratta and her friends joined those who marched in protest. Her grandson recounts that she was arrested and incarcerated, and only released after several of her prominent friends acted on her behalf. Although the extinction of El Salvador's cultural heritage had begun long before, now the crisis was even more severe. Perhaps not coincidentally, this was when de Baratta began to compose some of her most extensive musical works. The horror of La Matanza could, perhaps, only find outlet in this way. The compositions of the 1930s were indigenist dance dramas: *En el teocalli* (In the temple); *Ofrenda a la elegida: Danza ritual* (Offering of the selected one: Ritual dance); and *Nahualismo* (shamanism, sorcery).[17]

These titles compare to Chávez' earlier indigenist ballets *El Fuego Nuevo* and *Los Cuatro Soles*, both of which depict ancient Mesoamerican rituals. *Nahualismo* premiered on national radio of El Salvador in 1936, the same year that Chávez' *Sinfonía India*, featuring indigenous melodies, premiered on Boston radio and Colin McPhee's *Tabuh-Tabuhan*, featuring Balinese melodies, premiered on Mexican national radio. Evidently the international trend for such music helped the Salvadoran dictatorship to forget its differences with de Baratta.

While her compositional themes appear to be consistent with those of her peers, in no way did her indigenismo celebrate the government's efforts to establish national identity in El Salvador, which had long sought to eliminate traces of non-Hispanic culture. Her music featured aspects of her country that the government sought to bury. If she wanted to identify with nationalist composers, she did so in a way that contradicted national policy. The nation had nothing to do with her muse. Rather, the costumbres of Cuzcatlán, land of the past and imaginary land of the future, named for its geography rather than its conquerors' savior, ignited her creativity. Cuzcatlán was a Pipil name, and the Pipil lived alongside Lenca and Pokomam Maya, revering similar yet distinct deities and traditions.

De Baratta's impetus to preserve indigenous lore went beyond a desire to use it for aesthetic or identity-forming purposes; it transcended both art and politics. It was based upon what she felt was an internal mandate, upon her personal esteem of indigenous ways:

> *Cuzcatlán*, the Indian virgin, adorned with her symbolic necklace, sowing indigenous seeds in the fertile birthplace of her race . . . we must learn to see with eyes of the spirit . . . in order to experience the beauty of simple, humble things . . . we have to access the indigenous sector, where the most pure and original vernacular music, customs, legends, etc. always are . . . Obeying the mandate of the racial sap that I carry within, I have dedicated myself to study, to procure in any way, to deeply analyze the music of the Indian.[18]

Nahualismo: A Dance Drama about Doubling

A closer look at the idea and architecture of *Nahualismo* provides insights into how it artistically sought to resolve the composer's conflicts and contradictions—between admiration for indigenous culture and being raised in the Western church; between life as a privileged artist and caring about human rights; between the duties of wife and mother and those of a professional; and between indigenismo as tribute to indigenous cultures and as appropriation of those cultures for purposes unrelated to their own.

De Baratta's known compositional portfolio is exclusively indigenist. It includes the three 1930s dance dramas noted above, extant scores of which reside in the Fleisher Collection at the Free Library of Philadelphia. The piano score, *Danza indigena*, appears in Rafael González Sol's 1940 *Datos históricos sobre el arte de la música en El Salvador.* In addition, the San Salvador Ministerio de Cultura published the piano solo, *El zafa-caite: baile nacional: son*, in 1960; and arrangements of indigenous folk songs, *Estilizaciones folkloricas de Cuzcatlán típico* in 1952. An arrangement of the folksong *La Yegüita* is at the University of California–Berkeley's library. Another, *Los Tecomatillos*, appears in the Pan American Union's 1942 *Latin-American Song Book: A Varied and Comprehensive Collection of Latin-American Songs*. All of these works share indigenous inspiration.[19]

Nahualismo, as the most comprehensive of the known scores, provides a logical focus for investigation of de Baratta's compositional technique. Originally written for piano in 1934, it comprises fifteen sections, most of which bear programmatic titles related to the main theme. The length in performance is some twelve to fourteen minutes, similar to indigenist dance dramas by Chávez, Castillo, and others. Some catalogs give it the subtitle *Diabolus in Musica*, although the score from the Fleisher Collection does not. The orchestration fills fifty pages and 296 bars, and was rendered by Ricardo Hüttenrauch, who conducted the first performance by the *Orquesta de los Supremos Poderes* of San Salvador in 1936. De Baratta and Hüttenrauch presumably collaborated to produce the sonorities she intended. No known recordings are available. Nevertheless transcription (by this author) of the score into Finale has provided an audio track to facilitate analysis. The results are astonishing, insofar as they reveal a sophisticated, cabalistic scheme for depicting the subject matter and reflecting the composer's internal conflicts. An introductory discussion of Nahualism helps to frame how the topic facilitates expression and transformation of these concepts: http://unmpress.com/books/cultural-nationalism-and-ethnic-music-latin-america/9780826359759/audio.

The term "Nahualismo" refers to a variety of Mesoamerican beliefs and practices that date from before the conquest. In the words of the composer:

> One of the most entrenched sets of customs, in spite of the vigilance of the authorities, is Nahualism—witchcraft, sorcery, curses, spiritual curing and many other practices more absurd, that are found even now in the mid-twentieth century, throughout all of El Salvador and Mesoamerica . . . (of the customs that the indigenous people retained) the most curious and strongest was and is Nahualism . . . it subsisted many years after the Conquest, resisting the exhortations of missionaries and the severity of the Spaniards . . . The ancient chroniclers believed they had found in Nahualism the intervention of the devil. Nahualism had its

origin in an ancient Toltec law that prescribed the obligation to predict the horoscope of a newborn.[20]

While the term "nahual" may refer to a *bruja* (shaman or animal–spirit guide), it also represents other binaries. The Yaqui use the term "nawaa" to indicate all that is wild, as opposed to everything within the boundaries of a man-made pueblo.[21] An ancient Mayan glyph indicates both an individual's animal–spirit guide, and sleep-dream.[22] Nahualism, therefore, relates to bifurcation: of an individual into ego and animal guide; of society into the common man and the initiated bruja; of the world into the manmade and the wild; and of consciousness into the waking state and the dream state.

The term has been traced to the African-Arab root "na," which signifies wisdom and varied from one sub-region to another.[23] For example, in some cases, local shamans, who would undergo initiations and austerities to develop various powers, were referred to as nahual. Some purport to turn themselves into an animal double called a *nahual*. Nonshamanic individuals, too, usually have nahual animal guides, alter-egos, or protectors. Some think of a nahual as a malevolent being; others as a harmless trickster; and still others as a revered member of society, a *curandero*.[24] The practices of Nahualism include divination, prophecy, consulting deceased ancestors, healing ceremonies, exorcisms, prayers, incantations, music and dance, use of medicinal herbs, and propitiation of various deities including the Christian God and saints. De Baratta collected Nahualist lore from the Pipil, Lenca, and Pokomam that had individual variants.

Cuzcatlán Típico relates a gripping description of a Nahualist consultation, as told by a native of Nahuizalco, who had worked fifteen years for de Baratta's husband. The Nahuizalcan had "accompanied a friend" to consult a famous bruja of the region.

Arriving at her humble rancho, they found "miraculous herbs" and *copal* (resin incense) smoldering on a hot brazier, producing aromatic smoke. After the bruja performed lengthy incantations, waving a tule frond back and forth through the smoke, the Nahuizalcan reported a "dismal eddy shook the grounds and sent a shiver of terror" through him. Suddenly a huge frog jumped out of the stove, "croaking loudly." De Baratta concludes her retelling of the anecdote with "and as he told it to me I tell it to you, reader."[25] Its events appear to relate to a folk belief still held in parts of rural El Salvador that an evil eye or spell can cause a toad to grow in the stomach of an enemy, which can kill the enemy unless it is exorcised by a bruja.[26]

The composition *Nahualismo* seems to map to the Nahuizalcan's story. Its fifteen sections follow the contour of the tale. Their names, with translations such as "Divination," "The Spell," "Sorcery," "Bewitchment," and "Rise of the Nahual," occur in the same order as these concepts do in the anecdote. Table 6.1 compares de Baratta's music with the events of the tale, suggesting how musical devices depict them.

For example, the second section of *Nahualismo*, "Vaticinio," translates as Divination. Methods of divination vary from brujo to bruja, but may include astrology based on the Mesoamerican calendar, intricate systems of casting lots with native seeds, interpretation of omens and dreams, and reading crystals, among others. They involve mechanical application of learned procedures but are often accompanied by intuitive promptings.

The act of divination here combines the use of material objects—in this case seeds of a tree and quartz crystals—with narratives centering on the interpretation of the days within the indigenous pre-Columbian calendar, together with a shamanic gift called *copoya*, "sheet lightning," which races through the diviner's body resulting in "the speaking of the blood."[27]

The section contains musical gestures that could symbolize both mechanically performed technical procedures such as astrology, and "sheet lightning" intuition. It employs the Mesoamerican magic number thirteen in tuplets (groups of thirteen fast notes to one beat) and thirteen-bar phrases.

It features dramatic contrasts in dynamics. Its triplets suggest the lulling rhythm of the bruja's hand waving the tule frond, but sudden bursts to fifteen fast notes in the otherwise calm ground mimic flashes of intuition. The section ends with one of *Nahualismo*'s very few *ppp* (very soft) markings, as if, the divination or prophecy now complete, there is much to contemplate, nothing more to say.

The next section, "El Conjuro," refers to spell casting. The music seems to depict incantations. Its *pesante* (heavy) marking suggests deliberate utterance while visualizing an intended result. The subtitle, "Cuernos y Caracoles," refers to ancient indigenous wind instruments made from cattle horns and conches and used for ritual or magical purposes.

This and the *pesante* recall descriptions of certain Aztec ritual dances by sixteenth-century chroniclers Sahagún, as well as descriptions of certain

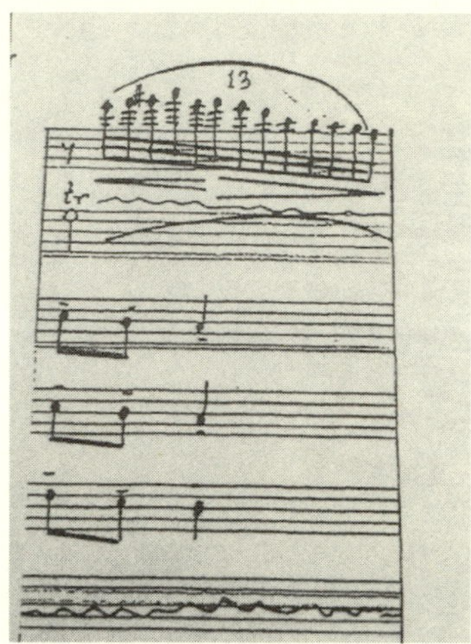

Examples of composition scores.

Mayan dances, in which the steps were close to the ground and very deliberately coordinated among the dancers.[28] Surely, both the music of these dances and Nahualist consultations were equally solemn.

"El Sortilegio" (Sorcery) technically signifies the casting of lots according to one of many systems. "Sorcery," in the vernacular, moreover, refers to invoking animal guides, spirits, or demons. This section appears at *Nahualismo*'s temporal midpoint. It presents the only change of key in the entire ballet, as well as the first use of a meter marking other than straight duple. Its compound duple character is that of a gently rocking *berceuse* (lullaby) or *barcarolle* (boat song), possibly suggesting the monotonous movements,

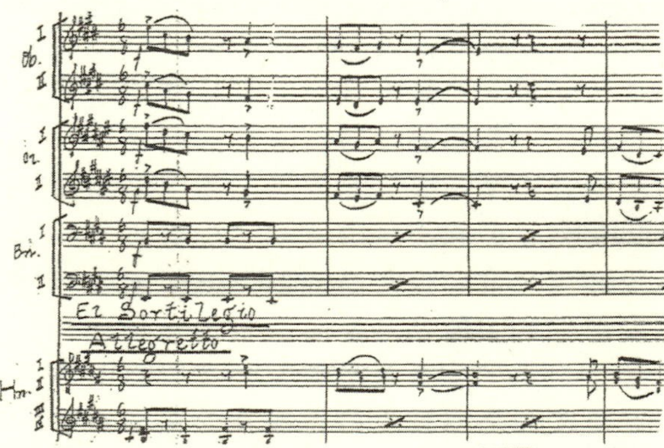

Example of composition score.

Example of composition score.

chants, and intoxicating smoke that lull client and brujo alike into a trance while wooing the double. After "El Sortilegio," "Vaticinio" returns exactly as it appeared before. This programmatically indicates another round of divination, evidently to further refine the findings of the first round.

The title of the next section, "Dance of the Cabala," is a bit enigmatic. This befits the sense of "cabala" as an occult, cryptic system. Indeed, certain ancient Mesoamerican glyphs function similarly to Cabbalistic tarot symbols, runes, or I Ching hexagrams, as agents for interpretation.[29] Dance, if not always associated with cabala, is often linked with brujería and *hechicería* (shamanism, witchcraft.) Three sequential sections of *Nahualismo* pertain to the "Dance of the Cabala" and, with diminishing tempi and characteristic dotted rhythms, suggest a serious tango or habanera.

"El Hechizo" (Bewitchment) ends with the occult dance. It and "El Sortilegio" are the only sections marked compound rather than straight duple. The rocking, lulling effect of this meter may evoke the trance of bewitchment. The melody seems to be a transfigured version of that which enters and exits abruptly in "El Sortilegio." This melody appears in other sections, disguised differently. The resultant start-interrupt-continue-interrupt-et cetera melodic contour presages Stockhausen's moment-form.

After bewitchment begins the denouement, "Surge el Nahual" (Rise of the Nahual). Descending, then ascending, arpeggios suggest text painting of something rising, perhaps the hopping of a frog. Similarly, in the following

Table 6.1. Programmatic scheme of Nahualismo

SECTION TITLE/ TRANSLATION	TEMPO	TEXT, IN ORDER IT APPEARS; TRANSLATION AUTHOR'S	EXPLANATION/MUSICAL DEPICTION
1-Andante con moto	Andante con moto	Processional, or arrival at ranchito and outline of problem to nahual "after advancing some money"	Arriving at ranch shrouded in smoke, paying money marks start of transition from one world to another. Music moves *pp* to tutti *fff*, in 2/4 processional, followed by contrasting theme of strings in stepwise 3rds alternating triplets/duplets. Harmonic in strings just before theme 2 could suggest eeriness of passing from one world to other. 2nd section finishes *fff* as if last attempt to remember world outside. Fermata may be breath before work.
2-Vaticinio (Divination)	Allegro ma non troppo	" . . . began the nahualist ceremony. In the rancho floated mystery; on a stake an owl looking on; in the middle . . . was a stove on which burned . . . copal . . . and magic herbs."	Formalities now handled, the bruja gets down to work, consulting a client's astrology and other prophetic omens, to determine causes and cures for complaint. Still in 2/4, but marked faster—allegro ma non troppo—the mechanical aspects of divination move like clockwork. The indigenous nature of divination is reflected in the septuplets and 11-tuplets in the flutes and clarinets, punctuated by a variety of sparse percussion, so similar to indigenous music idioms. Brass, too, makes interjections, and this sound is also familiarly indigenous. Fermata at end marks a shift to a less technical, more focused aspect of shaman's work.
3-El Conjuro: Cuernos y caracoles (The spell: horns and conches)	Pesante	"The owl fluttered as if obeying the rhythm of the dark hand waving a tule fan over the fire . . . saying chants to the rhythm of the swirling smoke."	Here the shaman would be conjuring the spell to bring about the needed cures. The marking here is Pesante, 2/2. The ornate wind figurations are gone and the music moves in steady quarter notes. The work at hand must be focused and serious—and the hand waves the tule frond steadily. Tutti winds and brass suggest cuernos (horns) and caracoles (conch shells), which in turn suggest the incantations. Fermata. 13 bars a magic number.
4-Marcato	No marking	"The eyes of the possessed jumped from their orbits."	The casting of the spell seems to intensify here: Shift to 4/4; more syncopation, more emphases. No fermata. Action is too intense to pause here.

5-El Sortilegio (Sorcery)	Allegretto	"The mouth contracted into a grimace of pain . . . while the bruja exhorted between her teeth . . . God for me, God for her."	Sorcery often refers to use of supernatural spirits to effect spells. 6/8 allegretto is a berceuse or barcarolle, a rocking meter a bit gentler for the dance between the person and the nahual. This is the first triple meter AND the first key change; again, indicating presence of nahual. Actually, the first gentle sections, p sections, for some time. Followed by fermata.
6-Vaticinio	Allegro ma non troppo	"The fire in the stove is dwindling, the shadows are lengthening."	Return to divination perhaps to fine-tune, checkpoint, or determine next step. This is exact duplication of the earlier Vaticinio movement, underscoring the somewhat mechanical nature of this activity. Ends ppp, fermata.
7-No name	No new marking		5 mm of 2/2 in straight quarters, recalls El Conjuro after the 1st Vaticinio but takes different direction without fermata into a dance.
8-Danza de la Cabala (Esoteric or occult matter)	No new tempo	"In the gloom the words of the exorcism in *cabala fanatica*."	3 mm of common time, no fermata over the double bar; the following Meno continues the dance, at a calmer, more stately pace. "Cabala" probably refers to a code or a cryptic jargon rather than a dance. Nevertheless, it suggests a witches' Sabbath.
9-Meno	Meno	"Low, drawn out . . . rolling"	Dance between bruja and nahua? Almost tango or habanera; no fermata.
10-Cadenza	No new tempo	"A dismal tremor shook the grounds, causing the Indian a chill of terror."	Rising wind glissandi could be word painting. No fermata.
11-No name but repeats 8	No new tempo		Da capo form when taken as one movement starting from section 8. Seems to be part of the framing of the dance.
12-El Hechizo (Bewitchment)	Allegro/rallen-tando	"Then to realize the bewitchment of the nahual"	This suggests a trance or hypnotic state at the very least Second of 2 triple (6/8) sections, suggesting the trance-like, lulled nature of bewitchment through a rocking lullaby meter. No fermata, but rallentando.
13-Piú mosso	Piú mosso	"..."	No more lull with 2/4, faster, and hocketing among the parts! Very intense.
14-Surge el Nahual (Animal spirit rises)	No new marking	"From the fire jumped a great frog."	Text painting with arpeggios down and then up the staves in strings and winds, ending very high in range, with no fermata before the final release.
15-La Carcajada (Loud Laughter)	No new marking	"croaking prophetically."	Hocketing may be croaking frog, laughing sorceress, etc. Hockets descend, followed by repeat of rising glissandi from10's shiver of terror and, almost as an afterthought, two repetitions of octaves on the "tonic" C.

Carcajada, "loud laughter," hocketing—a rapid exchange between multiple performers who each take successive notes of a melody line—seems to paint the events of de Baratta's anecdote's final section. The laughter might issue from a cackling witch, an observer's release of tension after an intense ritual, or, in the *Cuzcatlán Típico* tale, the "croaking loudly" of the frog itself.

Nahualismo's subtitle, while not always used, provides clues to its thematic and structural content. *Diabolus in Musica* is a double-entendre. It refers both to the demonic interpretation of Nahualism traditionally held by El Salvador's governmental and ecclesiastical authorities, and to a medieval European expression for the tritone, an interval of an augmented fourth, which was prohibited in church music at the time of the conquest. In addition to the clever title, De Baratta features the tritone prominently throughout *Nahualismo*, forming a musical pun with the dyad that a musical interval and a system of folk ritual represented the devil. Perhaps she found this to be as "absurd" as she had intimated she deemed Nahualism. Otherwise, would she have tempted the devil by featuring "his" tools in a work of art? Would she have used it in a pun? The rest of this section deals with cabalistic musical procedures that the composer employed in her dance drama; while they are ingenious, they involve terms that may be unfamiliar to those with little background in music; they are invited to skip to the next section, "Bruja Feminism."

The dualistic nature of the nahual is represented in several sets of binaries in *Nahualismo*. Not surprisingly for a ballet, some of the sections take a traditional binary or rounded binary dance forms. Two other binaries emerge as unique. One is the prominent gesture at the midpoint where abrupt changes in meter and key cut the work into halves. None of the sections have sharps or flats in their key signatures except "El Sortilegio," which abruptly introduces four sharps midway through the work. While the beginning and ending chords suggest the key of C, "El Sortilegio" establishes E with the sharps and a drone. In addition, here the meter makes its first formal shift, as noted above. The parts of *Nahualismo* that precede and succeed "El Sortilegio" are nearly equal in duration. An interpretation consistent with the midpoint of the anecdote in *Cuzcatlán Típico* is that here, the tension of the consultation undergoes a dramatic increase, having awakened the attention of the double, the nahual. The text reads, "The eyes of the possessed one jumped from their orbits, her mouth in a grimace of pain." This marks a pivotal fulcrum where

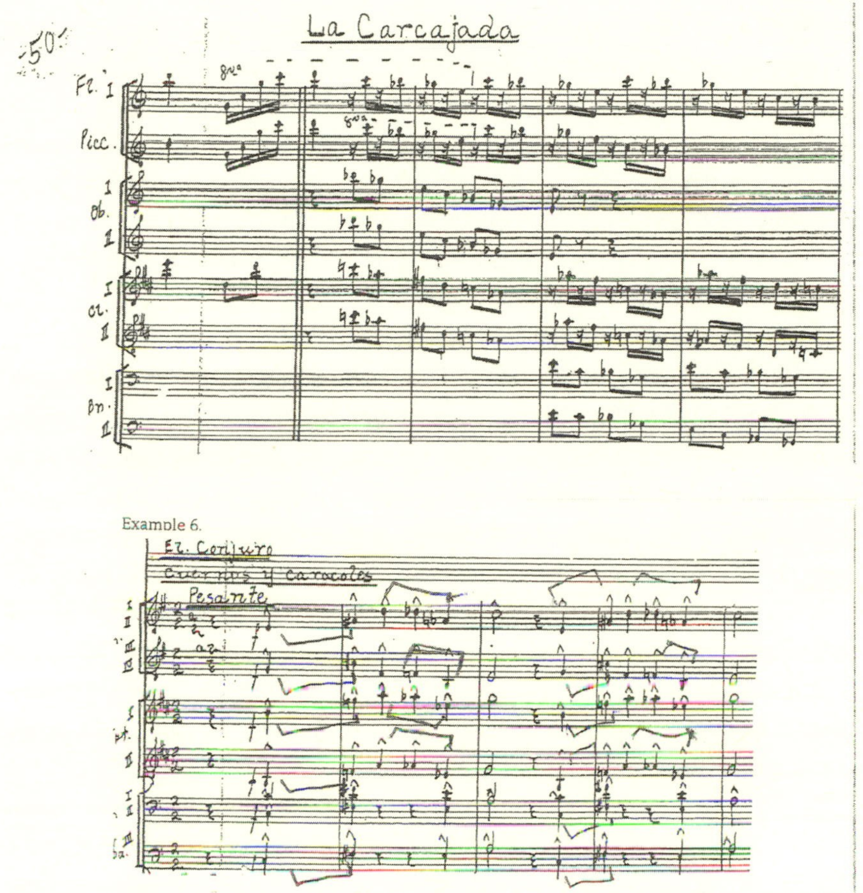

Examples of composition scores.

the episode tips away from the mundane, mechanical realm of payment and rote procedures, to the arcane realm of trance-induced materialization and shapeshifting.

The second unique binary that permeates *Nahualismo* is the interplay of two contrasting theme types. The "A" type is duple, relatively straightforward and prosaic, recalling the world of business, mechanical processes, and egos. The "B" type utilizes compound duple and lyricism, with asymmetrical groupings of quick tuplets, *hemiolae* (shifting metrical emphases between compound duple and straight triple), syncopations, and cross rhythms. It seems to represent the dream world of magic, spirits, and alter egos. The juxtaposition of theme types does not resemble classic-romantic musical forms that feature two specific themes, such as sonata-allegro form or minuet-trio; nor does it follow sonata-rondo form, although some aspects of the structure might be comparable. Rather, the two types interact unpredictably, sometimes appearing simultaneously, sometimes imitating each other, applying techniques of variation and moment-form.[30] This, combined with the midpoint shift, produces a genuinely original, cabalistic contour.

The appearances of the theme types correspond with the sequential events in the anecdote in *Cuzcatlán Típico*. The opening section presents two contrasting melodies that exemplify types "A" and "B." The first, featuring wide-spaced open chords in insistent duple, epitomizes type A; the second, with close thirds in triplets, demonstrates type B. "They arrived at her place, and after making payment, began the ceremony. In the dark grounds floated mystery; on a stake was an owl on a chain; in the middle of the prophetic habitation was a stove on which burned loaves of copal; miraculous herbs twisted below the hot coals of the small inferno."[31] The walking tempo and rhythm of type A could portray the clients arriving at the bruja's rancho, as she watches them. The triplets of type B could accompany the eerie motion of the bruja fanning the fire, seen through the clients' eyes.

In the next section, "Vaticinio," the bruja is performing diagnostic procedures to determine what types of spells or cures need to be conjured. Although the procedures might be relatively mechanical by nahual standards, they include intuitive flashes at random intervals that would appear exotic to a worldly client, and the theme is type B. The rhythm, while duple, is abundantly varied through use of groups of tuplets, and the down-up ostinato in the bass evokes the waving of a tule frond. "When the light flickers, rising from the shadows, behind the hand that fans the fire . . ." —refer again to example 1—"the *bruja* . . . recites chants to the rhythm of the swirling smoke." "El Conjuro" refers to the casting of a spell. It is slow, *forte*, duple, predominantly of the A theme type, exhibiting the focused assertiveness required to successfully cast a spell. After a *fermata* (pause) comes the "Marcato" section still in duple, louder, with more elaborate syncopations and cross rhythms, as the spell casting intensifies, and the characteristics of theme type B attempt to superimpose themselves. Several fermatae throughout this section suggest pausing to gasp or pant.

"El Sortilegio," again, arrives at the pivotal midpoint, possibly portraying the effective transition of the participants into the trance that abets the nahual's awakening. With its lulling compound duple *barcarolle* or *berceuse* rhythm, its theme type is B.

A programatic interpretation of the return of the Vaticinio that follows could be that another divination is needed to check the results of the spell and determine next steps; surely the conscientious Nahualist bruja often acts in stages. This also exemplifies Carlos Chávez's comment that magic is produced (both musically and extra-musically) through repetition.[32] "The fire in the stove is dwindling; the shadows are lengthening in the corners of the rancho." The second "Vaticinio" again precedes the first three bars of *El Conjuro*, the spell, "In the gloom, the words of the exorcism." The theme types are, respectively, B and then A, as the bruja once again incorporates herself to apply the serious focus of spell casting, "In cabala low, drawn out, mysterious, rolling in the sonorous waves of smoke: 'What leaves the nahual, what frees from evil, I ask it of the god Tecunal.'" "Danza de la Cábala" mimics a lugubrious tango. Aspects of both theme types create the ambiguity of a cryptic and occult dance. A rhythmically free Cadenza follows, suggesting the freeing of supernatural energies. The music is free, too, of the character of either theme type. Rather, the *glissandi* (rippling runs) text paint, in onomatopoeia, "A dismal eddy shook the boundaries of the rancho, sending through the Indian that witnessed this a chill of terror." "Then to realize the bewitchment of the nahual." "El Hechizo," bewitchment, is the only compound duple meter section other than "El Sortilegio." It is theme type B.

The following "Piú mosso" (A little more) raises the suspense and shifts back to faster duple, with hocketing. This lively alternation of notes between two parts symbolizes the duality of the nahual's established presence. The duple meter indicates the intensity of theme type A, "a large frog jumped from the stove." "Surge el Nahual," again, suggests unleashed forces rising and falling precipitously, as if jumping. As in the Cadenza, text painting takes a break from the constraints of theme types. Finally, "La Carcajada" (Loud laughter) serves as a codetta. The text concludes: "croaking prophetically. (And as he told it to me I tell it to you, reader)."

The overall thematic contour of *Nahualismo* follows in Schematic 1, in which types A and B are plotted against the sections, and "T" represents text painting in lieu of the dual theme types. Rather than perfect symmetry, this

Table 6.2. Schematic 1, theme types arrangement of *Nahualsimo*

THEME TYPE:	A B	B B	A A	B B	B B	A A	B T	B A	T T
SECTION #:	1 1	2 2	3 4	5 5	6 6	7 8	9 10	12 13	14 15

illustrates a general balance of the two types. The slight dominance of type B, the magic world, over A, the mundane, is consistent with the title of the work. The dissolution into text painting in the "T" sections suggests an abandonment of abstract logic for a more intuitive or magical modality.

These compositional procedures differed from the indigenismo techniques applied by de Baratta's contemporaries. While Chávez and Castillo, Moncayo and Roldán borrowed melodies, instruments, rhythms, or textures they found in the folk music of their lands, de Baratta addressed her subject matter in a more abstract, cabalistic way. *Nahualismo*'s indigenismo involved the architecture of the piece, its overall structure and contour, as a reflection of dualistic indigenous ontology. Such procedures might arguably be more acceptable to those who object to appropriation of indigenous art by bourgeois artists, as well as to bourgeois critics who object in general to folk and indigenous art.

The compositional binaries in *Nahualismo* also reflected the dualities and contradictions the composer confronted. De Baratta musically traced a Nahualist proceeding that involved activities she had verbally labeled "absurd." Nevertheless, while some of the B-type themes of the nahual's world contain arguably grotesque gestures, they are often also gentler and more lyrical than the worldly A-type themes. De Baratta subtitled her work "Diabolus in Musica." Rather than a condemnation of her own piece, this was more likely a "devilishly clever" pun on the use of a musical interval condemned by the Western church within a ballet on a topic equally condemned. While she used the interval frequently throughout the piece, it was often in association with the worldly theme type A rather than with the magical theme type B. If the tritone represented the devil, the composer made no choices as to which realm best deserved it.

De Baratta enjoyed the comforts of an affluent life, but often experienced more satisfaction when participating in the half-hidden rural world of festivity and magic. The assertive complete repeat of only the Dionysian "Vaticinio" section reflects this preference.

She socialized with prominent artists who were nominally respected by the elites, but who shared her outrage at society's treatment of indigenous people, or engaged in spiritual practices that fell outside of the strictures of the dominant religion. *Nahualismo*'s transitions between theme types reflect these contradictions, sometimes so smooth as to befuddle the listener as to when they have transpired; at other times they were abrupt, as if expressing a need to be ready to instantaneously switch guises when operating in multiple spheres. The composer admitted to indigenous blood and a mandate to preserve indigenous music, even while the hegemony preferred both the blood and its musical traces to vanish. She lived a double life—as a proper wife and mother and as a professional; as a member of society's elite and as a political dissident; as a public skeptic of indigenous ways and as a private admirer of them; as a composer and instrumentalist and as an ethnographer. The extent of her achievements reached proportions that were easily magical for their time and place. Not only was María de Baratta postnational, but in her own way, she also was a nahual—a bruja.

Bruja Feminism

De Baratta lived until 1978, but her formation was too early to qualify her as a second-wave feminist. She might have fit into the first wave: according to her grandson, she did march with the *sufragistas* (suffragettes).[33] Yet, feminism was not her focus; rather, she cultivated research, music, artistic society, and human rights activism. Feminism might have comprised a byproduct or even de facto precondition of these activities, but it was not the fundamental impetus. She moved with that which interested her, that which invoked her passion. She did not allow traditional gender roles to prohibit other pursuits. She chose her activities according to what mattered to her. These included childrearing, but were not limited to it. In a sense, she resembled a master of dissimulation, of shapeshifting as she plied several vocations; when one became impractical, she would turn her attentions to another, such as researching the brujas of Nahualismo. These shapeshifting professionals resemble de Baratta in more ways than one. They take care of people; she was a mother, hostess, and human rights activist. They operate outside of societal norms; so did she. They take ancient lore and create "magic" in the present. In the senses of art and overall work product, so did de Baratta. Her style of feminism was perhaps Kantian, presenting a public face different from the private.

The constraints within which de Baratta worked and the reception she received explains her need for a bruja approach. This term implies wisdom, just as nahual does. Chicana feminist theory recently has provided a framework for bruja feminism. Despite her economic class, the composer had obstacles to overcome as a woman and she has received only slight acknowledgement for her contributions and the prizes she won. Three publications about her stand out and she was praised especially for research "of vernacular expression" and "true revelations of the musical soul of the Pipiles, Lencas and remaining Maya-Quiché of El Salvador."[34] Perhaps she has been ignored because the quality of her music does not reach the repertoire options that musicians have. Even Chávez, whose quality as a composer seems still to please a consensus of critics, had difficulty mounting performances of his indigenist ballets, in part due to the associated expense. Nevertheless, one trait appears in a good deal of de Baratta's output: the use of danceable rhythms and textures reminiscent of popular music of her era. Parts of *Nahualismo*, such as "Danza de la Cabala," recall tango. In the latter half of the twentieth century, dance influences became unpopular among critics and acquired the condescending modifier "light." Still Chávez wrote several dances in his early career; Ravel's *Bolero* is a standard. Stravinsky's *Tango* of the 1940s and the tango portions of *Nahualismo* demonstrate "light" music informing that of "classical" composers. When Argentina's Astor Piazzolla went to Paris to study composition with the legendary Nadia Boulanger, he wrote several "serious" compositions that did not please the *maestra*. Then, on a whim, he gave her a tango; she responded enthusiastically that, from that time forward, he should write only tangos. During the early twentieth century, tango was immensely popular in Europe, where it transformed from a lascivious underground genre of resistance into a fashion avidly followed by a mix of classes. A 2012 novel, *El Tango de la Guardia Vieja*, includes the story of a composer of the 1920s who writes a tango. It describes his compositional process:

> It amuses him to work by copying other styles more than creating original ones; making winks here and there, in the manner of Schumann, Satie, Ravel . . . to *disguise himself* adopting manners of pastiche. Even parodying, and over all, parodying those who parody . . . Make no

> mistake. He is an extraordinary composer who deserves his success. He pretends to seek when he already has found, or to disdain details that he has already dealt with fastidiously. He knows how to be vulgar, but even then it is a distinguished vulgarity.[35]

This same text could be used to describe de Baratta. She disguised herself, she made parodies, she embraced vulgar gestures that her contemporaries might avoid, and she fastidiously mapped the details of her composition, as seen in her structural binaries and other symbolic techniques. In the novel, the composer is world famous. The woman at issue here is little known.

At various times, her musical works have been revived within El Salvador, but some bloggers have objected to her style of prose about Cuzcatlán, especially her dated terminology for the Indios she loved. Moreover, the *Oxford Dictionary of Music* is direct, if not ruthless, in claiming "her research suffered from conceptual limitations and has been criticized for inaccurate transcriptions."[36] It is rare, and thus possibly gender-related, to make such a sweeping criticism in an encyclopedia entry without providing examples and identifying sources. De Baratta's writing style was no worse than Chávez referring to indigenous music as "primitive."[37] While Jesús and Ricardo Castillo's publications managed to avoid such language, a closer analysis of any research of Jesús's type would likely reveal some "conceptual limitations" in hindsight. Perhaps his gender is more worthy of professional courtesy and willingness to forgive temporal markers in his writing.

Still, female ethnographers of the United States, such as Frances Densmore, receive ample attention for their contributions in spite of inaccurate transcriptions such as those which Densmore claimed as improvements.[38] Could the singular treatment of de Baratta be less related to gender and more to the status of the country from which she hailed? El Salvador is very small and relatively poor. Critics of affluent nations have probably had as much a tendency to filter out such nations' art as they have had to filter out women's. *Cuzcatlán Típico* references Henrietta Yurchenco, the vaunted ethnomusicologist of New York, as one of the colleagues with whom de Baratta interacted. Although Yurchenco was a generation younger, her goal of preserving endangered Mesoamerican music was similar to de Baratta's. Fortunately, she had the advantage of recording equipment, albeit cumbersome and rudimentary, to avoid criticism for transcriptions she did not have to make. She wrote little beyond program notes for her recordings, which avoided criticism for "conceptual limitations." Still, in her autobiography, Yurchenco did use prose consistent with usages of de Baratta and Chávez in her references to the Other, and inconsistent with today's norms.[39] Yet, this is not how her immense contributions are prominently remembered, nor how Chávez's are, nor Castillos.' Perhaps the public lost interest in de Baratta's music because she did. After the 1930s, she produced few known original compositions. During the 1940s, after the military dictatorship fell, she worked with a government committee to publish a collection of children's folksongs. Not satisfied,[40] in 1951, she followed it up with her monumental ethnography. In 1960, she published *Zafa-Caite*, a folk-inspired piano composition. Little has been documented about the rest of her life. Her grandson affirms that she remained a popular hostess and that she took up writing poetry, which has remained unpublished. While her total known compositions are relatively few, this is not the case with her ethnographic findings, which are extensive, unduplicated elsewhere, and similarly neglected. Still, the number of endeavors in which she was involved diminished her ultimate production in any one of them, and thus likely limited public awareness of her. Moreover, the exigencies of motherhood have often rendered the output of female composers greater in quality than in quantity.[41]

The bruja operates in occupations and sectors of society other than those prescribed by the bourgeoisie. Women composers have long shared this condition, as is seen in memoirs such as those of Fanny Mendelssohn Hensel.[42] At times, the bruja is a shapeshifter. Thus, it is striking the extent to which Gloria Anzaldúa's theory presents an analogy to the composer's techniques in *Nahualismo*. Consider that ecclesiastic authorities deemed Nahualism, animal-spirit doubling, of the devil, and that the etymological origin of "devil" *is* "double." Magical procedures involving doubling are, effectively, what Anzaldúa engaged for resolving binaries of working as a woman in a man's world, as a person of color in a white world, as a Spanish speaker in an English-speaking world, a bisexual in a world of opposing genders. Similar conflicts informed the puzzling dualities of *Nahualismo*. Anzaldúa entered her borderlands third space to resolve contradictory needs and identities with ancient mothers as guides—Coatlicue, the fearsome Mesoamerican mother goddess dressed in snakes and skulls; La Llorona, a mythical mother even more fearsome for having drowned her children in colonial reinterpretations, but whose actual origins extend before the conquest to the mother whose water breaks as her body is rent asunder in giving birth, causing deadly floods along with the very rain that grows food to give life to her children.[43] La Malinche, the mother of the mestizo race, feared for betraying her indigenous ancestors by her marriage to Cortez, and the Virgin of Guadalupe, whose dark face transformed prior racial conceptions of this famous mother. Just as Anzaldúa called upon mother guides, brujas call upon nahual guides, spirit doubles, and Mesoamerican and European gods to perform their tasks. De Baratta portrays such invocations and her parallel personal experiences in *Nahualismo*. In addition, Anzaldúa employed a therapeutically transcendent and transformative code switching by shifting between languages in her writing; de Baratta similarly used musical puns and binaries. Both constructed unique identities with the assistance of these methods. The identities that Anzaldúa and De Baratta constructed involved performing several identities in one body.

Cuzcatlán was María de Baratta's imaginary home. Its historic specifics long had been ravaged by subsequent authorities, yet she re-imagined them through her painstaking ethnographic research and her artistic style of writing about her findings. Thus, she created a vision for what might be a better present or future for El Salvador. Conscious construction of an imaginary reality requires dedication, perseverance, and mental focus, as does the bruja's spell casting in "El Conjuro." The fruits of such toil are, moreover, irrelevant to hegemonic objectives. They assist the individual or the subaltern collective to find identity and agency.

Martha González, musician and professor of Chicana studies, won a 2013 Grammy for the Smithsonian Folkways album by Quetzal, *Imaginaries*. In it are compositions dealing with the power of the imaginary. *Nahualismo* and *Cuzcatlán Típico* deal with this, too.

In María de Baratta's life were love for indigenous people and folk traditions, love for music and art, and love for family and friends. Sandoval expands love to include that which moves people beyond incorrect, fixed perspectives through invoking systems other than the brain, such as the heart. She references Roland Barthes's assertion that such love may be accessed through poetry, music, or spirituality—all of which Maria de Baratta practiced.

> But the differential is not easily self-consciously wielded, inhabited, named or achieved . . . the class instinct of the middle class and "*thus of intellectuals*" must undergo a painful transformation.[44]

Perhaps to modern positivist critics de Baratta's work seems romantic or awkward in some ill-defined "feminine" way.[45] Sandoval revolutionizes such a perspective, reiterating Haraway's observation that when differential consciousness is accessed, communication tends to become awkward or "stutter"; as a rational response to the awareness that many courses of action are possible. Thus, to enter the differential takes a certain egolessness and courage.

> To fall in love means that one must submit, however temporarily, to a state . . . of not being subject to control or self-governance . . . Once one recognizes this abyss *beyond dualisms* . . . then stereotypes (of love as a site of jealousy, possession, and hurt) are shaken. This form of love is not the narrative of love as encoded in the West; it is . . . a *synchronic* process that punctures through traditional, older narratives . . . that *ruptures everyday being* . . . this love . . . acts as "a punctum," as a *coatlicue* state.[46]

Love as a differential movida requires communicating from an unsure position, perhaps speaking discursively in search of the most resonant core. It requires relinquishment of the goal of embodying the Western definition of a proper intellectual, in favor of intellectual honesty. It requires invoking, possibly embodying, the archetype of the fearsome, unpredictable, and self-sacrificing mother goddess Coatlicue, who resides in the third space borderlands. This movida may appear unattractive to affluent Western eyes, but its power to help provide identity, agency, and organization for the oppressed is immense. Sandoval explains:

> Conquered and dominated populations can be incorporated into dominant society, even when this happens negatively by distributing their possibilities onto its binary rationality (male/female, heterosexual/homosexual, white/black, human/nonhuman, active/passive, same/different, etc.) But . . . There are cultural and human forms that do not slip easily into either side of a dominant binary opposition. They are the remainder—unintelligible to the dominant order—that is submerged and made invisible (to recognize them would be to upset the binary order of the same and different).[47]

In El Salvador, La Matanza went far to eliminate human forms who would not slip easily into a homogenous mestizo proletariat under the control of an elite hegemony. While many intellectuals disagreed with the authorities' methods, few stepped far outside of their comfortable situations into the differential, where they could actually make an impact. To the extent that María de Baratta did do so, she had to access the Coatlicue state of awkward-appearing love. Even if she did not proactively undertake this movida, her "internal mandate" sent her to the protest lines, sent her time and again to rural villages, impelled her to work out her conflicts through musical cabala, and propelled her to publish, after almost three decades of research counter to government objectives, an ethnography named after an imaginary, preserving lore that the authorities had sought to eliminate.

To step into the bruja's crucible of the differential is to access a space of agency and risks sacrifice of the approval of mainstream society. It turns away from bourgeois intellectual values in favor of return to earth wisdom, honesty, and originality. It seeks the aid of arcane guides and role models, as well as art, music, and poetry. It empowers Sandoval's "remainder" who do not fit hegemonic binaries. In addition, while it seems to invoke such binaries, it in fact abolishes them. It follows the "heretical" bruja full circle, to the space where the meek inherit the earth, in the words of El Salvador. Such is bruja feminism. Such was María de Baratta.

Conclusion

Around 1950 or slightly before, many composers abandoned this nationalistic approach, with varying degrees of rancor over the cooptation of their production for political ends. Carlos Chávez abandoned indigenismo for more abstract compositional procedures. Ricardo Castillo repudiated Guatemala's appropriation for identity building of his indigenist dance dramas such as *Estellas de Tikal* and *Quiché Achi*, decrying lively interpretations that had lost what he felt was a crucial Mayan sense of melancholy.[48]

María de Baratta wrestled with dualities and contradictions in her life. She employed a variety of techniques to derive power from the friction created by these conflicts. Her methods link her posthumously to postnational and third-wave feminist theory, as well as to bruja wisdom. They included inhabiting an imaginary, postnational Cuzcatlán that celebrated the indigenous culture of El Salvador; constructing her identity without undue regard for societal norms; engaging with problematic topics in her research, composition, and writing in a way that would appease authorities while foregrounding the values in the topics; employing cabalistic code switching in her composition to reveal the logical flaws in condemnation of Nahualism; and leading a life in which differential movidas such as love, music, and poetry claimed and provided agency. Perhaps her greatest legacy is as an example, even a mother guide, for future women, artists, marginalized, and lovers. De Baratta's Cuacatlán was a not national world: named for the environment, not the government; welcoming a diversity of cultures; and reaching beyond borders to corroborate and expand understanding of that diversity. Such a multiplicity of cultures befits postmodern thought that vaunts diversity, the subaltern, and the transnational. It is postnational.

Notes

1. Mirella Caceres, "Maria de Baratta: una vida de amor por el folclor," *Hablemos Online*, 2002.
2. María de Baratta, *Cuzcatlán Típico* (San Salvador: Publicaciones del Ministerio de Cultura, 1951), 263.
3. Nicolas Slonimsky, *Music of Latin America* (New York: Da Capo, 1972).
4. de Baratta, *Cuzcatlán Típico*, 5.
5. Roy Boland, *Culture and Customs of El Salvador* (Westport, CT: Greenwood, 2001), 22.
6. Jésus Castillo, *La Música Maya-Quiche* (Quetzaltenango: Editorial Piedra Santa, 1941), 78; de Baratta, *Cuzcatlán Típico*.
7. Sydney Hutchinson, "The Ballet Folklorico de México and the Construction of the of Mexican Nation Through Dance," in *Dancing Across Borders*, ed. Olga Najera Ramirez et al. (Urbana: University of Illinois Press, 2009), 206–25.
8. Gérard Béhague, "Indianism in Latin American Art Music," *Latin American Music Review* 27 (2006), 28–37.
9. de Baratta, *Cuzcatlán Típico*, front matter.
10. Caceres, "Maria de Baratta: una vida" (translation mine).

11. Virginia Tilley, *Seeing Indians: A Study of Race, Nation and Power in El Salvador* (Albuquerque: University of New Mexico Press, 2005).
12. de Baratta, *Cuzcatlán Típico*, preface.
13. Boland, *Culture and Customs of El Salvador*, 52.
14. Boland, *Culture and Customs*, 110.
15. de Baratta, *Cuzcatlán*, 263.
16. de Baratta, *Cuzcátlan*, 6.
17. Caceres, *Hablemos Online*.
18. de Baratta, *Cuzcatlán*, 5 (translation mine).
19. Sources such as Mirella Caceres's article in *Hablemos Online* and de Baratta's biographical summary in *Cuzcatlán Típico* suggest there may have been other unpublished works.
20. de Baratta, *Cuzcatlán Típico*, 263 (translation mine).
21. Edward H. Spicer, *The Yaquis: A Cultural History* (Tucson: University of Arizona Press, 1980), 169.
22. Michael D. Coe, *The Maya* (New York: Thames & Hudson, 1999), 229.
23. Ivan Van Sertima, *They Came Before Columbus* (New York: Random House,1974), 97–100. Van Sertiam proposes this link in conjunction his argument that West African traders had visited Mesoamerica well in advance of Columbus.
24. Hugo G. Nutini and John M. Roberts, *Bloodsucking Witchcraft* (Tucson: University of Arizona Press, 1993), 43.
25. de Baratta, *Cucatlán Típico*, 263 (translation mine).
26. Boland, *Culture and Customs*, 89.
27. Barbara Tedlock, "Divination as a Way of Knowing: Embodiment, Visualization, Narrative and Interpretation," *Folklore* 112, no. 2 (October 2001), 194. As an ethnomusicologist and SUNY Professor of Anthropology she was trained in Mayan divination.
28. Gertrude Kurath and Samuel Martí, *Dances of Anahuac* (Chicago: Aldine Publishing, 1974), *passim*.
29. Coe, *The Maya*, 199–229.
30. To provide examples here is prohibited by length constraints, but are available on request.

31. All of the quotations from the anecdote in de Baratta, *Cuzcatlán Típico*, 263, have been translated by me.

32. Carlos Chávez, *Musical Thought* (Cambridge, MA: Harvard University Press, 1961), 60.

33. Caceres, *Maria de Baratta: una vida*.

34. Rubén H. Dimas, preface, in de Baratta, *Cuzcatlán*.

35. Arturo Pérez-Reverte, *El Tango de la Guardia Vieja* (Doral, FL: Santillana USA, 2012), 85 (translation mine; italics mine).

36. T. M. Scruggs, "El Salvador," in *Grove Music Online*, *Oxford Music Online*, accessed November 10, 2008, http://www.oxfordmusiconline.com.ezproxy2.1ibrary.arizona.edu/subscriber/article/grove/music/08745.

37. Chávez, *Musical Thought*.

38. Robin Sacolick, "María Mendoza de Baratta: Ethnographer, Composer, *Nahual*" (paper presented at the annual meeting of Rocky Mountain Council for Latin American Studies, Santa Fe, New Mexico, March 1–5, 2009).

39. Sacolick, "Maria Mendoza de Baratta."

40. Ronald Smith, "Latin American Ethnomusicology: A Discussion of Central America and Northern South America," *Latin American Music Review/Revista de Música Latinoamericana* 3, no. 1 (Spring–Summer, 1982), 1–16.

41. Marcia Citron, ed. and trans., *The Letters of Fanny Hensel to Felix Mendelssohn* (Stuyvesant, NY: Pendragon, 1987).

42. Citron, *Letters*.

43. Gonzalo Aguirre Beltrán, *Pobladores del Papaloapan: Biografía de una hoya* (México, DF: Ediciones de la Casa Chata, 1992).

44. Sandoval, *Methodology*, 181.

45. A prominent historian with whom this author shared pieces of de Baratta's writing deemed it "romantic."

46. Sandoval, *Methodology*, 141. All italics mine except "*coatlicue*."

47. Sandoval, *Methodology*, 150.

48. Ricardo Castillo, *Recopilación de sus escritos publicados en El imparcial 1960–1966* (Guatemala: MK Ediciones, 2004).

CHAPTER 7

Cumandá: A Leitmotiv in Ecuadorian Operas?

Musical Nationalism and Representation of Indigenous People

Ketty Wong

Nationalism, understood here as a series of attitudes that unite people and shape sentiments of belonging to one nation, is commonly believed to have emerged in Europe in the aftermath of the French Revolution. In this period, a country's folklore was first regarded as a regional expression and began to be considered a national art. According to eighteenth-century philosopher Johann Gottfried von Herder, the artistic sources for the creation of a national expression are to be found in the "spirit of the people" (*volksgeit*). With the passing of time, composers began to view the folk melodies and dances of their countries as prime material for the construction of a musical nationalism.

Basing musical nationalism on folk melodies and genres is problematic because not every composition that employs folk elements implies nationalist attitudes, in the same way that not every piece of music assumed to be nationalist is based on folk elements.[1] Musical nationalism has an "aesthetic factor" that depends on the collective view and shared attitudes of both composers and listeners. Therefore, musical nationalism should be studied as a category that examines the reception and intention of people rather than a manifestation simply defined by the sound and use of folk music.

As in other Latin American countries, musical nationalism in Ecuador emerged in the first decades of the twentieth century as a result of social, artistic, and political movements. In each country, it manifested according to particular cultural and historical factors. In Mexico, for example, Carlos Chávez forged a national sentiment through a music that evoked the Aztec civilization and its glorious past. In his *Sinfonía India* (Indian symphony), he used melodies of pre-Hispanic origin to embody as he sought to express in music the nation's soul. Likewise, Ecuadorian composers expressed their national sentiment through an indigenous musical nationalism that presents a romanticized view of the past.

Although Ecuador achieved its independence in 1822, its artistic expressions continued to flourish under the Spanish cultural influence for most of the nineteenth century. Only at the end of that century did the first nationalist themes begin to appear in Ecuadorian works of art—a portrait of Indian people, a highland landscape, a novel about the life of native people, a musical theme based on an indigenous melody. Nonetheless, academic composers approached indigenous material in the first half of the twentieth century differently from writers and visual artists in terms of the temporality of historical accounts. This can be demonstrated by examining representations of indigenous people in Ecuadorian art music and comparing them with those portrayed in Ecuadorian literature and painting in the 1930s and 1940s.

Particularly, three indigenous operas serve as primary examples. They were composed by Pedro Pablo Traversari (1874–1956), Sixto María Durán (1875–1947), and Luis Humberto Salgado (1903–1977), each titled *Cumandá* and based on Juan León Mera's 1879 novel of that name. None of these operas have premiered, yet they are often heralded as expressions of academic musical nationalism; that is, the construction of sonic representations of the nation by Ecuadorian composers with conservatory training, and their employment of indigenous and *mestizo* rhythms and melodies in their works. These Ecuadorian composers' depiction of indigenous people in the first half of the twentieth century reflected *costumbrismo* and pre-Hispanic–themed images that reinforced romanticized views of indigenous people. These images stand in stark contrast with those depicted by the indigenismo and social realism literary and artistic movements in the 1930s and 1940s, which denounced the exploitation and abuse of indigenous people by landowners.

This study, based on the analysis of music scores and archival research, begins by comparing the aesthetics of costumbrismo with those of 1930s indigenismo and social realism. A discussion follows of the emergence of musical nationalism in art music and the role of *Cumandá* in the musical production of nationalist composers. The essay concludes with an exploration of Ecuadorian composers' depiction of indigenous people that is divorced from that of progressive writers and painters of the time. Understanding this phenomenon requires discussion of the social, cultural, and musical contexts in which these operas emerged.

Indigenous Operas

In the nineteenth century, several Latin American composers wrote operas narrating the encounter between Europeans and Indians. These included in Brazil, *Il Guarany* (1870) by Antônio Carlos Gomes, and in Mexico, *Guatimotzin* (1871) by Aniceto Ortega, and *Atzimba* (premiered in 1900) by Ricardo Castro. *Cumandá* continues this tradition of indigenous themes set to opera, although in this case based on a work of romantic fiction rather than on actual historical events. Published in 1879, not only did this novel open the way for the formation of a national literature with its thorough descriptions of the Ecuadorian jungle and native people, but its story also became a recurrent theme for nationalist operas.

The novel portrays the tragic love story of Cumandá, an Indian maiden from the Amazonian region who falls in love with Carlos, the son of a wealthy landowner. After Carlos's father loses his infant daughter and wife in a fire that was started during an Indian uprising, he decides to become a missionary priest as an act of penitence for his previous ruthlessness toward his Indian servants. The church sends him to a remote village in the Amazon region, and Carlos accompanies him. Carlos falls in love with Cumandá, unaware that she is his younger sister who did not, in fact, perish in the fire, but was rescued by Pona, a Palora Indian woman, who then raised her as her daughter. Their relationship is not approved and Tongana, Cumandá's purported father, forces her to marry Yahuarmaqui, an old chief from a neighboring tribe. Marked by the specter of incest, this encounter of an Indian maiden with a white man ends with the death of Cumandá who, following an indigenous ritual after Yahuarmaqui's death, is sacrificed and buried with her husband. Carlos also dies.

Like other nineteenth-century Latin American writers searching for a way to distinguish their literature from that of Europe, Mera wrote this romantic novel with Indian main characters. This literary trend from the late nineteenth century is known as Indianismo. The tragic love story of Cumandá and Carlos symbolically portrays the racial and cultural encounter of European and indigenous people and, in the impossibility of the young couple's love, the racial views of the period. According to literary critics this novel also portrays the civilization-barbarianism dichotomy prominent in late nineteenth-century literature, which is observed in the depiction of a jungle untouched by civilization and inhabited by "savage" Indians.

Indianismo differs from indigenismo and social realism, both literary and artistic trends in which writers and artists strive to provide realistic ethnic representations of the nation in their works. Indigenista writer Jorge Icaza, for example, describes in his novel *Huasipungo* (1934) a world of degradation and abuse of Indians by landowners in the highlands. In the same decade, the Guayaquil Group, formed by Enrique Gil Gilbert, Demetrio Aguilera Malta, Joaquín Gallegos Lara, José de la Cuadra, and Alfredo Pareja Diezcanseco, turned their attention to the social struggles of *montubios* (peasants), workers, and *cholos* (urbanized indigenous people) in the coastal region. By employing the colloquial language of these groups in their writings, these authors made visible sectors of society that had been neglected in the official imaginary of the nation.

In the fine arts, the paintings of Eduardo Kingman and Oswaldo Guayasamín provide analogous representations of indigenous people's anguish and misery through images of deformed faces and hands, which symbolize centuries of abuse and exploitation. With its dark tones, Guayasamín's paintings seek to provoke anger and, in Handelsman's words, "capture the horror of a society that allowed Indians to be abused."[2] These Indigenista paintings greatly contrast with the works of nineteenth-century costumbrismo painters, which take an unproblematic view of the treatment of Indians in their depictions of the landscape. An example of this trend is the watercolors of Juan Agustín Guerrero (1818–1886), a musician, writer, and painter who depicted indigenous people in social settings in everyday life, such as dancing and playing musical instruments, cooking native food, or simply walking through the streets.

Ecuadorian composers also sought to create a distinctive nationalist expression in a period in which European operas, salon music, and military marches dominated local music. They employed indigenous melodies and musical genres as well as indigenous themes referencing Ecuadorian precolonial history, although relying on European musical forms (symphonies, operas, and suites) and instrumental ensembles (symphony orchestra). This nationalist trend dominated the Latin American art music scene in the first half of the twentieth century, as the musical output of Heitor Villa-Lobos in

Brazil and Carlos Chávez in Mexico exemplify. Some composers borrowed folk melodies collected at the site of origin; others created new melodies based on stylized folk music.

According to Ecuadorian music researchers, Italian composer Domingo Brescia, who was an instructor at the National Conservatory of Quito from 1903 to 1911, was the first to encourage young Ecuadorian composers to incorporate indigenous melodies into their works.[3] He is often cited as the founding father of Ecuador's academic musical nationalism; nevertheless, it must be noted that before Brescia's arrival in Ecuador, both Traversari and Durán were already researching and writing about the particularities of indigenous music.

In 1902, Traversari wrote *El arte en América o sea historia del arte musical indígena y popular* (Art in America, that is, the history of indigenous and folkloric musical arts), a manuscript that describes indigenous and creole musical genres in several Latin American countries. His collection of Andean panpipes, ocarinas, and flutes, housed in Quito's Museum of Musical Instruments that bears his name, is impressive and indicative of a keen interest during that period in indigenous cultures. On the other hand, Durán, in his writings, was especially interested in drawing a close relationship between the Andean pentatonic scales with those of China, Japan, Indonesia, Laos, Egypt, and some European countries. He believed that "primitive races" in the Americas had their origin in Mongolia.[4] Several years later, Salgado also focused on defining the role of vernacular music in creating a symphony with Ecuadorian musical characteristics.

Traversari, Durán, and Salgado played an important role in developing an academic musical nationalism based on indigenous themes with their compositions and writings. They all held leading positions as directors of the National Conservatory of Quito and of various regimental bands from the country's military. They also wrote essays and newspaper articles commenting on musical performances held in the capital, thus orienting the public's opinion on musical matters. Likewise, they were either members of, or worked closely with, the Casa de la Cultura Ecuatoriana. This institution was founded in 1944 by writer Benjamín Carrión with the goal of strengthening a national culture after Ecuador's loss of half of its territory to Peru in 1941.[5] To overcome the psychological trauma following this loss, Carrión put forth his thesis of the "gran nación pequeña" (great small nation), which held that if Ecuador could not be a great nation through its military forces, politics, and economy, it would be one through its culture and arts.[6] Traversari, Durán, and Salgado contributed to the consolidation of this thesis with their compositions and writings.

The first self-conscious nationalist compositions for large orchestra portrayed salient rituals and historical episodes prior to the Spanish conquest, such as the consecration of the Sun's Virgins, the celebration of the Inti Raymi festivity, the decline of the Tahuantinsuyo empire, and the death of Atahualpa, the last Inca in power. Likewise, piano miniatures were often stylized renditions of indigenous and *mestizo* dances such as the *sanjuanito*, the *yaraví*, and the *albazo*, which were often grouped in a cyclic form known as Ecuadorian suite. Such suites were large-scale compositions made up of contrasting Ecuadorian dances and were modeled after the Baroque suite.[7] Their titles, such as *Escenas serraniegas* (Highland scenes) and *El páramo* (The northern highlands), often recall scenes of nature and everyday life that are reminiscent of nineteenth-century costumbrismo and Indianismo aesthetics in Ecuadorian literature and painting.

The existence of three indigenous operas based on the novel *Cumandá* may suggest an active opera tradition in Ecuador, but this is far from true. Although in the late nineteenth century Quito and Guayaquil had theaters for opera performance by foreign troupes, the country did not have the infrastructure to produce operas locally. Ecuador lacked professional music schools to train opera composers, singers, and instrumentalists for the orchestra. Founded in 1870, the National Conservatory of Quito closed its doors seven years later, only to be reopened in 1900 during the government of President Eloy Alfaro. Since the level of performance in the first decades of the conservatory's existence was still incipient, the three *Cumandá* operas were never actually performed on stage.

The loss of some of the scores for these operas has contributed to their ongoing neglect. Of the three, the only one for which the complete score survives is that of Salgado; indeed, conducted by Salgado, students of the National Conservatory of Quito performed some of its choral sections in the 1950s. Traversari's opera is frequently mentioned in biographies of him, but the actual score has yet to be found. From Durán's opera, only the manuscript of the vocal parts with piano accompaniment is preserved. In some cases, the scores are difficult to read due to the poor penmanship on the part of the composers.

JUAN LEÓN MERA

MIEMBRO CORRESPONDIENTE DE LA REAL ACADEMIA ESPAÑOLA

CUMANDÁ

Ó

UN DRAMA ENTRE SALVAJES

SEGUNDA EDICIÓN

MADRID

LIBRERÍA DE FERNANDO FÉ

Carrera de San Jerónimo, 2.

1891

Cover of the novel *Cumanda*, written by Juan Leon Mera in 1877 and the inspiration for three Ecuadorian operas.

Traversari's *Cumandá*

Because of his interest in indigenous music, Traversari is often cited as a member of the first generation of nationalist composers. He was born in Quito to a well-to-do family and studied the rudiments of music with his father, a flutist and one of the founding teachers of the first National Conservatory (1870). At ten years of age, his family moved to Chile, where Traversari received his formal music education at the local conservatory. He studied piano and cello, and had a keen interest in music theory and history. He continued his music studies in Italy, France, and Switzerland; concurrently, he began to collect ancient musical instruments from all over the world.

Traversari was a well-known public figure in Ecuador since he held important administrative positions. In 1900, he was hired as a music teacher at the refounded National Conservatory of Music in Quito; in 1903, he was appointed its vice director. In 1908, he became the army's General Director of Music Bands, and two years later was elected mayor of Quito. He was also the founder of the Academy of Fine Arts in Riobamba (1927), and the following year was appointed director of the National Conservatory of Guayaquil (1928–1936; 1944), which bears the name of Antonio Neumane, the composer of the Ecuadorian national anthem.

As mentioned earlier, little is known of Traversari's opera *Cumandá*, except that the composer himself wrote the libretto based on selected scenes from Mera's novel. While his writings and his catalog of the Museum of Musical Instruments can be found in music archives, his music scores are yet to resurface.

Durán's Cumandá

Durán was a well-known and highly esteemed figure in Quito, as this description of him in a local newspaper demonstrates: "He is the best-known person in Quito, not only because of his well-lived years, but also because he has held many public positions, carried out many duties, defended many clients as a lawyer, educated hundreds of people at the School of Arts and Handicrafts, and trained generations of artists from all social sectors."[8]

Born to a poor family, Durán was a self-taught musician who composed operas, salon music, and works for piano and orchestra in the early twentieth century. Some of his compositions received prestigious awards in Ecuador, Colombia, Peru, Argentina, and the United States.[9] In 1900, he was hired as a piano teacher at the National Conservatory of Quito, and went on to become its music director at three different points. A man of great erudition, he was an honorary member of the French Society of International History and, in recognition of his cultural endeavors, Ecuador's government gave him the Medal for First-Class Merit. Durán excelled in all the positions he held. He became a judge of the Supreme Court of Justice and also Quito's General Intendant for the Police.

Durán was appointed Director of the School of Arts and Handicrafts at a critical moment when this institution was experiencing serious economic problems and threatening to fold. At that school, students from lower-class families learned basic skills in carpentry, shoemaking, tailoring, printing, and other manual skills that would let them work and earn a living. In 1918, Durán had an unfortunate accident in which he lost the four fingers of his right hand. This tragic accident, which abruptly changed his life, made headlines in the newspapers, showing people's concern for his health and also praise for his various accomplishments. According to one newspaper account, the accident occurred when he tried to help a student who was unfamiliar with the functioning of an electric chainsaw the school had just acquired. The newspaper indicates that the student would have lost his arm had Durán not had intervened on time to remove it away from the chainsaw. Needless to say, the accident had tragic consequences for the composer because his career as a pianist ended abruptly. The government designated special funds to help Durán get medical treatment in Europe; the composer did not accept the offer.

Although his opera *Cumandá* was never performed in public, it was often cited (and still is even today) as "a great musical work that has brought glory to Ecuador's performance arts."[10] In 1916, two years before his tragic accident, *Cumandá* received warm reviews by Emilio Murillo, a renowned Colombian composer who heralded this opera as being "poised to bring at last to the old world a reconstruction of the drama, rhythms and instruments of the magnificent Inca civilization. . . . Additionally, this work will serve as a living book that will engage the erudite as much as the illiterate people in the vast field of Inca research, perhaps the last remaining line of inquiry in sociology and the arts yet to be explored."[11]

These comments situating *Cumandá* within the purview of Inca studies needs to be examined against an increasing interest in non-Western cultures in the late nineteenth century, as the emergence of world fairs in Paris, London, Philadelphia, and Chicago shows. Two specific events drew attention to the culture of the Incas. The first was the discovery of Machu Picchu in 1911 by the US explorer and historian Hiram Bingham, which spurred research and interest in this ancient civilization. The second was the premiere of the Peruvian *Zarzuela El cóndor pasa* (The condor flies, 1913) by Julio Baudouin y Paz (lyrics) and Daniel Alomía Robles (music), whose finale included a melody that became a hit straightaway and is arguably the best-known Andean melody.[12] Its pentatonic-flavored melody and the indigenous flutes in the instrumentation were the kind of exotic elements Europeans were seeking to incorporate into their works, which had come of age in the early twentieth century. These aesthetic changes are evinced in the emergence of impressionism, primitivism, expressionism, and neoclassicism in Western art music. The famous ballets that Sergei Diaghilev premiered in the early 1910s in Paris (e.g., *Prelude to the Afternoon of a Faun* by Claude Debussy, and *The Rite of Spring* by Igor Stravinsky) are but few examples of this approach.

Murillo went further in his review of *Cumandá* and compared Durán's indigenous opera with Giuseppe Verdi's *Aida* in terms of exoticism and renewal of Western European musical elements. He highlighted in *Cumandá* "the integration into the modern symphonic poem of traditions, refinements, language, costumes, rhythms, scales, modes . . . in a word, the Inca universe may be destined to disappear from the record of History."[13] Finally, he ended his review by calling on both Ecuadorians and Colombians to make sure that Durán's opera be performed and known abroad. He believed this to be an important step toward the consolidation of an Americanist art (*arte americanista*) that expresses itself through its own voice rather than by replicating Western European models.

As Durán's opera could not be performed in Quito due to the lack of resources, there were serious attempts to take the music scores to an opera theater in New York and have it performed in the United States. According to one newspaper account, enthusiasts collected a considerable amount of money to send the scores to New York City with Emilio Murillo; however, there is no evidence that a performance had ever occurred.

Structured in four acts, Durán's opera *Cumandá* is supposedly based on Traversari's libretto with additions made by Enrique Escudero, an intellectual from a well-to-do family in Quito. The libretto introduces several changes to the storyline, some of which are not historically possible. For example, Yahuarmaqui, who in Mera's novel is an elderly Jíbaro chieftain, is celebrated in the opera as an Inca king. Historical evidence shows that neither the Incas nor the Spaniards were able to conquer the Jíbaros. Yahuarmaqui's depiction is thus questionable.

Durán's opera reveals a style clearly influenced by the Italian operas that he may have heard performed by touring companies that visited Quito. Musical example 1 is a march, sung by a choir, in which indigenous warriors praise Yahuarmaqui. The melody has a clearly diatonic style, which recalls

Example of composition score.

the majestic melodies of Verdi's *Aida* rather than the indigenous pentatonic melodies that Durán employed in other nationalist works, such as the *Leyenda Incásica*, for violin and piano.

Indigenous instruments such as *quenas*, *zampoñas*, *bocinas*, and *tunduis* (drums) are introduced in the first act, and at times these are combined with the orchestra. This is a technique that other Latin American nationalist composers have employed in their works, such as Carlos Chávez, who used the *teponaztli* and the *huehuetl* (Aztec sacred drums) in his *Indian Symphony* (Béhague 1983).

Salgado's *Cumandá*

Born in 1903, Luis Humberto Salgado was a composer, pianist, teacher, and music critic of the second generation of nationalist composers. He is arguably the most outstanding and prolific Ecuadorian composer with his numerous symphonies, concertos, chamber music, piano pieces, and songs. He studied piano and composition in the 1920s at the National Conservatory of Quito and was its director for three different periods. He was also the director of the Casa de la Cultura Ecuatoriana's Music Section and conductor of the conservatory's student orchestra. He was known for his music reviews published in the local newspaper, which covered a variety of topics, such as recent trends in European art music and his views on what an Ecuadorian nationalist music ought to be.

Luis Humberto Salgado, Ecuador's most prolific composer. Courtesy of the Ecuadorian Musical Archives.

Salgado lived in a period of nationalist exaltation in the arts and set the basis for the construction of a musical nationalism in Ecuador with his writings and compositions. Unlike other fellow composers who employed folk melodies in their works, Salgado was an experimentalist who combined Ecuadorian folk music with European musical features in idiosyncratic ways. In the 1940s, for example, he combined indigenous pentatonic melodies with the twelve-tone series developed by Arnold Schoenberg, the leading figure of expressionism in Western art music. Notably Salgado never cited an indigenous melody in his musical works, although he was well acquainted with Andean folklore due to his frequent excursions to the countryside. This exposure allowed him to store in his memory vernacular melodies that enabled him to create his own music themes in that style.

Although Salgado was a well-known figure and actively participated in Quito's musical life as a pianist, his music was little known because it was seldom performed in public. Not only did his symphonies require a large orchestra that did not exist in Ecuador at the time, his compositional style was too avant-garde for musicians, who were unfamiliar with the complex harmonies derived from Salgado's application of the twelve-tone series. The public seemed similarly unprepared to hear his music, which may have sounded strange to their ears. Finally, Salgado's reserved personality did not help promote his music as it deserved.

It took Salgado approximately fourteen years (1940–1954) to complete *Cumandá*, his only indigenous opera from a total of four he composed.[14] Salgado himself wrote the libretto and structured the opera in three acts. His students from the conservatory performed a few choral fragments, which did find a small audience and were performed with the accompaniment of a piano transcription played by the composer himself.

The period in which Salgado wrote *Cumandá* was a time of experimentation and searching for national idioms. Known for his eclectic musical style, the composer utilizes a variety of musical languages—from indigenous pentatonic scales to diatonic scales to octatonic scales to the twelve-tone series—in order to depict the opera's main characters. He employs pentatonic melodies to represent Cumandá and the Indian warriors; diatonic scales for Western characters, such as Carlos and his father; and the octatonic scale and twelve-tone series to represent mystical scenes, such as the blessing by the *brujo* (indigenous sorcerer or shaman) in act 1. The indigenous characters are often depicted using the rhythm of the *sanjuanito*, the most representative indigenous musical genre in Ecuador.

The brujo scene in act 1 deserves special attention due to the inclusion of a dodecaphonic theme to portray the indigenous sorcerer. The scene describes the moment in which the brujo blesses the union of Yahuarmaqui and

Example of composition score.

Examples of composition scores.

Cumandá, a marriage that had been arranged by Tongana, Cumandá's Indian father. He has offered her daughter as a spouse to the old Indian chief in order to separate her from Carlos, and also to reinforce the friendship between their communities. The scene starts with a twelve-tone theme on a sanjuanito rhythm played by the piano.

One characteristic of the twelve-tone series technique is that none of the tones can be repeated until all twelve have been played once. Through the use of parallel thirds as interval components of the series, it is obvious that the series is arranged in sequences of notes that highlight the pentatonic structure of indigenous music. Then, the brujo sings the lyrics "the good spirits bless this union, you will be the great victorious people of the region" to a melody that is an inversion of the twelve-tone series just heard on the piano. A sequence of tritone intervals played by the orchestra adds a sense of mysticism to the scene, followed by a group of descending arpeggios playing an octatonic scale.[15] These are the kinds of compositional techniques Salgado employed to fuse European and vernacular systems.

In the love scene that takes place on the banks of the river in act 1, Cumandá and Carlos each have their own musical themes. Carlos is rowing his boat and looking forward to meeting Cumandá, while she too dreams of the coming encounter, singing to the birds and palms that surround her. Cumandá's theme in C# minor is composed of a pentatonic melody with a rhythmic accompaniment of sixteenth notes, which seems to resemble her heartbeat and symbolically expresses the anxiety she feels in anticipation of the meeting with her beloved. The high register of the accompaniment seems to represent the birdsong (musical example 3). On the other hand, Carlos's part is made up of triplets, which sonically depict the rowing of his boat and whose tempo increases parallel with his desire to see Cumandá. His vocal

Example of composition score.

part is accompanied by a harmony made up of notes that conform to a pentatonic scale, though in a different tonality from that of Cumandá (musical example 4). The music beautifully portrays the emotions and nature surrounding the young couple.

Indigenous People in Ecuadorian Art Music

As mentioned earlier, none of the nationalist composers from the first half of the twentieth century explored indigenista or social realism themes in their music, and it is worth asking why this is so. It is understandable that Traversari and Durán, both born in the mid-1870s, had each written an opera based on a classic novel of Latin American romantic literature. Nevertheless, Salgado, who was a member of the Casa de la Cultura Ecuatoriana and began to compose *Cumandá* in the early 1940s, was aware of the indigenismo aesthetics that permeated the other arts.

Nationalist composers may have felt compelled to employ themes that glorify the country's indigenous past because Amerindians were the original dwellers of the lands before the arrival of Spaniards and are thus considered the "essence of the nation." This idealization of an "archaeological" Indian who lived in current Ecuadorian territories is removed from the life experienced by contemporary Indians. On the other hand, writing an opera based on a subject critical of the ruling class, as was *Huasipungo* or any other literary work by the Guayaquil group, would have been inappropriate for an elite musical nationalism that emphasizes European aesthetics and values rather than indigenous struggles. Nonetheless, we can see an early example of critical indigenismo aesthetics in *El cóndor pasa*, the Peruvian zarzuela that denounces the exploitation of indigenous miners under British owners. Although the main hero dies in the struggle, the flight of the condor in the last scene symbolizes the Indians' hope for freedom. This kind of plot was atypical for Ecuadorian nationalist composers of this period, who preferred to set Greek and Roman tragedies to music.

Although Salgado was traditionalist in his choice of indigenous plots for a musical drama, his compositional techniques were avant-garde. Rather than addressing contemporary social issues, as his literary peers did, he was more concerned with experimenting and finding a nationalist expression that blends together Ecuadorian folk music and European modernist trends. The use of complex harmonies and a twelve-tone melody in the brujo's theme, for example, is a novelty in Ecuadorian nationalist music even by today's standards. Other nationalist composers of the period, such as Segundo Luis Moreno, Francisco Salgado, and Durán, have been conservative in their compositional methods by sticking with stylizing existing indigenous melodies.

If *Cumandá* has been a leitmotiv in Ecuadorian operas, the figure of Atahualpa, the last Inca emperor, has been a leitmotiv for instrumental compositions. It is interesting that subsequent generations of Ecuadorian nationalist composers have continued to focus on the Indian past, the most recurrent theme being the Incas' encounter with the Spanish conquistadors. Examples include Salgado's symphonic suite *Atahualpa* (1933); Durán's *Leyenda Incásica*, a chamber piece for piano and violin; *El ocaso del Tahuantinsuyo*, a symphonic poem by Corsino Durán Carrión; and *Danza Incaica*, a piano miniature by Juan Pablo Muñoz Sans. Atahualpa is such a pervasive theme in Ecuadorian art music that even in the late twentieth century, Ecuadorian conductor Álvaro Manzano composed the symphonic poem *Rumiñahui*, a programmatic orchestral piece dedicated to one of Atahualpa's generals who bravely fought against the Spaniards in Ecuador after Atahualpa's death.

Conclusion

Musical nationalisms point to particular ways of imagining the nation through music. By choosing Juan León Mera's novel *Cumandá* as inspiration for their operas, nationalist composers perpetuated images of "savage" Indians from the Amazonian jungle who are far removed from the social reality in the urban areas. In so doing, their musical nationalism was divorced from the aesthetics of indigenismo and social realism that permeated the other Ecuadorian arts in the same period. Rather than denouncing the misery and oppression of contemporary indigenous people, Ecuadorian nationalist composers were creating sonic representations of a romanticized indigenous life, which is reminiscent of the nineteenth-century Indianismo and costumbrismo literary trends. Costumbrismo can be observed in the titles of their works and in the treatment of indigenous and folk melodies as prime material for their works. Albeit different in their portrayals of indigenous peoples, both Indianismo and indigenismo depictions have greatly contributed to the construction of an Ecuadorian national art. It must be noted that although Traversari and

Durán did extensive research on the particularities of indigenous music, their operas lack the pentatonic flavor typical of Andean music, which they praised so much in their writings.

According to ethnomusicologist Gérard Béhague (1995), Latin American musical nationalism in the twentieth century continued to be generally equated with the use of national musical styles; but, as we have seen in this study, what really defines musical nationalism is a series of collective and individual attitudes toward a set of cultural values perceived as embodying images of the nation. The three Ecuadorian operas based on Mera's novel *Cumandá* are examples of this nationalistic perception that moves beyond the use of folk melodies. Even though the three operas have never been performed and their compositional styles, in terms of the use of folk melodies, differ from each other, they are all assumed to be representations of an Ecuadorian national character. This is the dominant social imaginary not only for people interested in Ecuadorian art music, but also for those who seek a national voice in the arts. Discourses about the beauty and uniqueness of these operas have been repeated so many times in conversations, newspapers, and other means of communication that many Ecuadorians seem to have a connection with it.

Thus, the question of whether the use of folk melodies defines the national character of a piece is irrelevant for understanding how Ecuadorian musical nationalism is constructed in the particular case of the three *Cumandá* operas because none of these operas have ever been performed and, therefore, the music remains unknown for most Ecuadorians. In the past decade, there have been several unsuccessful attempts to set Salgado's and Durán's operas on stage, foiled by a number of formidable structural issues. These attempts show an ongoing desire to create musical icons for the nation in the realm of classical music. This study suggests that musical nationalism may also be constructed beyond the actual sound through verbal discourses that shape collective perceptions, social imaginaries, and a sense of national pride among Ecuadorians. The prestige and legacies of Traversari, Durán, and Salgado beyond their operas greatly contributed to this construction of musical nationalism.

Notes

1. For example, indigenous music from the Amazon provinces in Ecuador is considered "ethnic" rather than national music. An anthem is considered nationalistic music, though it is rarely based on folk music.

2. Michael H. Handelsman, *Culture and Customs of Ecuador* (Westport, CT: Greenwood, 2000), 17.

3. Willi Apel, *Harvard Dictionary of Music* (Cambridge, MA: Harvard University Press, 1969), 253.

4. Durán presented his thesis at a music congress that took place in 1914 in the city of Göteborg, Sweden.

5. After the invasion of the Peruvian Army in 1941, Ecuador accepted the Protocol of Rio de Janeiro, a treaty signed in 1942 to resolve a long-standing and bitter border dispute between Peru and Ecuador. Rafael Quintero and Erica Silva, *Ecuador: una nación enciernes* (Quito: Editorial Universitaria, 2001), 190.

6. Israel and Greece were good illustrations of this thesis with the enormous influence their cultural legacies have had on modern times.

7. The Baroque suite was a cyclic composition made up of a series of dances of distinct European origin (*allemande*, *courante*, *sarabande*, and *gigue*).

8. "Es el hombre más conocido en Quito, no solo porque cuenta con muchos inviernos bien vividos, sino porque ha estado en muchos puestos públicos, ha desempeñado muchos cargos, ha defendido a muchos clientes en el ejercicio de su profesion de abogado, ha educado a centenares de muchisimos del pueblo en la Escuela de Artes y Oficios, ha formado generaciones de artistas de uno y otros sectores sociales."

9. His *Marcha Ecuador* (Ecuadorian March) won first prize in a composition contest organized by the Pan-American Union. His *Vals Colombia* was awarded first prize in a Colombian competition. In 1924, he won first prize in Peru in a contest held in honor of the centenary of the Ayacucho Battle. His *Sanjuanito* was warmly received at the Olympics in Paris in 1924.

10. "La ópera 'Cumandá,'" *El Comercio*, August 30, 1916.

11. Collection of newspaper articles about Sixto María Durán. Archivo Histórico del Ministerio de Cultura, Quito.

12. This song became popular in the 1970s in the interpretation of Simon and Garfunkel's English version "If I Could."

13. Ibid.

14. His other three operas form a trilogy about the history of Rome in the first years of Christianity: *Eunice* (1956–1957), *El Centurión* (1959–1961), and *El Tribuno* (1964–1971).

15. An octatonic scale is a scale made up of six whole tones.

CHAPTER 8

Dueling Bandoneones

Tango and Folk Music in Argentina's Musical Nationalism

Carolyne Ryan Larson

The Academia Nacional del Tango in Buenos Aires, in December 2003, inaugurated the Museo Mundial del Tango, dedicated to the "indispensable effort to safeguard our most precious cultural heritage."[1] On display in the museum, and featured on its webpage, are material objects that capture the essence of tango's cultural meaning for many Argentines: Carlos Gardel's (1890–1935) fedora, costumes of famous tango performers, and a *bandoneón*, described by the museum succinctly and tellingly as tango's "symbolic instrument."[2] The bandoneón is a kind of concertina, a relative of the accordion. Bandoneones were carried to Argentina by German, Italian, and Lithuanian immigrants in the nineteenth century, and have become the hallmark of tango music, which in turn has often been seen as the centerpiece of Argentina's musical identity. Juan Perón used tango imagery to connect with *porteño* workers; Jorge Luis Borges recognized in the *milongas* of Buenos Aires a hatchery of national spirit and poetry; and travelers to Buenos Aires today attend tango shows, purchase postcards of Carlos Gardel's beatific smile, and even try their hand at the dance's cuts and turns. Tango's power to represent Argentine culture has become transnational. Londoners and Parisians embraced tango as emblematically Argentine in the 1910s; today's Hollywood films feature sensual tango scenes; and tango clubs and festivals take place around the world, from Tokyo to Helsinki.[3]

This image of a tango-dancing Argentina is also a product of Buenos Aires's consciously cultivated centrality within Argentine culture, politics, and economics. Scholars have widely acknowledged that tango often privileges Buenos Aires over the rest of the country by asserting that a cultural icon of the port city represents the rest of the country.[4] This power has never been unrivaled, and tango's place in national iconography has always been a contested one, revealing internal cultural tensions that have shaped Argentina's twentieth century. This essay aims to outline briefly the parallel histories of tango and another important Argentine musical form, northern folk music.[5] Tango and folk music have each been understood as repositories for nostalgia about the past, as emblems for contemporary political issues and movements, and often as a combination of each. This flexibility to embody both nostalgic and political meaning has made folk music and tango historically viable identity markers throughout the tumultuous twentieth century and beyond.[6] In particular, tango and folk have each responded to crises in national identity prompted by the movements of new populations in Argentina, notably Italian and Spanish immigration in the late nineteenth and early twentieth centuries, and internal migration to Buenos Aires in the mid-twentieth century. These human movements proved unsettling to many Argentines, prompting questions about how to assimilate these "other" populations into a national community, or—conversely—how to exclude them from it.

The imagery, musical style, and instrumentation of tango and folk consciously crafted distinct national heritages. Tango, with its syncopated rhythms and dramatic dance steps, virtuosic guitars, violins, and bandoneones, has woven passionate stories of star-crossed love affairs and roguish *compadritos*, focused in Buenos Aires's urban landscape. The music and lyrics of tango reflect common porteño anxieties in the later nineteenth and twentieth centuries, and desires in the capital to craft a national origin story that was tied to the creole culture of the pampas and its urbanized expression in Buenos Aires. Early in its history, the tango was reimagined by creole nationalists as an authentic musical form, in opposition to the European immigrants flooding the city. The bandoneón offers a powerful example of this narrative's inner contradictions as an instrument imported by European migrants and appropriated to symbolize an "authentically Argentine" creole genre. Northern folk music, meanwhile, has turned some of the same musical elements—including bandoneones—to very different musical themes, including mountainous landscapes, the hardships of rural life, and the timelessness of creole and indigenous traditions. Folk music also incorporates Andean indigenous instruments, including pan flutes, the *bombo legüero*, the *erkencho*, and the *baguala*, invoking images of a timeless past and cultures connected with the land, though most folk musicians of the twentieth century have not self-identified as indigenous.[7] The different Argentinas represented by tango and folk music point out ongoing tensions in Argentina's cultural nationalism as well as how music has expressed and shaped that tension. The origins of folk music and tango, while much debated, are most interesting not in search of a single "true" version of these stories, but rather in that they reveal dense layers of highly motivated myth-making. As folk and tango dueled over centrality within twentieth-century iconographies of nationalism, they helped to shape the contested meanings of creole identity and the tangled relationship between authenticity and modernity.

Perhaps unsurprisingly, when music becomes connected with nationalism, questions arise over where that music came from. Scholars have focused considerable effort on identifying the origins of tango and Argentine folk music; both musical forms have been widely attributed with indigenous or African roots and with later creole adoption and nationalization. This type of racialized gentrification, from non-European cultural creation to creole appropriation, is hardly unique to Argentina. The twentieth century witnessed culturally appropriative nation-building projects across the Americas: in revolutionary Mexico, indigenous cultures were glorified as part of *lo mexicano* and yet state projects aimed to assimilate and Westernize indigenous communities; in Peru, the Inca became a symbolic, spiritual foundation of the nation and yet to identify as mestizo often meant far greater social privilege than to identify as indigenous; in Brazil, African culture surged to the national cultural forefront in samba and Bahiana musical style and costume, and yet the country's "racial democracy" failed to redress the strong correlation between African heritage and poverty.[8]

Florencia Garramuño has argued that musical nationalism in twentieth-century Argentina tapped into emerging aesthetics of what she calls "primitive modernism." Intellectuals like painters, poets, and musicians rejected nineteenth-century associations between primitiveness and savagery, instead understanding primitiveness as an autochthonous expression of the modern nation, and the essence of what made Latin American nations unique.[9] As Garramuño contends, the central question in Latin America's early-twentieth-century cultural nation-making was not whether the primitive is modern, but rather *which* expressions of the primitive were *most* modern and most emblematic of a national spirit. Tango and folk music engaged in this struggle as in twentieth-century Argentina. Both were creole-born projects of identity-making, which drew certain "primitive" elements from African and indigenous cultures and transformed them into modern national icons. The differences between these musical forms and the national projects they came to represent emerged from the contrasting kinds of primitivism they embraced as well as the kinds of creole nation they came to represent.

During the late nineteenth and early twentieth centuries, tango and folk music became vehicles for selectively embracing and adapting non-Western elements, including rhythm, melody, steps, style, instruments, and imagery. Creole nationalists celebrated the "primitive" origins of these musical traditions as reminders of an authentic national past and self, even as they appropriated them and reimagined them as "creole" musics. Hermano Vianna and others have argued that understanding the origins of nationally symbolic music like tango and folk sheds light on how these musical forms were transformed into national symbols. Such studies have highlighted the idea of "invented traditions" and "imagined memories," contending that a perceived need for tradition and identity leads to conscious appropriations of existing cultural forms as national emblems.[10] Tango and folk music, from this perspective, become cultural forms that are "about" the past—creating it, re-envisioning it, savoring it, connecting with it.[11]

Tango's origins have been the subject of particularly contentious debate. Scholars have argued that its roots lie in African music and dance, or in Spanish-Cuban *habaneras*, or in the influence of European *polkas*, or in the lower-class *orillas* of Buenos Aires, where urbanizing gauchos incorporated one or all of these musical influences into their own dances and songs.

Some scholars argue that tango first gained popularity in the brothels of Buenos Aires; others maintain that this is only urban legend or an unfair generalization that stigmatizes tango's early years. Some contend that the upper classes did not embrace the tango until after its reinvention in 1910s Paris and London; others insist that the elites of Buenos Aires had already been dancing the tango for decades before its European tour. As noted tango historian Simon Collier has observed, the question of tango's origins cannot be answered "with absolute precision," and yet this remains a prominent component in studies about tango, creating a kaleidoscopic array of possible origins and early histories.[12] By contrast, histories of Argentine folk music tend to begin not with the origins of folk music but rather with the beginnings of academic interest in folk music in the late nineteenth century. Early folklorists understood folk music as a timeless element of northern culture, harking back to Spain's golden age and honed by generations of creole pastoralists

Carlos Gardel.

living in the North's wild spaces. This perspective has persisted in recent historiography to the extent that scholars focus on the folklore movement, rather than the origins of folk musical traditions.

The potential drawback to focusing on tango or folk music's origins as a source of "invented traditions," as Eric Hobsbawm has shown, is that this approach implies conscious action by identifiable actors and that the process of making something "national" was to some degree controllable by the inventors.[13] If, as Collier contends, the origins of tango (and folk) may well be impossible to identify definitively, then it becomes more profitable to ask why and how these musics have been the subjects of such intense reinvention, and what agendas and perspectives those reinventions capture. These origin stories speak to the efforts of a group—in this case, predominantly creole nationalists—to look backward to a time before tango or folk music were of interest to them, in order to give that musical form a comprehensible prehistory to its modern adoption into the national fold. This nostalgia for an idealized national past has been expressed materially in both the past and the present through the objects in museums, private collections, and retail stores that are upheld as emblematic of Argentina's musical identity; in Buenos Aires, tango shoes and portraits of Carlos Gardel; in the North, reed flutes and images of Atahualpa Yupanqui.

Tensions between tango and folk as nationally iconographic musics also capture broader regional tensions between creole identity projects in Buenos Aires and the North. Over the course of the later nineteenth and early twentieth centuries, Northerners and porteños disagreed over what it meant to be creole. Northerners couched creole identity in connection with colonial Spanish heritage, along with selective indigenous influences that were often coded as cultural rather than genealogical. Mestizos and indigenous people formed a prominent demographic portion of the North's population, but these groups were often culturally subordinated to the idealized, ethnically Spanish creole in Northern *criollismo*, which celebrated the rural traditions of creole farmers, shepherds, and village life. Porteños, by contrast, understood creole identity in connection with the pampas and gaucho culture, as well as cultural connections with Northern European countries like Great Britain and France, meanwhile downplaying the overwhelming demographic influence of Spanish and Italian immigrants in Buenos Aires. Porteño creoles often saw the North as an unprogressive region that rejected modern civilization and culture in favor of backward colonial Spanish tradition, and labeled the mostly darker-skinned northern migrants arriving in Buenos Aires by the mid-twentieth century in racialized and derogatory contrast to the port city's whiter population. Northerners conversely dismissed porteño creoles as decadent sellouts to foreign influence who had forgotten their true cultural roots, their national identity hopelessly diluted by immigration and the superficial attractions of European consumerism.[14]

Both of these regional creole identities underscored the importance of Argentine birth, separating themselves from the European immigrants flooding the country in the later nineteenth and early twentieth centuries. And yet, both identities also prioritized European cultural and ethnic connections, albeit with very different parts of Europe, separating themselves from other Argentina-born groups like Afro-Argentines and indigenous populations. This overlap shows an important source of tensions between Northern and porteño creole identity projects during the twentieth century; to be creole was to be authentically Argentine, and to define what it meant to be creole directly translated into control over visions of Argentina's true nature. The ongoing tensions between creole identity projects in the North and Buenos Aires begin to illustrate why origin stories have been so crucial and so contested in histories of tango, folk music, and other nationally meaningful music. Origin stories, whether or not they are factually confirmable, capture the meaning that these musics have had for many Argentines and the flexibility of the past as a reshapeable source of legitimacy.

Tangled up in histories of musical nationalism is the question of authenticity. Both folk and tango nationalists—musicians, politicians, journalists, intellectuals, and others—have argued consistently that one or the other represents the "authentic" or "real" Argentina, raising questions about what it means to be authentic. As Zoila Mendoza has shown, Western intellectuals defining national authenticity in relation to non-Western cultural elements often struggle with a shifting balance between creating a shared and unique heritage, and yet also distancing the nation from the corruptive influence of "backward" people or practices.[15] Argentina's twentieth-century musical nationalism embodied this tension, as tango and folk music engaged in ongoing, unresolved conflict over which music represented the "real" Argentina, and which "primitive" influences were truly compatible with national creole identity. Tango has been embraced by porteños as an emblem of Buenos Aires's cultural ascendancy, used by politicians and intellectuals to politically leverage port-oriented models of *argentinidad*, even as the Afro-Argentine populations who played such an important role in the inception of tango and its "primitive modernity" were discursively erased from the urban landscape.[16] Meanwhile, folk music has been appropriated by a contradictory array of political and cultural identity movements, including a conservative northern regionalist movement in the early twentieth century, and later leftist protest movements beginning in the 1960s that politicized folk music as a vehicle for social commentary and resistance. In both cases, creole Argentines embraced non-Western cultural elements as a part of their own national heritage, while simultaneously arguing that these musics had become emblematic of an autochthonous creole nation. The contest between the different Argentinas represented by tango and folk music continued unresolved throughout the twentieth century, shifting alongside political, economic, and social currents. Exploring the histories of these musical forms side by side offers points of connection and contrast over the broad time frame of the long twentieth century, illustrating shifts of national mood and identity, and the power of music to represent them.

Tango and Folk Music: Parallel Histories and Unresolved Tension

Tango and folk's parallel histories of national musical symbolism begin in the late nineteenth century, when each began coming to the attention of creole musicians, intellectuals, and politicians. The early tangos played in the *orillas* of Buenos Aires began to move downtown during these decades, into mainstream Buenos Aires dance halls and urban culture. This transformation—so contested in its details—reflected growing social interest in identifying a national culture, in tandem with changing attitudes toward gauchos. Gauchos, the pampean cowboys who began migrating to Buenos Aires in increasing numbers toward the end of the century, had been marginalized throughout the mid-nineteenth century by the Argentine state, targeted by vagrancy laws and stereotyped as rowdy ne'er-do-wells who fled the confines of civilization in the open spaces of the pampas, living lives of random violence, dissipated alcoholism, and chronic womanizing. By the 1880s, however, the image of the gaucho was being rehabilitated by *gauchesque* literature and art that increasingly valorized gauchos for these very qualities, while the open-range cattle-grazing landscape that gauchos had occupied was slowly disappearing. Thus, gauchos became embraceable national figures as they ceased to be a potential threat to national progress.[17] José Hernández's two-part epic *El Gaucho Martín Fierro* (1872) and *La Vuelta de Martín Fierro* (1879) became emblematic of the romanticized gaucho. Through the character Martín Fierro, Hernández painted a romantic image of the gaucho:

> A son am I of the rolling plain,
> A gaucho born and bred;
> For me the whole great world is small,
> Believe me, my heart can hold it all;
> The snake strikes not at my passing foot,
> The sun burns not my head.[18]

As romanticized visions of traditional gaucho culture gathered iconographic momentum, gauchos themselves were being pushed off the pampas and settling in ever greater numbers at the fringes of Buenos Aires. These communities of urbanized gauchos took on a new and also highly symbolic identity, transforming from rough, rural nonconformists into slick, urbanized toughs called *compadritos*. Although historians generally acknowledge that Afro-Argentines played a crucial role in developing the rhythms, dance, and instrumentation of tango, as tango became increasingly connected with national culture, creole nationalists soon identified compadritos as the iconic source of "true" Argentine tango. Compadrito anthems of love and loss became the subject of countless tangos, including *El choclo*, written by Ángel Villoldo in the first decade of the twentieth century. Like many popular tangos, *El choclo* has been the subject of lyrical reinvention over time, but as it is most commonly sung, the song begins "Con este tango que es burlón y compadrito / se ató dos alas la ambición de mi suburbio" (With this tango that is playful and flashy / two wings tied ambition to my neighborhood). The narrator of *El choclo*, a compadrito who sings a love song to the tango itself, describes tango's "conjuro extraño de un amor hecho cadencia" (strange spell of a love made into rhythm) as a "mezcla de rabia, de dolor, de fe, de aucencia / llorando en la inocencia de un ritmo jugetón" (mixture of rage, of pain, of faith, of absence / crying in the innocence of a playful rhythm). The narrator cries, "tango querido / siento que tiemblan las baldosas de un bailongo / y oigo el rezongo de mi pasado" (beloved tango / I feel the shaking of the tiles of a dance hall / and I hear the rumble of my past).[19]

As tango emerged as a recognizably national cultural form on the coast, northern folk music also attracted increasing interest in the North. A wave of academic studies, travel writings, and other texts appeared in the last decade of the nineteenth century that called attention to Northern folk culture as a repository of *argentinidad* untouched by the corrupting influences of foreign immigration or cosmopolitan dissipation. Scientists like Juan B. Ambrosetti, Samuel Lafone Quevado, Adán Quiroga, and others published monographs, conference papers, and articles in museum and university journals, and their works were taken up in magazines and newspapers for a wider public readership that expressed growing interest in northern folklore as an exploration of the national past.[20] Moreover, folkloric studies were paired with—though carefully separated from—archaeological studies of ancient indigenous cultures of the Northwest like the Calchaquí and Santa María, whose striking ceramic, metallic, and other artifacts captured Argentine imaginations.[21] Folklore and ancient indigenous archaeology both suggested the ancient pedigree of the human landscape in the North, but, as scholars like Oscar Chamosa have noted, early folklorists focused their attention on the colonial Spanish elements of northern folklore, glossing over indigenous influences in present-day folk culture as romantic and abstract aesthetic contributions to a fundamentally creole tradition. Chamosa underscores the "Eurocentric agenda" of folklore study, arguing that folklorists "usually lumped all the villagers [under study] into a single ethnic category."[22] Thus, northern folklore—including folk music and instruments—emerged during this early period as a flexible symbol of an authentic Argentina that was located not in Buenos Aires but in the heart of South America, and which was identified as essentially creole with strong European connections, its links with mestizo or indigenous cultures subsumed within a focus on Spain's colonial past.

The 1910s–1920s witnessed an explosion in both tango- and folk-oriented Argentine musical nationalisms, in response to a political and social climate that increasingly valorized creole culture. By the 1910s, the civilizing promise of European immigration that had driven state policy during the later nineteenth century was tarnishing in the face of urban overpopulation, immigrant poverty, and political radicalism. Nativism intensified especially after World War I, and *criollista* cultural projects like tango and folk music played an important role in efforts to construct an autochthonous national self, even as their proponents clashed over what that national self entailed.[23] Also during these decades, Argentina's national politics changed dramatically. Escalating socialist, anarchist, and union agitation reached a breaking point in 1910 with a wave of strikes and government repression. In response to a general strike in May 1910, President Figueroa Alcorta declared a state of siege and unleashed a combined force of police and civilian militia against the strikers, resulting in a series of imprisonments, deportations, and the destruction of Anarchist and union operational headquarters in Buenos Aires. When angry Anarchist agitators bombed Buenos Aires's prominent Teatro Colón in response, Congress quickly passed legislation banning Anarchist associations and instituting six-year prison sentences for interfering with laborers willing to work during a strike.[24] In 1912, national elections were opened to mass participation through the Sáenz Peña law, which established universal male suffrage, and in 1916 the anti-oligarchic Unión Cívica

Radical gained the presidency with the election of Hipólito Yrigoyen (1916–1922; 1928–1930).

Tango enjoyed its first full flower in Buenos Aires during this period, capturing a nostalgic vision of the past and romanticizing the compadrito culture of the late nineteenth century as a vanishing class of authentic *criollismo*. While tangos expressed a nostalgic tradition, creole tango musicians and aficionados also deployed this nostalgia against the unwelcome tide of southern European immigrants, which politicized tango's nostalgia and captured the sharpening nativism of the time, especially among the city's middle and upper classes. Even as tango was becoming connected with creole resistance to unwelcome immigrant influence in the city, the immigrants also danced the tango, and some of tango's most influential early musicians were newcomers to Argentina.[25]

Meanwhile, the tango mania that gripped Paris, London, New York, and other cosmopolitan Atlantic cities in the mid-1910s contributed a transforming gentility and sleekness to the tango in Buenos Aires, offering a stark contrast between what many porteños perceived as the elevating power of Parisian enthusiasm for the tango, on one hand, and the corrupting foreignness of Italian and Spanish immigrants in the city, on the other. By the 1920s, as social unrest in Buenos Aires cooled, the national economy stabilized, and political radicalism declined, the tango attracted porteños of all classes, forming what Pablo Vila has called a tango of agreement between the sociopolitical oligarchy and the lower and middle classes.[26] Tangos were now danced in upper-class ballrooms and nightclubs by a cross-class clientele, composed especially of upper-class men and lower-class women. This clandestine intimacy on the dance floor fed the rise of tango lyrics about forbidden love affairs between upper-class men and lower-class *milonguitas*, the seductive and dangerous charms of tango dancing, and hearts broken over the tango. Among the most famous tangos of all time, *La cumparsita* was written during the late 1910s by Gerardo Hernán Matos Rodríguez, and tells the story of a doomed romance and the despair of a man abandoned by his lover:

Si supieras,	If you knew,
que aún dentro de mi alma,	that in my soul,
conservo aquel cariño	I keep that affection

que tuve para ti . . .	I had for you . . .
Quién sabe si supieras	Who knows if you knew
que nunca te he olvidado,	that I have never forgotten you,
volviendo a tu pasado	returning to your past
te acordarás de mí . . .	if you remember me . . .
. . . .	. . . .
yo siempre te recuerdo	I always remember you
con el cariño santo	with the divine affection
que tuve para ti.	I had for you.
Y estás en todas partes,	And you are everywhere,
pedazo de mi vida,	part of my life,
y aquellos ojos que fueron	
mi alegría	and those eyes that were my joy
los busco por todas partes	I search for them everywhere
y no los puedo hallar.	and I cannot find them.

Aficionados embraced tango's imagined landscape of dimly lit milongas and clandestine love affairs, lamenting vicariously the sadness of life and remembering their largely imagined urban, creole past with nostalgia and fondness.

Meanwhile, folk music's importance to an alternative imagining of Argentina also grew during the 1910s–1920s, alongside a northern regional identity movement that valorized folk culture as a seat of authentic argentinidad. While many porteños saw the North as isolated from the coastal center of Argentine culture, northern regionalists reimagined the region's distance from Buenos Aires as a strength and even a blessing, and its landlocked location in the core of the continent was recoded as not peripheral, but central. Juan B. Terán, a member of Tucumán's sugar elite and first rector of the Universidad Nacional de Tucumán, described the North in 1921 as a "geographical frontier," not because it constituted the outermost edge of civilization but because here "the mountain comes from the center of América and in Tucumán it smoothes itself out and [to the] south, the earth unfolding itself endlessly in the pampa, . . . the torrents lead into rivers and majestically soothe themselves; the brilliant sky of the tropics is profoundly chilled as it progresses; nature is less imperious, simpler the appearance of things and beings." From its position at this geographical crossroads, Terán argued that the North occupied the crux of the continent and the true seat of national "race and destiny," of argentinidad itself.[27]

During the 1910s and 1920s, northern intellectuals, educators, politicians, and others took up the task of exploring regional culture and fortifying northwestern identity through the celebration of its unique heritage. Historians have identified Terán and others as belonging to a group called the Generación del Centenario, which aimed, after the centennial of Argentina's independence statement drafted in San Miguel de Tucumán in 1816, to revitalize northern cultural identity and power within the nation.[28] This movement was organized and financed in large part by the region's rising sugar elites. The sugarcane agriculture made possible by northwestern provinces' pockets of semitropical climate was undergoing mechanization during the late nineteenth and early twentieth centuries, with resulting leaps in production and profitability. The region's sugar elites, as a result, were gaining greater social, economic, and political influence in the north, with an eye on the national stage as well. Attempts to rehabilitate and revitalize the North's reputation as a region were politically and economically useful to regional elites seeking power on a national level and prestige for their region.[29] Terán himself owned sugar mills in the region, and he participated in regionalist folklore promotion from a double position as wealthy mill owner and university administrator.

Folklore studies gained momentum in Argentine universities and museums during the 1910s–1920s; Juan B. Ambrosetti, Juan Alfonso Carrizo, Robert Lehmann-Nitsche, and others produced an increasing number of folkloric studies during these years, while magazines and newspapers picked up folkloric themes in the North and, increasingly, in Buenos Aires as well. Adán Quiroga expressed the deepening connections between folklore and national identity in a 1918 article titled "El folk-lore argentino," arguing that folklore "deals with a question whose foundations we also ascribe to the beginning of nationality."[30] The North also became a growing focus of Argentine literature during these decades, elaborating a Northern aesthetic of timeless culture and powerful nature; as Julio Aramburu wrote in his 1928 literary collection *Tucumán*:

> The ancient houses are familiar to me, the brown faces, the native costumes. In all the traces of the eternal things, endures a feeling of

> romance; in all the mystery of extinct things floats a sadness of legend. Oh, December nights, luminous and burning, that reveal to the acute spirit the legendary fascination of provincial life![31]

The romantic and mystical imagery developed here also appeared in traditional folk music and in new folk compositions of the twentieth century.

By the 1920s, regional elites also sponsored folk music and dance performances in theaters and festivals, increasingly describing the chacareras, zambas, and other folk songs and dances performed by lower-class creoles in these contexts as belonging to a shared regional culture, something to which elites belonged rather than something they simply observed.[32] This connection between folk music and regional identity revealed a strongly nostalgic tenor to northern regionalism during the 1910s–1920s. Northern frustrations against Buenos Aires's control over politics and economic resources also combined with a sense of nostalgia for what had been. Regional memory of the North's distinguished colonial past and illustrious heritage was widely felt and seen as closely connected to present concerns. In deliberately embracing folk dances and folk music as a part of *their* culture, northern sugar elites distanced themselves from porteño-centered visions of national culture and situated themselves as the champions of a marginalized people, despite the active role they often played in that marginalization as the region's largest employers and governmental representatives.

The 1930s witnessed economic depression and cultural conservatism throughout Argentina; cynicism about the elevation of European culture, which had begun to take root in Argentina shortly before World War I, grew into a crisis of modernism throughout the Americas and beyond during the later 1920s and 1930s, giving rise to antipositivist movements that sought truth beyond the bounds of Western culture. Psychoanalysis, surrealism, spiritualism, and other movements sought understanding in realms of illogic and non-Western cultures, rejecting the orderliness and optimism of modernity, embracing mystical and sometimes darker visions of humanity and everyday life.[33] In 1930s Buenos Aires, tango lyrics became "universally bleak," depicting a world mired in greed, injustice, and immorality, in which meaningful relationships between men and women were impossible.[34] Enrique Santos Discépolo typified the dark tangos of the 1930s in songs like

Cambalache, written in 1934, which describes the modern world as a "junk shop" where value becomes meaningless:

Que siempre ha habido chorros,	That there always have been thieves,
maquiavelos y estafados,	traitors and victims of fraud,
contentos y amargados,	happy and bitter,
valores y dublé . . .	precious and fake . . .
Pero que el siglo veinte	And that the twentieth century
es un despliegue	is a display
de maldá insolente,	of insolent malice,
ya no hay quien lo niegue.	no one can deny.
Vivimos revolcados	We live sunk
en un merengue	in a mire
y en un mismo lodo	and in the same mud
todos manoseados . . .	we are all stuck . . .

In the pessimistic tangos of the 1930s, nostalgia for a simpler and better past was sharpened by disillusionment with the present. The values of the past had become weaknesses in this Machiavellian world—hard work and morality were unprofitable because, as *Cambalache* lamented, "it's all the same":

Es lo mismo el que labura	He who works
noche y día como un buey,	Night and day like a mule,
que el que vive de los otros,	Is the same as he who lives off of others,
que el que mata, que el que cura	He who kills, he who cures
o está fuera de la ley . . .	Or is an outlaw . . .

The 1930s also witnessed greater commercialization of tango, as tango music and famous tango singers became the focus of porteño radio, music sales in recordings and sheet music, film, fashion, and an array of tango-themed commodities from cigarettes to perfume.[35]

Folk music also enjoyed rising popularity during the 1930s, in conjunction with the increasingly conservative national political climate. The crash of

Argentina's economy in 1929 helped pave the way for a September 1930 coup d'état against the radical government that toppled Hipólito Yrigoyen's presidency and returned an oligarchic, conservative regime to power. The 1930s, called the *década infame*, were marked by electoral fraud and political corruption, as well as a rising tide of conservative nationalism.[36] Liberal nationalism, which had championed progressive northern European countries like Great Britain and France as models for Argentine emulation, now increasingly gave way to conservative rehabilitations of Catholic and Hispanic traditions, reframing these elements as distinguished and authentic customs of Argentina's ancestral past. Conservative nationalists also restyled liberal narratives of Argentine history, vilifying previously heroized liberal statesmen like Bartolomé Mitre and Domingo Faustino Sarmiento as overly Europeanized, and locating the epitome of leadership in figures like the mid-nineteenth-century *caudillo* Juan Manuel de Rosas. Conservatives also took an anti-imperialistic stance against foreign involvement in Argentine affairs, and accused the liberal oligarchy of surrendering the nation's economic interests and natural resources to foreign interests.[37] Conservative nationalism of the 1930s was often antiforeigner, anticommunist, and antiliberal, with elements of profascist, anti-immigration, and anti-Semitic sympathies. In this new climate, many institutions created by earlier liberal governments—including many museums and universities—gradually lost state and popular support, becoming stigmatized as overly steeped in foreign intellectual traditions. As Nicola Miller writes, "From the 1930s onwards in Argentina, even to identify oneself as an intellectual was to invite accusations of supporting the *vendepatria* oligarchy and imperialism against the interests of the people."[38] Folk music became a positive embodiment of these broader currents of rising conservative political and cultural thought. Academic folklore continued to command the attention and funding of regional elites in the north and in museums and universities elsewhere, and folk music also entered the growing Argentine popular music scene, performed by an emerging set of professional musicians for a public audience rather than traditional creole performers who played for folklorists at public festivals and in their home communities.[39]

Atahualpa Yupanqui (1908–1992), a foundational figure of Argentina's folk music movement and one of Argentina's most internationally successful folk singers, began composing new folk music during the late 1920s and

1930s, inspired by traditional musical forms. One of Yupanqui's earliest songs, *Camino del indio*, was first recorded in 1936, though Yupanqui wrote it a decade earlier. *Camino del indio* painted a nostalgic landscape very different from cynical, urban tango lyrics, invoking the timelessness of indigenous Argentina, couched in the mountains of the northwest:

Caminito del indio	The Indian's Path
Sendero colla	Winding [colla] path
Sembrao de piedras	Strewn with stones
Caminito del indio	The Indian's Path
Que junta el valle con las estrellas	That joins the valley with the stars
Caminito que anduvo	The way upon which traveled
De sur a norte	From south to north
Mi raza vieja	My ancient race
Antes que en la montaña	Before in the mountain
La pachamama se ensombreciera	The Pachamama darkened
Cantando en el cerro	Singing in the hills
Llorando en el río	Crying in the river
Se agranda en la noche	Growing in the night
La pena del indio	The sorrow of the Indian
El sol y la luna	The sun and the moon
Y este canto mío	And this song of mine
Besaron tus piedras	They kissed your stones
Camino del indio	The Indian's Path
En la noche serrana	In the mountainous night
Llora la quena su honda nostalgia	The flute cries its deep longing
Y el caminito sabe	And the path knows
Quién es la chola	Who is the girl
Que el indio llama	Who the Indian calls

Se levanta en el cerro	It rises in the hills
La voz doliente de la baguala	The plaintive voice of baguala
Y el camino lamenta	And the path laments
Ser el culpable	To be the cause
De la distancia	Of the distance
Cantando en el cerro	Singing in the hills
Llorando en el río	Crying in the river
Se agranda en la noche	Growing in the night
La pena del indio	The sorrow of the Indian
El sol y la luna	The sun and the moon
Y este canto mío	And this song of mine
Besaron tus piedras	They kissed your stones
Camino del indio	The Indian's path

Yupanqui's generation of folk musicians, combining performances of traditional songs with their own original compositions in the style of northern folk music, would transform folk into an identity marker consciously embraced by a much wider cross-section of Argentines, in the North and beyond. The images invoked by *El camino del indio*—nature as an ancient and spiritual presence, indigenous culture in its connections with the landscape, longing and loneliness—proliferated throughout folk music, constructing an Argentine landscape of profound antiquity and natural beauty, nostalgia for a deep past and a simpler way of being. For both tango and folk, the 1930s marked large-scale processes of cultural appropriation, detaching these musical forms from the communities associated with their origins and early existence as national musics, and transforming them into nationalized consumable forms embraced by middle- and upper-class audiences on a massive scale through radio and film, sheet music and records.

During the 1940s and 1950s, the nationalist power of tango and folk music faced the political and cultural crucible of Juan Perón's first presidency (1946–1955); under Perón, national culture became a deliberate focus of state funding and control. Among Perón's most powerful support bases were the working classes in Buenos Aires, a diverse group prominently including porteños and northern migrants. Perón worked consciously to connect with these working-class constituencies—and to distance himself from the vendepatria oligarchy—by invoking northern and porteño imagery into his political rhetoric and by championing the culture of the lower classes as the "true" culture of Argentina. As Daniel James shows, Perón wove *lunfardo*—the much-vilified slang of Buenos Aires's lower classes—and gaucheque imagery into his public speeches.[40] Perón also codified the already-growing Argentine recording industry, mandating that stations play state-determined quotas of folk music and tango. Jan Fairley notes that "while this decree was supposedly never enforced it stimulated local musical production" that aimed to satisfy state guidelines as well as growing popular demand for "national" music.[41] The growth of a northern working class in Buenos Aires contributed to the rise of *peñas folklóricas* in the city, musical venues that also became restaurants and bars, where porteños and northerners rubbed elbows, sang, and danced to northern folk music.[42]

And yet tango and folk music during these years also revealed ratcheting social tensions in the port city. Pablo Vila has contended that porteños witnessing the growing influx of northerners into the city became uncomfortable, aware of "a clash between their idealized image of gauchos and the real ones arriving in the city,"[43] whose dark faces and indigenous customs did not align with creole culture as porteños imagined it. Middle- and upper-class opponents of Perón's new worker-based politics, in particular, rejected these migrants and interpreted their arrival in the city as a threat to "their" culture and society. Under Perón these tensions intensified; middle and upper classes, who self-identified as civilized creoles, began to racialize the cultural traits of internal migrants, labeling folk music as "musica de negros."[44] Meanwhile, northern migrants who found themselves excluded from Buenos Aires society sought solace in folk music and other regional cultural forms. Thus, while the Peronist years of the 1940s and early 1950s witnessed intensifying national feelings in association with both tango and folk, these projects were often pitched against one another, translated through languages of class and race into very different expressions of an authentic Argentina. The nostalgic images that these musics offered their audiences—tango's impassioned urban landscape and folk music's fusion between timeless culture and vast nature—became strongly politicized, especially within Buenos Aires, as expressions of social division, hostility, and mutual rejection. Folk music continued to be a focus of academic study during these decades; by the

1940s, northern folklorists working in a series of folklore institutes, university departments, and museums were publishing field guides like *Instrucciones generals para la recolección de material folklórico* in an effort to rescue folk culture before it disappeared into oblivion, in keeping with global practices of "salvage" ethnography.[45] Despite these fears that folk culture was waning, folk music also expanded its commercial presence enormously during the 1940s–1950s, performed and recorded by popular groups including *Los Chalchaleros* (formed in 1948) and *Los Fronterizos* (formed in 1953).

While tango continued to play an important role in porteño cultural identity, battling against newly ascendant musical movements like *rock nacional*, by the 1960s, folk music was enjoying an unprecedented explosion in popularity and political meaning. The *boom folkórica* of the 1960s crossed national borders, connecting Argentina's folk music scene with performers in Chile, Cuba, and elsewhere, and transforming folk music's associations with Argentine cultural traditions into a broader movement that spoke to political, social, and human values across Latin America. Scholars have connected folk music's broad-based success in later twentieth-century Latin America with a flexibility of musical expression, crises of urbanization and industrialization, and political protest against repressive military dictatorships, human rights abuses, and social injustice.[46] Atahualpa Yupanqui, who became one of the most influential figures in Argentina's folk movement of the 1960s—alongside figures like Mercedes Sosa, Jorge Cafrune, Facundo Cabral, and groups like los Huanca Hua, los Chalchaleros, and los Fronterizos—captured many of these impulses in songs like *El arriero*, recorded by Yupanqui in the 1940s and re-recorded and performed throughout the 1960s and beyond. In *El arriero*, the solitary figure of a mule driver becomes emblematic for many of folk music's political messages in its 1960s incarnation as *Nueva Canción*:

En las arenas bailan los remolinos,	Whirlwinds dance in the sand,
el sol juega en el brillo del pedregal,	The sun plays in the brilliance of the scree,
y prendido a la magia de los caminos,	And caught by the magic of the roads,

el arriero va, el arriero va.	The mule driver goes, the mule driver goes.
. . . .	. . . .
Las penas y las vaquitas	Sorrows and cattle
se van par la misma senda.	Take the same path.
Las penas son de nosotros,	The sorrows are ours,
las vaquitas son ajenas.	The cattle belong to others.

The melancholy of *El arriero* is paired with resolve in the face of injustice and adversity; this type of bittersweet, lovely, and yet pointed lyric writing typified music of the boom folkórica, such as *Gracias a la vida*, composed in 1966 by Chilean folk singer Violetta Parra and recorded by a wide array of Latin American vocalists (including Argentine artists, notably Mercedes Sosa) after Parra's suicide in 1967.

Gracias a la vida que me ha dado tanto	Thanks to life that has given me so much
Me dio dos luceros, que cuando los abro,	It gave me two eyes, that when I open them,
Perfecto distingo lo negro del blanco	Perfectly distinguish black from white
Y en el alto cielo su fondo estrellado	And in the sky above, its starry depths
Y en las multitudes el hombre que yo amo	And in the multitude the man that I love
. . . .	. . .
Gracias a la vida que me ha dado tanto	Thanks to life that has given me so much
Me ha dado la marcha de mis pies cansados;	It has given me the march of my tired feet;
Con ellos anduve ciudades y charcos,	With them I have traversed cities and puddles,
Playas y desiertos, montañas y llanos,	Beaches and deserts, mountains and plains,
Y la casa tuya, tu calle y tu patio	And your house, your street and your patio

. . . .	. . . .
Gracias a la vida que me ha dado tanto	Thanks to life that has given me so much
Me ha dado la risa y me ha dado el llanto	It has given me laughter and it has given me tears
Así yo distingo dicha de quebranto,	So I distinguish between joy and pain,
Los dos materiales que forman mi canto,	The two materials that form my song,
Y el canto de ustedes que es el mismo canto,	And your song that is my own song,
Y el canto de todos que es mi propio canto	And the song of all that is my own song
Gracias a la vida que me ha dado tanto	Thanks to life that has given me so much

Like the folklorists of the turn of the twentieth century, folk musicians of the 1960s and 1970s based their efforts on a sense of rediscovery, invoking a cultural past and tradition that could purify the corruption of the present. Unlike early folklorists, folk musicians of the 1960s and 1970s reinterpreted the sensibilities and message of folk music in connection with present-day political and social agendas rather than capturing it in frozen, academically measured recordings that sought to "rescue" vanishing cultures. These new folk musicians, by contrast, suggested that this music was the real heart of Argentine—or Latin American—culture, and that to listen to folk music was to rediscover one's true self. From Argentina and Chile, especially, South American folk music spread to Europe and North America, where it enjoyed a transnational vogue as had tango a half-century before.[47]

Conclusions

Tensions between the cultural identity projects that embraced folk and tango as representative of an "authentic" Argentina did not resolve with the boom folklórica of the 1960s; they continue today. Today, tango and folk are both vibrant musical genres; for example, milongas and peñas each attract devoted crowds, and while they play very different music, they each act as performances and declarations of a national "us." Museums like the Museo Mundial del Tango enshrine the material culture of tango and folk as relics of Argentina's historical self, and are visited by locals and tourists alike as emblematic windows into authentic Argentine cultural heritage.[48] The ability of tango and folk music to command powerful symbolism throughout the twentieth century and into the twenty-first has lain in their flexible capacity to embody cultural traditions that are both nostalgic and politicized. In capturing "primitive" and "authentic" cultural traditions, folk and tango could be turned in support of a variety of identities and agendas, especially in response to "new" populations like foreign immigrants and internal migrants, whose movements threatened to overturn the fragile balance of still-emerging Argentine identities. This chapter does not argue that either tango or folk music is *more* authentically Argentine, or even that one or the other has been more successful at capturing claims to authenticity. Rather, the existence of these dual national musics facilitates the study of ongoing divisions of region, class, race, politics, and other identity markers as they have changed over time. As Florencia Garramuño argues, enduring tension between different musical identity movements reveals the complexities of modern nationalism; their unresolved dialogue is itself an entry point into historical understanding.

Moreover, while the social movements that inspired tango's and folk's cultural iconographic power during the early decades of the twentieth century are very different, these movements and the identities they represented also had much in common. Tango singers including the inimitable Carlos Gardel incorporated folk elements into their repertoires, and many musicians today fuse elements of both genres, meeting over common ground like the instrumental voices of the guitar and the bandoneón. Moreover, both tango and folk have promoted national identities that emphasize the value of the cultural heritage inherited by European-descended creoles—gauchos transformed into compadritos in the pampas, creole peasants in the North. It would be deceptively clean-cut, then, to suggest that folk and tango represented truly opposite or incompatible sensibilities of argentinidad; rather, the conflict between these musical models of national identity shows the importance of interpretation and of control over shared identity categories like creole heritage. Tango and folk dueled, in fact, because they competed over the right to define musically shared ground.

Websites for Further Reading, Listening, and Watching

Todo Tango: www.todotango.com
Academia Nacional del Tango: www.anacdeltango.org.ar/
Fundación Atahualpha Yupanqui: www.atahualpayupanqui.org.ar/
YouTube: www.youtube.com

Notes

1. "Inauguración de Museo Mundial del Tango," Academia Nacional del Tango, accessed October 21, 2013, http://www.anacdeltango.org.ar/museo_inauguracion.asp. This link, the original source for this information, is no longer active. For comparable information, see http://gardelysusmonumentos.blogspot.com/2008/12/en-el-museo-mundial-del-tango-buenos or html https://www.welcomeargentina.com/ciudadbuenosaires/museo-mundial-tango.html.
2. "Interior del Museo," Academia Nacional del Tango, accessed October 21, 2013, http://www.anacdeltango.org.ar/museo_interior.asp. This link, the original source for this information, is no longer active. For comparable information, see https://www.facebook.com/Academia-Nacional-del-Tango-104683766346981/.
3. US-made films have often employed the tango as an outlet for forbidden attraction, sensuality, and even romance coupled with violence. These films vary widely in subject and tone. See Martin Brest, *Scent of a Woman* (1992); James Cameron, *True Lies* (1994); Martin Campbell, *The Mask of Zorro* (1998); Peter Chelsom, *Shall We Dance* (2004); Robert Duvall, director, *Assassination Tango* (2002); Liz Friedlander, *Take the Lead* (2006); Doug Liman, *Mr. and Mrs. Smith* (2005); Baz Luhrmann, *Moulin Rouge!* (2001); Alan Parker, *Evita* (1996). Also see television shows like *Dancing with the Stars* and *So You Think You Can Dance*, where tango dancing is a staple.
4. Marta E. Savigliano, *Tango and the Political Economy of Passion* (Boulder, CO: Westview, 1995), 4; Donald S. Castro, *The Argentine Tango as Social History, 1880–1955: The Soul of the People* (San Francisco: Mellen Research University Press, 1990), 6.
5. The northern regions of Argentina have given rise to the country's most well-known and commercially successful folk music, although other regions have produced their own distinctive folk music as well. In this chapter, I refer to the North in very broad, regional strokes for the sake of space. Northwestern provinces, including Salta, Jujuy, Tucumán, and Santiago del Estero, were especially active in shaping modern Argentine folk music, and

I refer the reader to more in-depth examinations of this region and its music in my references here.

6. Shelley Garrigan's recent work on object collecting in nineteenth-century Mexico argues that objects (or here, musical traditions) can be "emptied" of earlier meanings and reinvested with new meanings according to the needs of the present. Tango and folk music have each been the subject of ongoing reinvention of this kind. See Shelley Garrigan, *Collecting Mexico: Museums, Monuments, and the Creation of National Identity* (Chapel Hill: University of North Carolina Press, 2012), 13.

7. Film is a good way to learn more about how these instruments are played and how they impact folk music and tango. For instance, see Andrés Wood, director, *Violeta se fue a los cielos* (2011), which focuses on Chilean folk musician Violeta Parra but is nonetheless a good demonstration of South American folk music; Adam Boucher, director, *Tango: The Obsession* (2007).

8. See Rick A. López, *Crafting Mexico: Intellectuals, Artisans, and the State After the Revolution* (Durham, NC: Duke University Press, 2010); Marisol de la Cadena, *Indigenous Mestizos: The Politics of Race and Culture in Cuzco, Peru, 1919–1991* (Durham, NC: Duke University Press, 2000); Thomas E. Skidmore, *Black into White: Race and Nationality in Brazilian Thought* (New York: Oxford University Press, 1974).

9. Florencia Garramuño, *Primitive Modernities: Tango, Samba, and Nation* (Stanford, CA: Stanford University Press, 2011), 33.

10. Hermano Vianna, *The Mystery of Samba: Popular Music and National Identity in Brazil*, trans. and ed. John Charles Chasteen (Chapel Hill: University of North Carolina Press, 1999); Beatriz Dujovne, *In Strangers' Arms: The Magic of the Tango* (Jefferson, NC: McFarland, 2010).

11. Dujovne, *In Strangers' Arms*, 17.

12. Simon Collier, "The Popular Roots of the Argentine Tango," *History Workshop*, no. 34, Latin American History (Autumn 1992), 92.

13. The classic text remains Eric Hobsbawm and Terence Ranger, eds., *The Invention of Tradition* (Cambridge: Cambridge University Press, 1983). See also Garramuño, *Primitive Modernities*, especially her introduction.

14. See Oscar Chamosa, "Criollo and Peronist: The Argentine Folklore Movement during the First Peronism, 1943–1955," in *The New Cultural History of Peronism*, eds. Matthew B. Karush and Oscar Chamosa (Durham, NC: Duke University Press, 2010), 113–42, for an analysis of Northern *criollismo*.

15. Zoila S. Mendoza, "Defining Folklore: Mestizo and Indigenous Identities on the Move," *Bulletin of Latin American Research* 17, no. 2 (May 1998), 166.

16. See George Reid Andrews, *The Afro-Argentines of Buenos Aires, 1800–1900* (Madison: University of Wisconsin Press); and Jorge Fortes and Diego H. Ceballos, dirs. *Afroargentinos* (New York: Third World Newsreel, 2003).

17. Scholarship on gauchesque literature and identity in nineteenth-century Argentina is vast and far more complex than I can address here. For recent treatments, see Brian Bockelman, "Between the Gaucho and the Tango: Popular Songs and the Shifting Landscape of Modern Argentine Identity, 1895–1915," *American Historical Review* (June 2011), 577–601; Ariel de la Fuente, *Children of Facundo: Caudillo and Gaucho Insurgency during the Argentine State-Formation Process (La Rioja, 1853–1870)* (Durham, NC: Duke University Press, 2000); Kathryn Lehman, "The Gaucho as Contested National Icon in Argentina," in *National Symbols, Fractured Identities: Contesting the National Narrative*, ed. Michael E. Geisler (Middlebury: Middlebury College Press, 2005), 149–71; Richard W. Slatta, *Comparing Cowboys and Frontiers* (Norman: University of Oklahoma Press. 1997).

18. José Hernández, *The Gaucho Martín Fierro*, trans. Walter Owen (New York: Farrar & Rinehart, 1936), 1:1:14. There are many translations of *Martín Fierro* into English; the Owen translation cited here is not the most linguistically accurate of available translations, favoring meter over literal translation. I prefer this translation because of its rhythmic flow, but it is certainly not the only available option or approach. See, for instance, *The Gaucho Martín Fierro*, trans. Frank G. Carrino, Alberto J. Carlos, and Norman Mangouni (Albany: State University of New York Press, 1974).

19. *El choclo* is one of the most popular tangos of all time and has been recorded by many, many artists. It was also given English lyrics and performed by Louis Armstrong as *Kiss of Fire*. Readers interested in hearing *El choclo* and *Kiss of Fire*—or any of the other songs discussed here—can easily find video and audio recordings online, via popular websites like YouTube or TodoTango.com.

20. Many of these publications appeared in Argentine scholarly journals, most prominently the *Revista del Museo de La Plata*, the *Anales del Museo de La Plata*, the published proceedings of the *Congreso Internacional de Americanistas*, as well as individual studies published by printing houses in Buenos Aires like E. Coni, Juan A. Alsina, and Buenos Aires. For a helpful, if selective, bibliography of folklore produced during this period that also demonstrates the widely varied interests of many scientists during this period, see Juan B. Ambrosetti, *Trabajos Publicados* (Buenos Aires: Imprenta de Juan A. Alsina, 1904), for a complete list of Ambrosetti's early publications, including those on northern folklore and folk music.

21. See Carolyne R. Larson, *Our Indigenous Ancestors: Museum Anthropology and Nation-Making in Argentina, 1862–1943* (University Park: Pennsylvania State

University Press, 2015), for a discussion of this archaeological work in connection with Northwestern identity and Argentine national identity more broadly.

22. Oscar Chamosa, *The Argentine Folklore Movement: Sugar Elites, Criollo Workers, and the Politics of Cultural Nationalism, 1900–1955* (Tucson: University of Arizona Press, 2010), 3, 11, 27, 56, 184.

23. David Rock, "Intellectual Precursors of Conservative Nationalism in Argentina, 1900–1927," *The Hispanic American Historical Review* 67, no. 2 (May 1987), 273.

24. David Rock, *Politics in Argentina, 1890–1930: The Rise and Fall of Radicalism* (Cambridge: Cambridge University Press, 1975), 86–87.

25. Simon Collier, Artemis Cooper, María Susana Azzi, and Richard Martin, *Tango! The Dance, the Song, the Story* (London: Thames & Hudson, 1995), especially 55–65; Simon Collier, "The Popular Roots of the Argentine Tango," *History Workshop*, no. 34, Latin American History (Autumn 1992), 92.

26. Pablo Vila, "Tango to Folk: Hegemony Construction and Popular Identities in Argentina," *Studies in Latin American Popular Culture* 10 (January 1991), 107.

27. Juan B. Terán, *La universidad y la vida* (Buenos Aires: Imprenta y Casa Editora Coni, 1921), 35.

28. Elena Perilli de Colombres Garmendia, "Lo regional, instrumento de equilibrio de la nación," in *La Generación del Centenario y su proyección en el Noroeste Argentino, 1900–1950*. Actas de las III Jornadas, tomo I (San Miguel de Tucumán, Argentina: Fundación Miguel Lillo, Centro Cultural Alberto Rougés, 2000), 206.

29. Donna Guy, *Argentine Sugar Politics: Tucumán and the Generation of Eighty* (Tempe: Center for Latin American Studies, Arizona State University, 1980); Ian Rutledge, *Cambio Agrario e Integración: El Desarollo del Capitalismo en Jujuy, 1550–1960* (Tucumán: COOTGRATUC, 1987); Patricia Arenas, "Alfred Métraux: Momentos de su paso por Argentina," *Mundo de Antes*, no. 1 (1998), 121–36; Chamosa, *The Argentine Folklore Movement*, esp., chaps. 3 and 4, 64–116.

30. Adán Quiroga, "El folk-lore argentino," *Revista argentina de ciencias politicas* 15 (1917–1918), 590.

31. Julio Aramburu, *Tucumán* (Buenos Aires: M. Gleizer, 1928), 33.

32. For more on this period, especially in sugar-growing provinces of the Northwest, see Chamosa, *The Argentine Folklore Movement*, esp. chap. 3, 64–92.

33. I gesture here to a broad body of historical literature internationally. For a sampling of other discussions of this, see Patricia Arenas, "Alfred Métraux: Momentos de su paso por Argentina," *Mundo de Antes*, no. 1 (1998), 121–36; Silvia Eugenia Formoso, "Padilla, Rougés y la cultura folkórica," in *La Generación del Centenario y su proyección en el noroeste argentino (1900–1950)*, Actas de las IV jornadas realizadas en San Miguel de Tucumán del 3 al 5 de octubre de 2001, eds. Aráoz de Isas, Florencia, Elena Perilli de Colombres Garmendía, and Elba Estela Romero de Espinosa (Tucumán: Fundación Miguel Lillo, Centro Cultural Alberto Rougés, 2002), 171–81; Robert Wohl, *The Generation of 1914* (Cambridge, MA: Harvard University Press, 1979); Edward Lucie-Smith, *Arte Latinoamericano del siglo XX* (Barcelona: Ediciones Destino, 1993), esp. chaps. 1–4; and histories focused on antipositivist trends in society and culture like Mariano Ben Plotkin's *Freud in the Pampas: The Emergence and Development of a Psychoanalytic Culture in Argentina* (Stanford, CA: Stanford University Press, 2001).

34. Daniel James, *Resistance and Integration* (Cambridge: Cambridge University Press 1988), 23, 26–27.

35. Studies that explore the commercialization and consumer culture of tango include Pablo Vila, "Tango to Folk: Hegemony Construction and Popular Identities in Argentina," *Studies in Latin American Popular Culture* 10 (January 1991), 107, accessed August 1, 2013, http://web.ebscohost.com/ehost/detail?vid=3&sid=359f0e02-6774-41ba-8e74-2e1220facff3%40sessionmgr15&hid=28&bdata=JnNpdGU9ZWhvc3QtbG12ZQ%3d%3d#db=aph&AN=9612134274; Simon Collier, "The Popular Roots of the Argentine Tango," *History Workshop*, no. 34, Latin American History (Autumn 1992), 92–100; and Simon Collier, Artemis Cooper, María Susana Azzi, and Richard Martin, *Tango!*.

36. Rock, *Argentina*, chap. 6.

37. María Luz Endere, Plácido Cali, and Pedro A. Funari, "Archaeology and Indigenous Communities: A Comparative Study of Argentinian and Brazilian Legislation," in *Indigenous Peoples and Archaeology in Latin America*, eds. Cristóbal Gnecco and Patricial Ayala (Walnut Creek, CA: Left Coast, 2011), 159; Miller, *In the Shadow of the State*; Nicola Miller, *In the Shadow of the State: Intellectuals and the Quest for National Identity in Twentieth-Century Spanish America* (London: Verso, 1999); David Rock, "Argentina, 1930–1946," in *Argentina Since Independence*, ed. Leslie Bethell (Cambridge: Cambridge University Press, 1993), 173–242.

38. Miller, *In the Shadow of the State*, 224–25.

39. For a discussion of this period, see Oscar Chamosa, *The Argentine Folklore Movement*, chap. 6.

40. Daniel James, *Resistance and Integration*, 23, 26–27.

41. Jan Fairley, "La Nueva Canción Latinoamericana," *Bulletin of Latin American Research* 3, no. 2 (1984), 110.

42. Oscar Chamosa, "Criollo and Peronist: The Argentine Folk Movement during the First Peronism, 1943–1955," in *The New Cultural History of Peronism*, eds. Matthew B. Karush and Oscar Chamosa (Durham, NC: Duke University Press, 2010), 134–35.

43. Vila, "Tango to Folk."

44. Ibid.

45. *Instrucciones generales para la recolección de material folklórico*, Instituto de Historia, Linguística, y Folklore, Universidad Nacional de Tucumán (Imprenta "El Progreso," 1942).

46. Vila, "Tango to Folk"; Fairley, "La Nueva Canción Latinoamericana"; Steve J. Stern, *Reckoning with Pinochet: The Memory Question in Democratic Chile, 1989–2006* (Durham, NC: Duke University Press, 2010).

47. Fernando Rios, "La Flûte Indienne: The Early History of Andean Folkloric-Popular Music in France and its Impact on *Nueva Canción*," *Latin American Music Review* 29, no. 2 (Fall–Winter, 2008), 145–89.

48. Museums dedicated to folklore and folk music include, but are certainly not limited to, the Museo Folklórico in La Rioja, the Museo Folklórico in San Miguel de Tucumán, and the Museo de Motivos Argentinos "José Hernández" in Buenos Aires.

CHAPTER 9

Carnival as Brazil's "Tropical Opera"

Resistance to Rio's Samba in the Carnivals of Recife and Salvador, 1960s–1970s

Jerry D. Metz Jr.

Dance fosters social exchange and camaraderie. It heightens the sense of union. As [Ernst] Grosse put it so well, "During the dance participants are in a condition of complete social unification, and the dancing group feels and acts like a single organism."

—MARIA AMÁLIA CORRÊA GIFFONI[1]

Creation and Controversy

Alongside Argentine tango, Mexican mariachi, Cuban *son*, and Dominican merengue, the story of samba's construction as symbol of Brazilian identity reigns as a textbook case of Latin American cultural nationalism. Nevertheless, resistance to samba in two northeastern Brazilian carnivals involved mediation over the values and content that regional embodiments of an ostensibly national festival should present and also over the relations of cultural power and autonomy between region and metropole. The question of whether Brazilian carnival represents a moment of social inversion, as put forth by Roberto da Matta (through Bakhtin and Durkheim), or a top-down cementing of the political and social order increasingly takes regional variation into account.[2] Carnival is well suited as a site to explore these dynamics because, prior to the imperatives to unify the vast territory starting in the national period, carnivals across Brazil had long served to incorporate and redeploy

Parts of this essay were adapted from Jerry D. Metz Jr., "*Alegria:* The Rise of Brazil's 'Carnival of Popular Participation,' Salvador da Bahia, 1950–2000s" (PhD dissertation, University of Maryland, College Park, 2012). The author thanks Marc A. Hertzman.

an immense variety of manifestations understood as typical of local conditions, meanings, and experiences.

Well before samba music emerged from the hillside parties and downtown bars of 1910s–1920s Rio de Janeiro, the wide embrace of carnival across national territory offered a way to reach people, unite them in ritual time, and meld revelry to a sense of community (influenced by ethnicity, gender, and class as well other historical factors). The idea of a unitary, unifying Brazilian carnival, national in dimension and significance but rooted in Rio, has appealed to intellectuals. As early as 1924, four years before the rise of the term *escola de samba* in Rio to describe a parading neighborhood samba club,[3] modernist poet Oswald de Andrade (1890–1954) proclaimed in his iconic "Manifesto Pau-Brasil" that "the Rio carnival is the religious event of the race."[4] The line imagines a nation (the Brazilian "race") born and ritualistically reborn annually, through dancing and singing—a collective apotheosis in celebrating Rio's carnival.

Carnival began to take on a national character with the "discovery" of samba music and dance in lower-class Afro-Brazilian quarters of Rio, and their elevation as a unique, racially harmonious festival practice in Brazil's capital. These developments were hailed by the Getúlio Vargas regime, which in the 1930s and 1940s sought to harness both national public enthusiasm for Rio's carnival and the discursive frames of samba lyrics to patriotic ideals. Classic sambas from the period that praise Brazilian history and popular culture include "São coisas nossas" (Noel Rosa, 1932) and "Aquarela do Brasil" (Ari Barroso, 1939), as well as much of Carmen Miranda's early repertoire.

At the same time carnival, initially a festive period common to the Catholic world but unanchored to any specific traditional cultural practices, was resignified as a secular celebration of the nation-state, its new meanings, textures, and rhythms reinforced through popular culture and the mass media: recordings, movies, newspapers, magazines, and radio. Television broadcasts became an especially significant medium, linking the exciting spectacle of Rio carnival to the allure of new consumer technology. What viewers saw were the parades of *escolas de samba* (samba schools),[5] required since 1936 to develop song and float themes around nationalistic topics or historical figures.

By midcentury, the escolas were part of carnival in Brazil's major cities.

In São Paulo the first escola was founded in 1937,[6] and two decades later observers of local culture were looking to the condition of the escolas as a direct index of the health of the city's carnival.[7] It was claimed of carnival in the southern city of Florianópolis in 1958 that "one of the high points is its *escolas de samba*, all spectacular and well-rehearsed, identical to those in Rio."[8] There was samba at the mouth of the Amazon: in Belém do Para in the late 1950s, local escolas de samba were the most populous type of carnival entity, incorporating up to two hundred dancers each.[9] In 1979, in the northeastern city of Teresina, Piauí, locals were "thirsty for recognition from their compatriots as full-fledged Brazilians," so they created their own Rio-style carnival featuring sixteen escolas as a gesture of cultural alignment.[10] Rio's escolas became carnival's most recognizable manifestation, a national common denominator; one ethnomusicologist notes that there remains "strong pressure to copy this kind of carnival performance everywhere else"[11] in the country.

In emphasizing Rio carnival's significance to Brazilian identity, Roberto da Matta stressed the deep egalitarian *comunitas* it revealed (a national trait, he further argued, that becomes obscured by the hierarchies and clientelism ordering quotidian life). He called the festival a national rite of passage and asserted that it was the prototype for all other carnivals in the nation.[12] In 1994 another Brazilian anthropologist, Raul Lody, offered lyrical praise of the enduring national value of Rio-style carnival: "No matter how professionalism and entrepreneurialism increasingly orient their aesthetics, *escolas de samba* still pulse with civic sentiments, their parade of colors, flags, and emblems a ceremonial theater . . . they represent a sort of national *ópera tropical*."[13]

This all accords with Hermano Vianna's *Mystery of Samba*, which emphasizes a consensus embrace of samba both during and beyond carnival. Still, as he properly notes, "The great challenge for those interested in the cultural and political unity of Brazil was to select (or invent) national traits that the *largest number* of 'patriots' would accept as exemplifying an essential Brazilian identity."[14] So, it was not unanimous.

Indeed, a few midcentury "patriots" did raise objections to the national institutionalization of escolas de samba. Unpredictably, perhaps, these included folklorists—many of whom had problems with accepting carnival itself as a nationally authentic festival of folkloric merit (except narrowly for the Recife case).[15] Suggestions by Vianna, Bryan McCann,[16] and others that there was a generalized rush to fossilize the escolas as expressing Afro-Brazilian *favela* samba's "static, pure folkloric essence" misrepresent the orientation of the folklore movement itself, launched in 1947 with the Comissão Nacional de Folclore (CNF).

In the late 1950s Rio's escolas were the source of conflict between two of Brazil's most prominent folklorists, musicologist Renato Almeida (1895–1981) and ethnologist Edison Carneiro (1912–1972). Almeida, CNF director, insisted that the escolas were a popular culture phenomenon—that is, he saw them as fully integrated into the diverse, cosmopolitan, capitalistic milieu that produced modern samba, just as detailed by McCann and Marc Hertzman,[17] which meant by definition they were nonfolkloric. Carneiro, a CNF executive, disagreed. He claimed the schools demonstrated grassroots innovation and organic democracy, of great value to a country that was experimenting again with political democracy after 1951. He argued that they needed to be allowed to evolve without the constraints of enforced standardization and judged competitions. Thus, he saw them as "folklore" understood as a dynamic process of popular, proto-political, creative association. Almeida, however, maneuvered to prevent him from including them in a proposed CNF national study of samba.[18]

Pushback against the hegemony of Rio carnival also took regional contours. In 1966 none other than sociologist Gilberto Freyre—champion of Brazil as a model of creative and peaceful sociocultural assimilation, exemplified by so-called racial democracy—fired off a column to the Pernambuco state newspaper *Jornal do Commercio* raging against the "invasion" of Rio de Janeiro–style escolas de samba into the carnival of capital city Recife.[19] This was the same Freyre cast by Vianna as among the central protagonists in the "invention" of samba as a national music in the 1920s. Freyre's avid regionalism played no small role in this later outburst. Yet his antipathy to samba was shared by a range of musicians and culture administrators across the city, where the first escolas dated to the 1930s. But by the mid-1960s Recife carnival was facing numerous threats to its vitality, and its escolas de samba were taken, forcefully if briefly, as both symbol of and scapegoat for the ostensible precariousness of cherished "authentic" local traditions. Chief among these were the kinetic *frevo*[20] music with its parasol-twirling dance and the Afro-Brazilian *maracatu de nação*[21] musical procession.

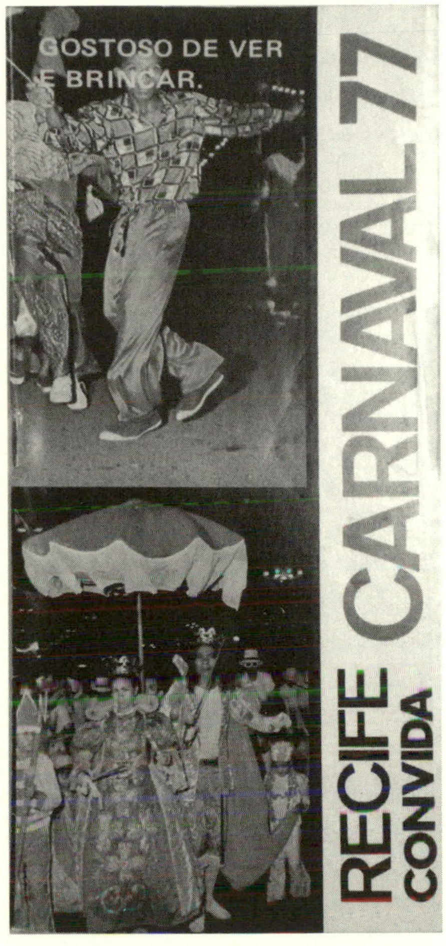

"Recife Invites You." 1977 carnival guide. Courtesy of Arquivo da Prefeitura da Cidade do Recife.

In Salvador da Bahia, another coastal city in the northeast, 675 kilometers to the south of Recife, circumstances differed. From the 1930s to the 1950s, diverse Afro-Brazilian groups such as *batucadas* or *blocos de sujo* brought the energy of samba percussion to street carnival. More formal escolas de samba—with allegorical floats and parades structured like those in Rio—rose to prominence in the 1960s and enjoyed a brief heyday until the late 1970s. Ultimately, they were crowded out by local innovations, losing space on the street as well as official support. At the time Salvador carnival was taking on a more localized character: *afoxés*,[22] a Bahian performative tradition (renovated from the late nineteenth century) mingling secular and profane aspects of Afro-Brazilian *candomblé*, were spearheading what would soon be termed the "re-Africanization"[23] of Salvador's carnival. In addition, the home-grown *trio elétrico* phenomenon[24] (starting around 1950, musicians playing amplified music atop ambulatory sound trucks while crowds freely danced along) was attracting tourists from around Brazil. A 1978 carnival exposé affirmed that representatives of the afoxês and the trios agreed with city tourism boosters: Salvador's festival was no place for so-called false escolas de samba.[25]

Performing Regional Nationalities

This naturally lent itself to tourism and place marketing. Tourism has not generally been seen as a complicating factor for carnival the way it has for Afro-Brazilian musical practice, as Béhague found in Bahia,[26] although it may contribute to the "spectacularization" of the festival: encouraging anaesthetics of scale, designed for visual impact rather than open participation, done for show. This has been a concern with Rio's carnival, since its central feature is a regulated, judged, televised parade.[27] But with the midcentury expansion of transportation infrastructure and the rise of a native travel industry, the presence of tourists—still nearly exclusively domestic ones in the 1960s and 1970s—became both a factor in organizing urban carnivals and an aspect of how the success of a given carnival was measured. Regional tourism's capitalist logic, its representational regimes, and its "fetishization of locality"[28] intervened in the nationalist project, but were largely absorbed as "heterogeneity is constantly rediscovered, and thus recreated, by a nation-building discourse that seeks to mold unity from diversity."[29] The various carnivals became privileged mediums to embody that diversity, situated within local history and local aesthetic parameters, and put proudly on display for residents and visitors.

This could involve marginalizing symbols associated with the nation's cultural, political, and economic power centers through selective assimilation or elusion. Rio-style samba might be rejected or abandoned; it might be integrated in forms adapted to local cultural norms. But the most provocative tactic, put to use differently in the cases of Recife and Salvador, was to suggest that escolas de samba did not belong outside of Rio because local carnival culture—whether traditional or new—better conveyed such national ideals as racial democracy, popular authenticity, and social inclusion.

Recife

In Recife, attempts to officialize carnival date to the mid-1930s, and folklorists took more interest in carnival there than in any other Brazilian milieu, resulting in comparatively rich historical archives in the city. The perceptions of carnival culture and the forms of carnival management established by the late 1930s would influence both Recife's carnival identity and the city's resistance against samba in the 1960s.

In 1934, several dozen prominent doctors, lawyers, politicians, artists, military officers, and businessmen came together in Recife, capital of Pernambuco, to form an organization called the Federação Carnavalesca Pernambucana (Pernambucan Carnival Federation [FCP], legally recognized in 1935). Their broad goals intended to stimulate patriotism, emphasize local pride, preserve and "dignify" traditions, boost the economy, and secure public order. The latter point was especially critical as rival carnival clubs frequently engaged in violent, bloody scuffles; the FCP hoped both to regulate and pacify carnival, then use it as the anchor of tourism campaigns.

In 1938, FCP president J. P. Fish, an American manager of Pernambuco Tramways, oversaw the publication of a carnival "yearbook," laying out the group's statutes and its vision of how carnival in Recife was properly celebrated. The 1938 *Anuário do Carnaval Pernambucano* reflected both the regionalist enthusiasm currently in vogue and the nation-based patriotism of Getúlio Vargas's New State regime.[30] Yet there is slippage when it refers to celebrating "things of the land (*coisas da terra*)." Which land was referred to? The Federation hoped to "imprint a highly nationalist character to our carnival" by encouraging the use of costumes based squarely on Pernambucan symbols: local historical characters or the state's agricultural exports. Illustrations advertising preferred costumes for the upcoming festival (marketed by local stores) recommend that men dress as Mauricio de Nassau, while women style themselves as tomatoes, pineapples, mangoes, cotton, even lobster or processed sugar.[31]

No ambiguity existed about the types of carnival organizations that reflected "our customs." In a carnival modeled directly on Rio's structure (registered groups received subsidies and competed for small prizes), escolas de samba were not listed among the five local forms recognized by the FCP—even though by 1938 Recife had at least one documented escola, and there may have been more.[32] The FCP list included *caboclinhos*, *blocos*, and *troças*, and the most prestigious, *frevo* clubs and *maracatus*. Samba received only negative mention.

Acknowledging the "universal fame" of Rio's carnival, the FCP described its samba dancing as "monotonous" and "languid," unlike that inspired by the music of local frevo orchestras where "everyone pulsates together in a contagious, captivating joy." An essay by writer Mário Sette sketches a Recife-centered history of carnival from the raucous Iberian *entrudo* (practiced since the mid-sixteenth-century and unsuccessfully banned in 1822) to frevo, and calls the latter a "typical signature" of local culture.[33] The mention of Rio's festival noted that it may have been more "luxurious and aristocratic" but lacked Recife's "popular flavor" rooted in "unique" frevo. In all, frevo's importance is underscored in a half-dozen sections of the *Anuário*. Additionally, the FCP's Statute 5 stated that the FCP would help ensure that clubs of frevo orchestras and dancers had their own assigned day during carnival to enjoy open street access in order to protect them from being run over by auto parades.[34]

Frevo's prestige over Rio's carnival samba in Recife could be justified in two ways, even beyond being locally unique. First, it was a working-class form that predated what was recognized as modern samba in Rio (or in Recife, where the first escola, Limonil, dated to the mid-late 1930s). Recife's oldest frevo clubs were Vassourinhas, founded in 1889, Pás Douradas in 1890, and Lenhadores in 1897. This gave frevo a clear advantage in disputes over the significant intangibles of traditional primacy and popular authenticity. Second, frevo's music and dance—the latter called *passo*, thought to be derived from practitioners of Afro-Brazilian *capoeira* who would clear the way for orchestras on crowded carnival streets[35]—had long been praised by regional boosters as expressing genuine mixed-race Brazilian identity. While some of the celebratory discourse of frevo's national significance was crafted in direct response to the tropes of samba-based cultural nationalism emanating from Rio, it still arises notably early in that process. In 1936, Dr. Arthur de Moura appealed to Pernambuco state government for the FCP's recognition as an "association of public utility," and said that Recife's carnival

> always had . . . the elements that enter in the formation of the Brazilian type. Masked balls or clubs and elegant dances, things common to

> European carnivals with no regional particularity, represent the ethnic element of the white race. Costumes and clubs fashioned on the aborigines, the *caboclinhos*, referencing their customs and tribal names, with flute music, hint at what Brazil was before the victory of the civilizers. Black clubs, the *maracatus*, parading African courts with their characteristic music performed on barbarous instruments, represent the negro element crudely imported for slave labor, but who contributed to our progress and to our blood . . . Finally, the wandering clubs mix and unite the three ethnic elements, with the creation of the *frevo*.[36]

Frevo music is highly syncopated, featuring elaborate horn lines over uptempo march rhythms given loose, playful verve; the passo is an individual (noncouples) dance, improvised through a repertoire of traditional moves, many of them requiring enormous agility. Folklorist Valdemar de Oliveira mused that frevo was a "genuinely *mestiço* product," performed and enjoyed by all races, and suggested the music had evolved alongside the acrobatic street dance into a unique creolized form that transcended explicit evocations of its origins in military marches, polka, and the quadrille.[37] Journalists came to adopt the trope of miscegenation to describe and advertise Recife carnival. They wrote that if whites, blacks, and indigenous could present discrete traditions from "their" cultures in carnival's multicultural kaleidoscope, the frevo was a medium to erase those distinctions and reveal "a fourth Brazilian race, embodying all the ethnic qualities of the Indian, white, and negro." This was "the new Brazilian generation, a new race, because just as *frevo* is a mixture, Nationality today also is the product of miscegenation of the three races that make up contemporary Brazilian character."[38]

The discourse of frevo's popular origin and triple ethnic integration, along with it being a unique local tradition, ultimately provided a bedrock of resistance to escolas de samba. Some observers saw them as based more narrowly on black-white cultural polarities. American ethnomusicologist Larry Crook has written that "unlike the samba, *frevo* was never a viable candidate to fulfill the role of the unifying emblem of Brazil's national consensus culture," in large part because its "authentic prototype" was not located "exclusively in Afro-Brazilian cultural roots."[39] This opinion sidesteps the powerful political symbolism of samba's discovery in Rio, the nation's capital.[40] Rio was also the center of Brazil's flourishing culture industry—and a city with very low indigenous demographics, unlike in Pernambuco or other parts of the northeast, the Amazon, or elsewhere, so including them in the cultural nationalist project was initially less strategically important to Rio's staff of functionaries, administrators, artists, and entrepreneurs. Also, Recife in the 1930s enjoyed relatively few of the modernist, globally cosmopolitan elements that led, in Vianna's analysis, to the diverse social interactions creating and justifying Rio samba as a national symbol.[41]

An argument could be made for frevo as expressing national identity, but it would be more challenging to make one for Afro-Brazilian maracatu de nação, which ranks with frevo among Pernambuco's most hailed carnival traditions. The procession incorporates ludic, performative elements of *candomblé*, with many *maracatus* being organized out of *terreiros*. The most traditional groups were, and still are, led by a *pai de santo* or even a *mãe de santo* (*candomblé* priest or priestess), with matriarchal leadership prominent. The maracatu likely originated from the colonial practice of electing a "Kongo king" among black lay Catholic brotherhoods, who would parade with a court on festival days. Elefante (founded in 1800) and Leão Coroado (1863), Recife's oldest groups, originated decades before the abolition of slavery in 1888.[42] In midcentury Recife it was common to refer to maracatus as representing an essentially "African part" of local culture brought over by slaves; the 1938 *Anuário* called maracatu "purely African." Conceiving of it as a manifestation of the Atlantic slave experience has been more recent. Still, maracatu checked the same ethnic box, as it were, that escolas de samba did for dominant classes in Rio. Recifenses could congratulate themselves for their lack of racial prejudice, proven by the prestige given to maracatus's carnival participation: "They bring to society, which does not make racial distinctions as it used to, some of the negro culture that contributed to the formation of our own."[43]

Between the 1940s and the 1960s, Recife carnival, unlike other Brazilian carnivals, was increasingly accepted by folklorists, culture managers, and journalists alike as a showcase of regional folklore anchored by frevo, maracatu, and the indigenous-themed *caboclinhos*, relative upstarts debuting in carnival in 1921.[44] The mid-1960s resonated with the earlier era of the FCP: a period of fraught politics (Brazil entered a military dictatorship in 1964 that lasted until 1985) and once again had an American at the helm of Recife's carnival management. Katherine Royal Kate (1927–2006), rendered Katarina

"Maracatu Nação Elefante, Recife carnival 1961." Photograph courtesy of Katarina Real / Acervo.

Real in Portuguese, arrived with impeccable credentials. Holding a 1960 master's degree in anthropology from the University of North Carolina, having researched Brazilian carnival (with fieldwork in five cities), she was recommended to lead Pernambuco's folklore commission (CPFL) by CNFL executive Renato Almeida; and Gilberto Freyre persuaded her to undertake an in-depth study of Recife's carnival.[45] That study became a book (*O Folclore no Carnaval do Recife*, first published 1968) that cemented the link between local carnival and folklore. It was during Real's brief tenure at both the CPFL and the FCP's Carnival Organizing Commission (roughly 1965–1968) that tensions in Recife reached their brief but intense boiling point over samba.

Real's book contains some romanticized concepts but is based on impressive research over five years among diverse groups, during and out of carnival. The festival had grown along with the city—Recife's population nearly tripled between 1950 and 1970—and Real described twelve categories of officially recognized carnival culture, compared to the FCP's five in 1938. "I doubt," she wrote, " . . . that any other carnival in Brazil or even in the hemisphere has such a great variety of groups," more than 150 of which were active throughout the year as well.[46] Part of the growth, she noted, was due to migrants bringing customs from the state's rural interior: carnival was "being enriched by continuous waves of new folkloric influences from other areas."[47]

But behind the enthusiasm, Real and others saw threats to traditional carnival. A principal source of concern was economic. Although local businesses had once been avid partners in sponsoring carnival events (detailed in the pages of the FCP's *Anuário*), their contribution had decreased considerably. Direct investment in carnival clubs was structurally discouraged through what Real called "one of the noteworthy characteristics of Recife carnival . . . the total absence of commercial (and political) propaganda."[48] Among the clubs, customs of informal public fundraising gradually faded as economic crises and mounting inflation cycled through mid-century Recife. These and other factors—population rise, increased mobility, ballooning real estate prices, and the growth of enclosed sky-rise apartment buildings—weakened communal sensibilities and dislocated groups from their longtime downtown headquarters out to the suburbs. The overall effect was near-total dependence on the government to underwrite carnival's cultural activities. Demand was excessive, and groups of all types were dropping out year by year: most shockingly, Recife's signature frevo clubs were affected. Vassourinhas took defiant public stands demanding municipal and state support in 1964 and 1965,[49] and Pás Douradas did not parade in 1966 or 1970.[50]

Meanwhile the maracatus seemed on the verge of disappearing. A practice sustained by poor Afro-Brazilians and led by its spiritual elders, the essence or soul of each maracatu resided in its aged leader, who provided a living link to tradition. But in the most prestigious groups those leaders were dying and were not casually replaced. Real had witnessed the demise of Elefante (founded 1800), when its queen Dona Santa died, and Estrela Brilhante (1910) disbanded after the 1964 carnival. She sadly considered Leão Coroado the only "legitimate" maracatu of the four then still active in the city.[51]

Against this alarming backdrop, the fact that Recife's escolas de samba were flourishing seemed to indicate careless disregard for local tradition and a transformation of carnival away from its roots, embracing the nonnative "invasion" of samba as Freyre put it. The following table, collating information from Real's book and various sources from her archive,[52] suggests the founding of escolas in midcentury Recife. It is not authoritative, but compiling specific sources should facilitate future research.

Table 9.1. Escolas de samba founded in Recife, 1930s–1970s

YEAR	NAME
1935/1938	Limonil
1940/1941/1942	Gigante do Samba
1943	Boêmios do Santo Amaro
1944	4 de Julho
1944/1954	4 de Outubro
1946/1947/1949	Estudantes de São José
1954	Unidos de Mangueira
1956	Labariri; Flamengo de Arruda
1957	Estudantes do Pina
1960	Unidos de Massangana
1961	Duvidosas*; Garotos Desamparados*
1962	Império do Asfálto; Unidos da Linha do Tiro
1962/1965	Sambista do Cordeiro
1962/1968	Galeria do Ritmo
1963	Geográficos do Samba
1964	Couro de Bode; Cruzeiro do Sul*
1965	Unidos do Salgueiro; Bafo da Onça; Amadores do Ritmo*; Acadêmicos do Ibura*; Aliados dos Remedios*; Burra Carnavalesca da C.I.T.*; Burra Brasileira*; Brotinho*; Baininha da Cidade*; Baiana da Sudan* ; Bandeirante do Samba* ; Galeria do Samba; Inocentes do Pina*; Macaco da Sede do Guararapes*; Unidos do Samba* ; Mocidade de Caixa D'Agua*; Camuré*; Portela*
1965/1968	Luar de Prata
1965/1969	Império do Samba
1966	Comandante do Samba* ; Portela*
1967	Almirante do Samba
1968	Vilela
1969	Unidos da Vila
1970/1972	Samarinas
1971	Alegria do Morro
1975	Gente Inocente
1976	Intimidade
1978	Unidos de São Carlos
1979	Formiguinha de Santo Amaro; Mocidade Alegre de Iputinga; Navegantes de Boa Viagem; Vai-Quem-Quer

Notes: 1. If more than one founding date was recorded, they will all be included. 2. Multiple escolas founded the same year will be listed on the same line. 3. An asterisk (*) indicates no founding date was found, but the escola was mentioned that year. 4. Real also lists the following as active between 1961–1965: Macombeba; Filhos do Mar.

The trends in Real's material may represent her growing attention to the escolas as she entered carnival management around 1965 as much as anything else, but it does appear that after moderate growth in the 1950s the escolas expanded rapidly. She wrote that they were the largest form of carnival group in Recife, often reaching 400 members, "but even the smallest rarely parade with fewer than 100"; and escolas made up fully 22 percent of the total carnival entities active between 1961 and 1965 (at forty groups, they were second most numerous out of twelve culture categories).[53] To critics, this spelled doom for the future of carnival's traditional character.

An early salvo against samba in Recife was fired in 1954 by Mário Melo (1884–1959), one of the city's most prominent journalists. He charged in his opening "good Pernambucans" to rise up against the "works of subversion" threatening local carnival's "originality," and goes on:

> They want to turn us into *cariocas* by force—some of them doing it consciously, some unconsciously. There never existed, in Pernambuco, *Escolas de Samba*. None of our music, even before *frevo*—which I can state as a witness, because I attended its birth—had a samba rhythm. But, because in Rio de Janeiro today the *Escolas de Samba* dominate, they want to force them on Pernambuco, for the degradation of our Carnival. And, what is lamentable if not condemnable, they want to establish prizes for this exotic species! Instead of repelling it as the weed it is, they want to offer prizes to what causes us harm! I have been a lonely voice against this, but I have to cry out in defense of what is ours. I shouted yesterday to impede the *Escolas*' affiliation with the Federação Carnavalesca Pernambucana, I shout today, I will shout tomorrow, in the hopes that once I am gone other voices will take up the message.[54]

While Melo lashed out at carnival samba in various forms, including orchestras from Rio playing local dances and record albums, it was the FCP's debates on recognizing Recife's escolas that most galled him. Melo had helped found the FCP, and, coincidentally or not, he left in 1955; he may have quit in protest or simply retired because of age. Soon after Melo's screed and departure, the escolas were allowed to affiliate, which meant official legitimacy as well as access to public subsidies. A January 1956 municipal decree states, for the first time, that judged competitions between escolas de samba would be part of Recife's carnival. But City Hall still mandated that the festival be "promoted and sponsored within folkloric parameters, preserving above all the frevo clubs, the maracatus in their primitive form, and the clubs of caboclinhos."[55]

A decade later, growing tensions between samba and frevo gained national attention, and the magazine *O Cruzeiro* characterized the situation as a sort of wary Russian / American "Cold War coexistence."[56] Nevertheless, it remained common in the early 1960s for escolas in Recife that otherwise resembled their Rio counterparts to include a small horn section, with trombones and cornets in a clear case of adapting samba to aesthetic conditions defined by frevo. The practice faded that decade, perhaps due to new concern with formal judging categories as the number of escolas rose; but Real perceptively noted that filming the escolas's parades for television (starting 1961) led to more homogeneity and fewer deviations from the Rio standard.[57] Unfortunately Recife's recording industry, centered on Fábrica de Discos Rozenblit (active roughly 1954–1984, although badly flooded and periodically inactive during the late 1960s), was focused on the annual carnival frevo competitions and on recording frevos and other manifestations of the "typically local" for export to Brazil's southeast, although I have yet to encounter an LP or 78rpm of Recife's period carnival samba.

Folklorist Roberto Benjamin, no admirer of "imported" escolas, asserted that they still could not help but produce a different form of samba than carioca escolas because of the preexisting cultural substrate of local percussive traditions (from maracatu), a preference for instrumental music over the escolas's sung *enredos*, and completely different physical qualities in the dance that characterize preexisting frevo versus samba.[58] That is, like a weak parasite, samba "infested" Recife but it lacked the power fully to take over its host. By contrast, Freyre saw the escolas as impacting local culture directly, and like Melo he blamed the FCP for legitimating their proliferation. He continued, "Here in Recife, re-creating and authorizing the *escolas de samba* is killing the *frevo*, the *maracatu*, the popular clubs, the spontaneity. Managers are imposing a false exoticism, this caricature of Rio's carnival, that is contrary to the spirit of our tradition and should be treated as a crime of treason in Pernambuco."[59]

Criticism of the escolas took three approaches. First, critics accused the escolas of being associated with mass culture. This was factually valid, since before it could be reproduced, Rio samba was consumed in Recife through radio, television, and commercial recordings. Given local carnival's symbolic importance as a showcase of folklore, notions of faddish, inauthentic pop culture had negative connotations. The increasing reach of television factored in samba's expansion in Recife, and radio and dance clubs became battlegrounds. In 1964, esteemed frevo musician Nelson Ferreira campaigned for a restriction on sambas in Recife carnival, proposing that four native songs should be played for each samba.[60] Another famous composer, Capiba, opposed prohibiting samba, but said that bandleaders should voluntarily refuse to play it (along with rock and roll) to set an example. He also declared that the dances of Rio's escolas were "nothing more nor less" than adaptations of the passo[61] (present with frevo in Rio among the Pernambucan migrant community since the 1930s).

Samba's links to the national music industry suggested ulterior profit motives to some. A journalist wrote in 1965, "Our radio stations and orchestras defend playing the music of the south by saying it's good business, risking bringing about the demise of the *frevo*."[62] The "popular" nature of the grassroots boom in *escolas de samba* would be cast in doubt if, as darkly alleged, Recife's radio stations heavily played samba on orders from distant bosses in Rio who wanted to make the music "popular" in the commercial, industrialized sense, to expand market share of the "samba racket" and at the same time homogenize the country.[63]

Second, Real and other carnival administrators found the escolas's relative autonomy disconcerting. Many escolas chose not to affiliate with the FCP, which precluded them from competing in the downtown route, but they could parade elsewhere in the city. This challenged the FCP's urge to centralize, regularize, and stabilize carnival festivities. Unaffiliated escolas received no public subsidy, but many carnival clubs considered the amounts too small. Certainly not all the escolas were financially secure—in 1964, five-time champion escola Estudantes de São José joined Vassourinhas and several other prominent groups in not participating in carnival, because their leaders said that subsidies were insufficient for the expenses they faced.[64] For the escolas that affiliated, gaining the subsidy could hardly have been a prime motive. The 1956 decree recognizing them as a carnival category also specified that 60 percent of the FCP budget should go to culture groups in the forms of assistance and prizes and, of that amount, the escolas share was only 5 percent. The FCP apparently wanted to include but not financially encourage escolas. That rule still existed in 1989, when Real returned to revisit Recife carnival. Thus, the escolas survived either on their own resources or they received patronage elsewhere. Freyre ponders whether the escolas represented a merely alienated "imitation of the exotic," or whether corrupt politicians hovered in the background, sponsoring escolas for votes: "It would be interesting for the Joaquim Nabuco Institute [today Foundation] to raise an investigation into the finances behind these infiltrations into the Carnival of Recife."[65]

Third, critics alleged that the escolas heightened racial disparities in the city. This provocative argument implied not only that the groups had a somehow inauthentic middle-class identity (unlike the local traditions seen as emerging from popular, miscegenated sectors), but also that, if escolas de samba symbolized racial harmony in Rio's carnival, they did not function that way when transplanted to Recife. Real, noting that the escolas were an "explosive topic," wrote that the "social and economic factors in their favor" in Recife came in part from leadership by middle-class, white families.

> They find Recife somewhat provincial, and admire anything from Rio de Janeiro; families of means are delighted to pay for luxurious costumes for their pretty daughters to appear at the front of a samba school . . . [W]hile the directors are often middle class and light-skinned, the dancers and drummers tend to be dark-skinned . . . [T]he drummers, nearly all of whom are poor black youths, are happy to participate in carnival for free, because they receive public applause along with a new suit and pair of shoes; the drummers will also earn a bit of money from the private shows that elite carnival clubs contract with the schools for private performances . . . Thus, surprisingly, it is in Recife's *escolas de samba* that one encounters the only traces of a certain separation of color or class.[66]

Real may have intended to aim her indictment narrowly at some of the newer groups.[67] Folklorist Manuel Nascimento Costa wrote in 1980 that three escolas—Estudantes de São José, Gigante, and Império do Samba—were traditionally led by Afro-Brazilian adepts of candomblé, and may (like the maracatus) even have gotten their start as recreational clubs in the terreiros.[68] Visiting Recife again in 1989, one year after Brazil's celebration of the one-hundred-year anniversary of the abolition of slavery, Real was struck by the black consciousness throughout Recife carnival and notes the "nearly constant glorification of Afro-Brazilian religions" by the escolas and the use of African dialects in enredo lyrics.[69] Yet this was not a wholly new phenomenon. For instance, in 1977, the escola Império do Samba presented its theme as the Festival of Iemanjá, a West African–Brazilian *orixá* associated with the ocean and motherhood. Spoken narration as the escola prepared to parade praised Iemanjá as the "most prestigious female entity of *candomblé*, *umbanda*, and *macumba*," stressed her Yoruba origins and notes that "the cult of Iemanjá is becoming very popular among Brazilian people."[70] But other influences on Recife carnival in the period of heightened Afro-Brazilian consciousness around the abolition centenary included Salvador's numerous afoxés, which were inspiring local versions, and a resurgence in maracatus (led by the somewhat theatrically influenced, nontraditional Nação Pernambuco, created December 1989).[71]

By the time Katarina Real left her offices in 1968, the conflict over samba had begun to wind down, although she and other observers later reaffirmed their displeasure with the escolas in Recife and critiqued their ostensibly negative aesthetic influences on frevo, which it seemed was growing more spectacular in their shadow.[72] Real's successor in the folklore commission, Valdemar Valente, publicly stated, "Samba is not really a threat to *frevo*, and may contribute to it. Anything the people naturally embrace is valid. We cannot control folklore, and samba is a national music."[73] Newspapers gave less attention to the clash, although in 1977 carnival, the mass disqualification of the largest escolas due to tardiness rocked the press, briefly threatening to reignite old tensions. That year, the cover of the city's carnival guide "Recife Invites You" featured pictures of frevo and maracatu with the caption "Delightful to see, and to play."

The escolas listed inside equaled in number the total of all frevo and maracatu groups combined and marshaled thousands more members.

Salvador

The story of escolas de samba in Salvador's carnival took a different trajectory from Recife. Two factors contributed to a somewhat thinner historical record here than for Recife: lack of perceived relations between carnival and folklore, and later (and unarchived) carnival centralization initiatives. Underlying those specifics, there existed a different attitude toward carnival in Salvador. Recife's festival was widely understood to both evoke and celebrate an earlier era through the embodiment of traditional, typical local culture that was consolidated into an idealized whole by the 1920s, just as the invented tradition of Rio's modern carnival looks nostalgically to the early 1930s, when the neighborhood escolas de samba joined a still vibrant street festival. While tradition mattered in Salvador, no particular golden age existed for the festival. It was a carnival in flux, looking forward as well as back.

Folklorists in Bahia and the rest of Brazil saw little in Salvador's midcentury carnival to inspire the sorts of studies (and conflicts) that Recife's festival did. In an early essay (possibly written in 1940), Edison Carneiro praised what he saw as the main distinguishing feature of Bahian carnival, the *caretas* (masquerade, using mask or costume or both, usually to cross-dress or appear as infants, doctors, strange creatures from nature and oral tradition, or Hollywood archetypes), and asserted that when the masks come off, Salvador's festival "cannot be distinguished from any other carnival."[74] Folklorists had limited interest in the afoxé tradition, reborn in 1949 with the Filhos de Gandhi who, parading with songs and handheld percussion instruments (especially the atabaque hand drum, afoxé gourd rattle, and iron agogô bells) from their candomblé terreiros, were modeled on late nineteenth century precedents such as Embaixada Africana, founded in 1895, and Pándegos da África, founded in 1896.[75] Nor did folklorists find interesting another principal feature of Salvador's carnival, the three so-called grand clubs—Cruz Vermelha (founded 1884), Fantoches (1884), and Inocentes em Progresso (1900). These private elite associations mounted extravagant parades with floats, music, and costume, all with a decidedly classical European aesthetic. The loud, gas-powered trio elétrico that appeared after 1950, also did not appeal to folklorists, although it profoundly altered how carnival was celebrated in Salvador.

Instead, it was religious festivals occurring throughout the carnival season that intrigued folklorists. These included the ritual public washing of the steps of Bonfim church on the second Thursday in January, and the festivals of Ribeira, the Monday after the second Thursday in January, and of Yemanjá,

February 2. Scheduling the upcoming 1953 Bahia Folklore Week, CNFL executive secretary Renato Almeida suggested, "We could take advantage of the Bonfim cycle, and hold it in January."[76] By the 1950s, some individuals saw carnival threatening the integrity of these popular religious rituals through its secular, nondefined nature, in which traditional cultural details could easily be submerged into an unstructured morass of licentiousness, drink, disorder, and ribald samba lyrics. This feared process, felicitously termed "carnival creep,"[77] was the opposite of Recife's experience, where carnival was understood to collect and redeploy the best, most authentic local culture. Things changed by the late 1960s and 1970s, when the traditional afoxés and the modernistic, amplified trios elétrico both flourished, and became, officially, the new face of Salvador's carnival.

Where were Salvador's escolas de samba in all this? An answer is complicated because the historical record is incomplete, in part because the city did not create an authority to regulate carnival until April 1959, fully twenty-four years after Recife had initiated its carnival administration, and its documents have disappeared.[78] In the 1950s, carnival unfolded through the city center around Rua Chile and Avenida Sete de Setembro to Praça da Sé and Baixa dos Sapateiros, but the city and local businesses promoted numerous neighborhood festivities. An early reference to escolas appeared in February 1954, when notable entertainers from radio station Rádio Sociedade da Bahia teamed with sponsoring beverage maker Fratelli Vita to produce Carnaval nos Bairros (carnaval in the neighborhoods). A traveling show of sorts in the days leading up to carnival, it featured diverse cultural groups (orchestras, singers, mascarados, batucadas, cordões, ranchos, and the famous trio elétrico). The program producers also hoped to stimulate neighborhood revelers by holding a competition for the best local batucada, cordão, and bloco carnavalesco. In 1954, it visited eight different localities across Salvador, including Barra and Liberdade, and included radio personalities and the samba orchestra of local musician Batatinha and the Escola de Samba Associada.[79] Although the program's acts included an escola de samba, it did not hold a competition for area escolas. Similarly, another neighborhood precarnival event on Rua Manoel Barros de Azevedo that year had judges to choose the best cordão, batucada, bloco, and rancho. No judging of the best escola de samba[80] suggests the practice was not common enough to warrant it. But another reference to escolas from 1952 appeared in a notice of precarnival festivities on Rua do Bângala, with "rich prizes" for local "batucadas and escolas de samba."[81]

These accounts imply a coexistence of batucadas and escolas de samba, but not necessarily that they were taken as the same exact phenomenon,[82] although the language of period newspaper reporting encouraged ambiguity. For example, a 1956 article praising the city's first downtown parade of cordões, blocos, and batucadas hails the latter as "similar to escolas de samba of the carioca carnival."[83] Certainly the two groups shared the use of many, although perhaps not all, the percussion instruments common to Rio's escolas. Archimedes da Silva, a founding member and president of Salvador's Federation of Carnival Clubs (1959), notes that the essential distinction between the two types of groups came in their percussion: "Batucadas did not use the loud surdo (large bass drum) or snare drum; they used smaller drums and lots of hand instruments instead."[84] Some batucadas were known to dress in costume, like escolas, and the largest ones carried banners; but it remains unclear whether they also presented allegorical floats like escolas, and they did not seem to have organized flanks of dancers.

How and when, then, did groups recognized as escolas appear? Some batucadas became escolas in the 1960s, many escolas emerged from other cordões. Adding to the complexity, an intermediate form called *charanga* appeared in the early 1960s that was half escola de samba, half other type of bloco. Katarina Real (then Katherine Cate), doing research on carnival, visited Salvador's festival in the late 1950s. Acknowledging a focus only on the city center, she notes the relative lack of "formally organized, or semi-specialized, dance groups" compared to Recife or Rio. She mentions neither batucadas nor escolas in Salvador's festivities, but points to blocos de sujo: "groups of teen-aged boys, numbering up to a thousand, dancing through the streets to the samba drums wearing swimming trunks and carrying large palm fronds in their hands."[85] She may have arrived too early to have witnessed many local escolas. The following table combines their references from Félix and Nery with those in a 1969 news report on carnival competition to sketch a portrait of the city's escolas de samba. The 1969 article included no founding dates.

While an incomplete picture with some questionable dates—Juventude do Garcia may have started in 1959[86]—this still captures Salvador's prominent escolas and allows three conclusions. First, the escolas were consolidating

Table 9.2. Escolas de samba in Salvador, 1960–1970s

NAME	YEAR FOUNDED	YEAR ENDED
Ritmistas do Samba	1950s–1960	?
Juventude do Garcia	1962	1973
Filhos do Tororó	1963	1973
Politeama	1964	1968
Diplomatas de Amaralina	1966	1978
Filhos da Liberdade	1969*	?
Filhos do Morro	Early 1960s*	?

Sources: Anísio Félix and Moacyr Nery, *Bahia, Carnaval* (Salvador? Brazil?: s.n., 1993?); "Vencedores," *Estado da Bahia,* February 19, 1969. Escolas listed here will be marked with (†).

Notes: An asterisk (*) indicates no founding date included, but the escola was called active that year.

Listed as participating in 1969 carnival: Filhos do Tororó,† Diplomatas de Amaralina,† Filhos do Morro,† Juventude de Garcia,† Filhos da Liberdade,† Bafo da Onça,† Juventude da Boa Viagem,† Calouros do Samba,† Filhos do Barbalho,† Ritmo da Liberdade,† Juventude do Vale do Canela,† O Abafa,† Mocidade em Mangueira,† Juventude da Cidade Nova e Politeama.†

at the same time as in Recife carnival, although in Salvador the resistance came slightly later, in the 1970s. Second, escolas increased in number during the 1960s; their membership had willingly traded informal modes of revelry for a highly regulated practice, including the advance delivery of enredo lyrics for assessment and consenting to be judged according to multiple categories.[87] Third, the escolas had brief careers. A major factor in their vulnerability, unlike in Recife, was the demographics behind the sponsorship of Salvador's new escolas de samba. Recife had sponsors from the financially comfortable, white middle class, but in Salvador they were lower-class Afro-Bahians. The names of the groups reflected their humble *bairros* of origin—Nordeste de Amaralina, Tororó, Liberdade, Cidade Nova.

They made a promising start by joining Salvador's nascent carnival regulatory project, the Federation of Carnival Clubs, founded in 1959. Representatives from Filhos da Liberdade and Filhos do Morro were early members alongside leaders of other culture groups such as batucadas and afoxés.[88] In this era the distinctions between batucadas and escolas became formal, and the category of batucadas gradually disappeared from publicly posted judging guidelines. Some may have been absorbed into blocos or *pequenos clubes*, although one 1970 article states that as a defined traditional form it no longer existed in Bahian carnival.[89] Over the 1960s the escolas entered a growth phase, depicted in newspaper coverage during carnival season featuring photographs of their drummers or dancers and often transcriptions of the year's *enredo* from major groups like Diplomatas de Amaralina. Diplomats performed at Bahia's first Carnival Song Contest in 1970 and was deemed by one reporter the high point of the evening, while another newspaper assured its readers that every year Juventude do Garcia "leaves their admirers, and the general public, transfixed at the judging stand in Praça da Sé because of the innumerable attractions they bring . . . They are the escola with the most passionate support in the state."[90] Garcia claimed a bateria of 110 men and 2,000 dancing participants (*figurantes*) in 1970.[91] Salvador's escolas de samba were among the local culture presented in homage to visiting Brazilian president Emílio Médici in 1972.[92]

The glory was brief. From fourteen competing escolas in 1969 they winnowed to seven in 1973, rose back to nine in 1975, but collapsed to three in 1979.[93] By 1983 only two escolas paraded in carnival, "down from four in 1981 . . . Bafo da Onça ceased to exist after the 1983 Carnival, a victim of disinterest."[94]

The decline resulted, according to the standard answer, from wider social processes in Salvador and other Brazilian cities. The influences of foreign black musical culture, notably from the United States and Jamaica, and the earlier 1960s black soul music trend in Rio, led to what Bahian writer Antonio Risério praised in 1981 as the re-Africanization of Salvador's carnival. This meant the fuller embrace of African-descended identity through diverse diasporic references embodied by the Afro-Bahian afoxés and blocos afro (starting in 1974 with Ilê Aiyê, these groups are less explicitly related to candomblé, and their percussive music draws more on African and Afro-Caribbean elements). In this analysis, samba has been co-opted by white aesthetics and ideologies. Rosério argues that samba represented a symptom of Afro-Brazilians' cultural and racial alienation that the afoxés and later the blocos afro redressed. When describing how the moves of Ilê Aiyê's dancers are based on individual interpretations of the dances of candomblé orixás, he added that there existed no imposed choreography, "There is nothing here that remotely recalls the rigid structure that defines the escolas de samba of Rio de Janeiro."[95]

Risério heralded a wave of critical reassessments of samba as the music of racial democracy, rooted in analyses of Rio-style carnival as a form of social control. His characterization of afoxés and blocos afro as better suited to Salvador's majority Afro-Brazilian population became paradigmatic. It is not coincidental that he refers to "the escolas de samba of Rio de Janeiro," ignoring their local manifestations outright as a regrettable chapter in recent Afro-Bahian history. The consciousness he valued was local as well as racial. In the magazine *Afinal*, writer Antonio Medrado took glee in 1988 in recounting how the pioneering bloco afro, Ilê Aiyê, helped eliminate the city's escolas:

> To give you an idea of the force of the movement they started, it's enough to observe that a decade later, the old escolas de samba—Diplomatas, Filhos do Tororó, Juventude do Garcia among them—had been swept from the street, them and their attitude of vassalage to their carioca counterparts, with all the vulgarity of their costumes and allegorical floats and monotonous rhythms.[96]

The rise of the blocos afro in mid-1970s–1980s Salvador may have been influenced by black youths' rejection in Rio and São Paulo of "traditional African-Brazilian forms such as samba, which they perceive as having been corrupted by white cultural dominance."[97] Nevertheless, in the late 1960s and early 1970s, escolas de samba were still among Salvador's most recognizably "black" cultural groups, along with afoxés, and analysis of their enredo themes might help complicate assumptions regarding their racial alienation. In 1973, for instance, Filhos do Tororó won the championship with a theme celebrating a historically prominent Afro-Bahian mãe de santo, Menininha do Gantois.[98]

Carnival also provided a medium to raise and explore the history of slavery. Song texts may not have been overtly confrontational, such as Filhos do Morro's 1970 "Life and Loves of Castro Alves," cheering the abolitionist poet; or the 1971 enredo of Juventude do Garcia praising Princess "Isabel, the redeemer / who abolished slavery."[99] On the other hand, in 1974, the Diplomatas de Amaralina paraded with "Casa Grande e Senzala," based on Gilberto Freyre's book.[100] This song declared, "Today there is no sadness / the Negro is happy / And can sambar and sing," but drew pointed attention to the "blood and sweat" spilled by African slaves that helped fertilize Brazilian soil. And it hailed the memory of runaway black rebels: "We also exalt / Those valiant warriors / Who entered into history / Searching for liberty / In their fortified quilombos." Textually, as a hybrid statement of racial awareness and reconciliation, little separates this message from bloco afro Ilê Aiyê's 1979 carnival song, "Most Beautiful Life": "Smiling in this most beautiful life / You all have to see / The happy creoles of Ilê Aiyê / Don't have color discrimination / Come with me to feel / the Negro singing in nagô / All the people will applaud."[101]

Larry Crook has posited another reason for the escolas's demise: the *blocos de índio* (groups based thematically on images of Hollywood Western Indians, starting in 1968). Risério characterized these *blocos*, which applied "war paint" and carried wooden tomahawks, singing samba songs over an escola-like percussion section, as "coming before" Salvador carnival's re-Africanization: a transitory step, controversial because of their disorder and lacking the peaceful inclinations of *negritude*, but a salutary assumption of nonwhite identity.[102] They may have been overturning the escolas from within:

> In 1968, participants from several of Salvador's samba schools founded new Carnival groups of this kind . . . The first bloco de índio formed was the Caciques do Garcia (Chiefs of Garcia), created by members of Juventude do Garcia. The second was the Apaches do Tororó, founded by members of Filhos do Tororó. The transformation of these samba schools to blocos de índio heralded the search for new forms of identity among Salvador's poor black youth.[103]

Two problems exist with this analysis. First, it does seem accurate that there might have been some overlap in escola and bloco de índio membership in the early years; and later, as the escolas were increasingly viewed as obsolescent, escola members may have migrated over. There is no clear evidence of a rapid transformation of one type of group to another. A 1975 newspaper feature on the Apaches do Tororó states that the idea for the group came from neighborhood residents who wanted to invent a different type of carnival group; it said nothing about escolas.[104] Tororó's escola and its bloco amiably held public rehearsals on different nights to not compete for audiences. Both Filhos do Tororó and Juventude do Garcia continued their carnival participation among the elite escolas in the late 1960s and into the 1970s; indeed, Juventude do Garcia had the prestige of winning the championship in 1968[105] and it is unlikely it would have simply converted into a bloco de índio just months afterward. Filhos do Tororó was champion in 1973. In 1974 when both these escolas announced they were no longer able to parade; the reason declared by both was lack of finances, not that they were losing members to blocos de índio (and at the time there were still six remaining escolas registered with the city).[106]

The second problem with the analysis above is more general. Often such post-Risério analyses are concerned with what may have enticed Afro-Bahians in Salvador's escolas de samba toward some other type of association, such as more compelling assertions of ethnicity. A carnival cultural climate favoring novelty and experimentation over the performance of tradition, as in Recife, was also likely significant. Neguinho do Samba (Antônio Luís Alves de Souza, 1954–2009), percussion director for Olodum, Salvador's most commercially successful bloco afro, got his start in Ritmistas do Samba and Diplomatas de Amaralina.[107] He once remarked that he rejected the whistle common to escola bateria leaders as "something for a traffic cop," implying that in samba the priority is following rules and policing deviations rather than experimenting or innovating.[108] That also suggests questions about what pushed people away from carnival samba in Salvador. To close, I will address three interrelated factors working against local escolas by the early 1970s that helped lead to their abandonment.

Most obvious is the rising costs associated with parading. For a competitive performance medium valuing increasingly sumptuous spectacles year after year, Salvador's escolas de samba had a precarious economic base. In 1970, Diplomatas director and noted geographer Milton Santos sighed that "victory is expensive"[109] after Diplomatas invested 60,000 *cruzeiros novos* (US $13,274.34) overall and as champion won only 1,000 cruzeiros novos (US $221.24). The next year, Juventude do Garcia spent the small fortune of 25,000 (US $5,530.97) cruzeiros on just one costume. Salvador's escolas lacked both the personal resources enjoyed by most of Recife's new escolas and the patronage relationships with organized crime that kept many of Rio's escolas afloat.[110] In 1973 Valdomiro Conceição, a leader of Diplomatas, warned that the escolas were in crisis.[111] They needed to unite to lobby for more resources, and they needed to hold regular, admission-charging public rehearsals. Nevertheless, many escolas lacked the infrastructure of a headquarters to do so (Filhos do Tororó was said to have the best). In addition, subsidies to the escolas were shrinking. In a wan gesture of protest in 1976, the president of Acadêmicos do Ritmo returned its small sum to the state tourism board while admitting that without such support the group was doomed.[112]

Whatever else their enticements, the blocos de índio were certainly cheaper to outfit with simple war paint and wooden tomahawks. But carnival's content and spatiality were changing in other ways, principally around the effects of the trios elétrico.[113] Started as an electric duo by inventor-friends Dodô and Osmar in 1950, and parading as a trio in 1951 with the addition of a third amplified guitar player (while percussionists marched beside the vehicle), the trios had proliferated in Salvador through commercial sponsorships and were reshaping how carnival was celebrated. The music they played in the early 1970s was still mostly fast-paced frevo, inflected with influences from rock to classical; Dodô and Osmar's 1975 LP *Jubileu de Prata* situated melodies from Liszt, Mozart, and Paganini into celebratory songs with distinctly northeastern Brazilian thematics.[114] The music had no associated traditional dance steps, and people were free to *pular* (jump, leap) along in any way they chose. The surging masses of revelers could be physically dangerous, but the trios represented novelty, modernity, autonomy, and spontaneity. Mounted on huge sound trucks, they roamed about nearly at will, often thwarting the judged parades of carnival groups. Juventude do Garcia complained that the trios were overwhelming them with crowds and decibels.[115] As spontaneity and popular participation became significant descriptors of Salvador's evolving carnival, its formally judged component was compressed from two or three days in the late 1960s to one day in 1976, while the area reserved for judged parades was displaced from the central, larger avenues.

Finally, tourism officials, city boosters, and the media came to embrace the trios as representing true local identity, suggesting that the carnival experience they generated was uniquely defined by popular creativity and equitable inclusion. Bahian musician Caetano Veloso drew national attention to the trios in 1969 with a song in the trio style, "Atrás do Trio Elétrico," which declared "it's only the dead who don't follow the trio elétrico."[116] In these discursive contexts, the escolas became unwelcome, inauthentic vestiges of Rio's carnival. A 1972 opinion piece dismissed Rio-style escola parades and bragged:

> By now we can say we have an export-quality carnival, because of its fame throughout and beyond Brazil which attracts more and more tourists each year in search of something different, less standardized . . . Our carnival is on the street, a carnival of people, with all the warmth and energy that only a trio elétrico is capable of generating as one of the most authentic carnival creations on earth. We must strive to ensure that carnival keeps its Bahian character, a carnival of Bahia that only exists here.[117]

Waldeloir Rêgo, Afro-Bahian activist and author, vociferously rejected local escolas, "The spirit of the Bahian carnival reveler is eminently participative, and it is clear that our escolas de samba are poor spectacles copied from Rio's . . . they got off to a graceless start around 1957 and remain inconsequential today."[118] Reversing the charge levied by Juventude do Garcia, the escolas were accused of getting in the way of all the unstructured merriment fostered by the trios, annoying "the people" by imposing obstacles on their "rights to circulate."[119] A 1973 roundtable sponsored by the newspaper *A Tarde* asked whether the escolas should be allowed to "pass into extinction" since they did not fit into Salvador's innovative, popular street carnival.[120] Prior to the debate, Antonio Tourinho, director of the city's tourism department, had made his opinion clear:

> I think that our escolas de samba should go away. They are to blame for the disappearance of the grand batucadas that were such a strong point of Salvador carnival. Our festival is driven by complete popular participation, and the escolas here are nothing more than a poor imitation of Rio's . . . Many cariocas come to Salvador to enjoy carnival on the streets, the trios-elétricos, the animation, because they are accustomed to paying to watch escolas parade like spectators at the theater. Here no, the people participate and really enjoy themselves.[121]

The trios had another advantage. While they received lucrative contracts to advertise on their vehicles, they also got public funds; some threatened to leave Salvador for other cities in order to ensure them. (Their privatization through associated blocos charging revelers admission began later in the decade.) In 1976 each escola received 2.4 percent of the sum given just to Dodô and Osmar's trio.[122] Compared to trios, Tourinho called the escolas dysfunctional and decadent. A decade or so later, they were gone.

Conclusion and Afterward

The rise of domestic tourism from the urban south to the northeast coincided with the demotion of Rio de Janeiro from national capital in 1960 and the onset of the national military dictatorship (1964–1985). Thus, a range of factors may have led northeastern carnival proponents to invert discursively national cultural geography in the 1960s–1970s, dislocating Rio de Janeiro from the symbolic center of local festivals by pushing back against the escolas de samba they contained. This played out differently in the carnivals of Recife and Salvador, with distinct outcomes.

In mid-1960s Recife, urban growth, economic instability, and increased mass mediation led cultural observers to hunker down, fearing that local tradition was under siege. Recife's escolas seemed to thrive despite a socioeconomic milieu detrimental to frevo and maracatu, and they appeared to introduce dangerous racial distinctions to a festival long regarded by boosters as racially equitable. That young Afro-Pernambucans were joining escolas de samba rather than acting to preserve maracatu was especially distressing to folklorist Katarina Real (who intervened to help create a new maracatu group in 1967). But the public controversy was short-lived. In 1989 a new threat emerged—this time, carnival culture from Salvador[123]—and old suspicions of the escolas were mostly forgotten as Recife circled its collective wagons to again protect its festival from copycats and foreign invasions. Once a foe, the escolas were embraced as allies. Yet a recent video documentary on the history of Recife carnival, prepared by a subsidiary of the newspaper *Jornal do Commercio*, ceded roughly sixty seconds of its forty minutes to the presence of escolas de samba.[124]

In Salvador, formal escolas de samba emerged around twenty years later than in Recife. They enjoyed wide acceptance while Recife's escolas were under attack. But by the early 1970s the escolas were cast as contrary to the spontaneity of the evolving festival; joined with the economic constraints faced by their lower-class proponents, this proved too much to surmount and the practice faded. Samba itself was not rejected by state tourism and culture managers—only carnival samba modeled on Rio's escolas. The state tourism authority boasted in 1976 of the city's unique blocos de índio, who performed samba.[125] And it took advantage of Bahia's rural samba de roda (circle samba), an influential predecessor of Rio's urban samba, featuring it through the 1970s and 1980s in year-round tourist folklore shows. Local events were also staged for Brazil's Samba Day (December 2), with musicians like Gilberto Gil and Paulinho Camafeu. By the first decade of the 2000s, samba was growing in prominence, partly as a grassroots reaction to the commercial hegemony and artistic homogeny of Salvador's globalized carnival music, known as axé music[126] (the state blamed lack of musical innovation for a drop-off in carnival tourism after 2004).[127] In 2009 a batucada paraded on Bahian Independence Day (July 2) with a banner reading "Don't Let the Samba Die." But the city had heard the call. In a drive to make Salvador carnival simultaneously more diverse

"Don't Let the Samba Die." *Batucada* parade, Salvador's Centro Histórico, July 2, 2009. Courtesy of Jerry D. Metz Jr.

and more conventionally Brazilian, it installed a samba stage at the festivities at Praça da Sé, and additionally in 2009, nineteen samba blocos paraded in carnival, fifteen with public subsidy.[128]

Both Salvador and Recife carnivals came to emphasize populist values: the people make the festival. They embraced national ideals of social inclusion and popular agency, in part to distinguish themselves from Rio's judged, regulated, spectator event. Recife carnival, encompassing many specific traditions which tourists can enjoy but not join conceded the tag "popular participation" to Salvador and is advertised as "multicultural." Salvador's carnival is now the world's largest street festival. Samba persists in these carnivals as a resource of both national and local identity, strong because simultaneously traditional and adaptable to new contexts—having endured earlier rejections by culture managers and producers as racially, culturally, and regionally alienated. The cases explored here represent specific challenges to Hermano Vianna's thesis on samba's nationalization in Brazil, but ultimately Vianna's conclusion is reaffirmed. Nonetheless, this chapter suggests that the mystery of samba still remains greater than has been fully appreciated.

Notes

1. *Danças Folclóricas Brasileiras e suas Aplicações Educativas*, 2nd ed. (São Paulo: Edições Melhoramentos, 1964), 19.
2. A helpful essay situating Brazilian carnival in both regional and global frames is Michaeline A. Crichlow and Piers Armstrong, "Carnival Praxis, Carnivalesque Strategies and Atlantic Interstices," *Social Identities* 6 no. 4 (July 2010), 399–414.
3. The first group to adopt the term was Deixa Falar, founded in 1928 in Estácio. However, Deix Falar did not join the carnival escola parades, which started in 1932 and were increasingly officialized through the mid-1930s. Mangueira, founded 1928 or 1929, is considered the first actual escola to join Rio's carnival and is still among the dominant groups today. Amaury Jório and Hiram Araujo, *Escolas de Samba em Desfile: Vida, Paixão e Sorte* (Rio de Janeiro: Poligrafica, 1969).
4. Oswald de Andrade, "Manifesto Pau Brasil," *Correio da Manhã* (Rio de Janeiro), March 18, 1924.
5. Live footage from 2013 carnival shows the scale of contemporary escolas,

framed by the bleachers of the Sambadrome: http://www.youtube.com/watch?v=NDphdusk_jg.

6. André Diniz, *Almanaque do Carnaval* (Rio de Janeiro: Zahar, 2008), 241.

7. "São Paulo esta vivendo o carnaval mais melancôlica da sua história," *Folha da Manhã* (São Paulo), March 4, 1957.

8. "Florianópolis na cadência do samba," *A Gazeta* (São Paulo), April 2,1958.

9. Katharine Royal Cate, "The Brazilian Urban 'Carnaval': A Discussion of its Origins, Nature, and Ethnological Significance" (Master's thesis, University of North Carolina, 1960), 152.

10. Julie Taylor, "Carnival, Media, and Regional Traditions: Integration and Manipulation in Brazil," *Studies in Latin American Popular Culture* 7 (1988), 191–97.

11. Tiago de Oliveira Pinto, "The Pernambuco Carnival and its Formal Organisations: Music as Expression of Hierarchies and Power in Brazil," *Yearbook for Traditional Music* 26 (1994), 20–38.

12. Roberto da Matta, *Carnavais, Malandros e Heróis: Para uma sociologia do dilemma brasileiro* (Rio de Janeiro: Zahar Editores, 1979); Matta, "Carnaval como um Rito de Passagem," *Ensaios de Antropologia Estrutural* (Rio de Janeiro: Vozes, 1973).

13. Raul Lody, "O fazer da folia," *Diário de Pernambuco*, February 10, 1994.

14. Hermano Vianna, *The Mystery of Samba: Popular Music and National Identity in Brazil*, trans. John Charles Chasteen (Chapel Hill: University of North Carolina Press, 1999), 113 (emphasis added).

15. Metz, "*Alegria*," 37–38.

16. Bryan McCann, *Hello Hello Brazil: Popular Music in the Making of Modern Brazil* (Durham, NC: Duke University Press, 2004), 46, 62–63, 93–94.

17. Marc A. Hertzman, *Making Samba: A New History of Race and Music in Brazil* (Durham, NC: Duke University Press, 2013).

18. Metz, "*Alegria*," 65–74.

19. Gilberto Freyre, "Recifense, sim; sub-carioca, não!" *Jornal do Commercio*, February 27, 1966.

20. One popular carnival frevo is "Hino do Elefante de Olinda," http://www.youtube.com/watch?v=RGQ7-fSKVkU. Samples of the dance are demonstrated in this short news feature, http://www.youtube.com/watch?v=yUzxN5yR8MI, Portuguese voiceover.

21. Footage of maracatu Estrela Brilhante parading during 2012 carnival is available at http://www.youtube.com/watch?v=L60wPfftGjw.

22. A four-part documentary in Portuguese on Salvador's oldest afoxé, Filhos de Gandhi starts here: http://www.youtube.com/watch?v=9Y-xBSDotpc.

23. Antônio Risério, *Carnaval Ijexá* (Salvador: Corrupio, 1981).

24. Images and sounds from the pioneering trio, Dodô e Osmar, ca. 1982, can be found at http://www.youtube.com/watch?v=KUWdE6BJMB0.

25. "Povo encontra a medida no Carnaval-participação," *Jornal da Bahia*, April 21, 1978.

26. Gerard Béhague, "The Effects of Tourism on Afro-Bahian Traditional Music in Salvador, Bahia, Brazil," in *Come Mek Me Hol' Yu Han': The Impact of Tourism on Traditional Music* (Kingston: Jamaica Memory Bank, 1986).

27. As a revenue generator, in recent years foreign tourists have been able to purchase the opportunity to accompany some of Rio's escolas during carnival, regardless of their abilities to keep up with the singing and dancing.

28. John Connell and Chris Gibson, *Sound Tracks: Popular Music, Identity and Place* (London: Routledge, 2003), 143.

29. Peter Wade, *Music, Race, and Nation: Música Tropical in Colombia* (Chicago: University of Chicago Press, 2000), 7.

30. A good account of Recife's carnival during the first Vargas regime is Mário Ribeiro dos Santos, *Trombones, Tambores, Repiques e Ganzás: A Festa das Agremiações Carnavalescas nas Ruas do Recife, 1930–1945* (Recife: SESC, 2010).

31. *Anuário do Carnaval Pernambucano* (Recife: Federação Carnavalesca Pernambucana, 1938). Pages are not numbered.

32. *Recife Convida 1977* (carnival guide; no publication information). Katarina Real Archive, KRMp2 cap 4 doc 2 (KRMp2cap1/14), Fundação Joaquim Nabuco, Recife.

33. Mário Sette, "Entrudo e Frêvo," *Anuário do Carnaval Pernambucano*, np.

34. "A Federação Carnavalesca e seus Estatutos," *Anuário do Carnaval Pernambucano*, np.

35. Possibly hinting at frevo's "pacification," the small parasols twirled by dancers are thought to have replaced brooms and sticks once wielded by capoeiristas. Valdemar de Oliveira, *Frevo, Capoeira e "Passo"* (Recife: Companhia Editôra de Pernambuco, 1985).

36. Dr. Arthur de Moura, "O Reconhecimento da Federação Carnavalesca

Pernambucana como Associação de Utilidade Pública," *Anuário do Carnaval Pernambucano*, np.

37. Valdemar de Oliveira, "Frevo acrobata," printed essay archived without publication information, Katarina Real Archive, PIpdoc32 (FJN).

38. "O carnaval de Pernambuco e suas atrações folclóricas," *Última Hora*, February 8, 1974; Paulo Viana, "Carnaval de Pernambuco," in *Antologia do Carnaval do Recife*, eds. Mário Souto Maior and Leonardo Dantas Silva (Recife: Fundação Joaquim Nabuco / Massangana, 1991), 305.

39. Larry Crook, *Brazilian Music: Northeastern Traditions and Heartbeat of a Modern Nation* (Santa Barbara, CA: ABC-CLIO, 2005), 170.

40. Thomas Turino, "Nationalism and Latin American Music: Selected Case Studies and Theoretical Considerations," *Latin American Music Review* 24 no. 2 (2003), 179–94.

41. Vianna, *Mystery of Samba*, 112.

42. The question of whether these groups represented accomodation of or resistance to Pernambuco's sugar-centered slavocracy is debated today. Jerry D. Metz Jr., "Cultural Geographies of Afro-Brazilian Symbolic Practice: Tradition and Change in Maracatu de Nação (Recife, Pernambuco, Brazil)," *Latin American Music Review* 29 no. 1 (Spring–Summer 2008), 64–95.

43. "Maracatu Leão Coroado: Tradição que só sai âs ruas no Carnaval," *Jornal do Commercio*, February 20, 1977.

44. The message was spread nationally, e.g., "Rio e Recife: Últimos redutos do carnival," *Revista Visão* (São Paulo), March 1, 1957; "Carnaval do Recife: Material imenso e rico para os estudios de nosso folclore," *A Gazeta*, April 29, 1958; "Carnaval de Pernambuco: Frevo, Caboclinhos e Maracatu," *Revista Senhor* (Rio de Janeiro), February 1962.

45. Metz, "*Alegria*"; Clarisse Quintanilha Kubrusly, "Katherine Royal Cate (1927–2006) e os Maracatus do Recife" (Masters thesis, Federal University of Rio de Janeiro, 2007).

46. Katarina Real, *O Folclore no Carnaval do Recife, 2nd Edição* (Recife: Fundação Joaquim Nabuco, 1990), 133–37.

47. Real, *O Folclore no Carnaval do Recife*, 138.

48. Real, *O Folclore no Carnaval do Recife*, 250.

49. Katarina Real Archive, KRJp6 docs 510, 518 (FJN, KRJp6doc.501/600).

50. Waldemar Valente, "Carnaval sem Pás Douradas," *Diário de Pernambuco*, February 8, 1970.

51. Real, *O Folclore no Carnaval do Recife*, 60–61.

52. *Recife Convida 1977*; "Notas atribuidas pela Comissão Organizadora do Carnaval de 1961," KRMp2cap8doc1 (FJN, KRMp2cap1/14); "Escolas de Samba 1965," KRMp1cap7doc1 (FJN, KRMp1cap1/11); "Escolas de Samba 1966," KRMP1cap10doc1 (FJN, KRMp1cap1/11); "Textos para Divulgação: Carnaval de 1966," KRPIp4doc52 (FJN, KRPIp4doc34/52); field research notes, KRPIp1doc1 (FJN, KRPIp1doc.1).

53. Real, *O Folclore no Carnaval do Recife*, 51, 136.

54. Mário Melo, "Crônica da Cidade: O Folclore no Carnaval," *Jornal do Commercio*, March 4, 1954. In 1952, he published a lengthy reader's letter that rejected samba in Recife: Melo, "Crônica da Cidade: O Frevo e o Samba," *Jornal do Commercio*, March 9, 1952.

55. "Decreto n. 1351 de 23 Janeiro de 1956," Departamento de Documentação e Cultura, Recife, KRPIp4doc35 (FJN, KRPIp4doc34/52).

56. "Pernambuco: Samba e frevo de mãos dados," *O Cruzeiro*, February 22, 1964.

57. Real, *O Folclore no Carnaval do Recife*, 50–51. A photograph in her book (between pages 46 and 47) shows a trombone player in Estudantes de São José in 1961 carnival.

58. Roberto Benjamin, *Folguedos e Danças de Pernambuco* (Recife: Prefeitura da Cidade do Recife, 1989), 118–19.

59. Gilberto Freyre, "Recifense, sim; sub-carioca, não!"

60. "Compositores aplaudem concessão de prêmio oficial para maracatu," *Jornal do Commercio*, 7 January 1965.

61. "Em terra de frêvo não se dança Rock'n Roll," *Diário de Pernambuco*, February 24, 1957.

62. "Meta carnavalesca: Esforço comum é para que carnaval seja autêntico," unsourced newspaper clipping. KR Jp 5 doc 440 (FJN, KRJp5doc.401/500).

63. "Samba recebe ajuda de compositores locais em prejuízo do nosso frêvo," *Jornal do Commercio* (Recife), 19 Dezember 1965.

64. "Carnaval 64: Clubes não saem," *Última Hora*, January 16, 1964.

65. Freyre, "Recifense, sim." Real found in 1961 that while the FCP received funds from the city, an independent fund-raising organization for escolas was taking donations from the state governor (*O Folclore no Carnaval do Recife*, 178).

66. Real, *O Folclore no Carnaval do Recife*, 52–53.

67. Only further research could validate or challenge the claim as to how Recife's escolas experienced and expressed race as a dimension of performing carnival samba, and of social life more broadly. On one occasion it was sexuality, not race, that some escolas took an exclusionary attitude to. In 1978, Gigantes do Samba decided to expel its members who were known transvestites or transsexuals, charging that they parade in a drugged state—but alleged corruption in the voting process for the year's enredo was seemingly part of the dispute. Several other escolas followed their lead. "Boneco de Mola contra travestis durante carnaval," *Diário de Pernambuco*, October 14, 1978.

68. Manuel Nascimento Costa, "Candomblé e Carnaval," in *Antologia do Carnaval do Recife*, 245–51.

69. Real, *O Folclore no Carnaval do Recife*, 202.

70. "Escola Império do Samba apresenta A Festa de Iemanja," typed program and research material for the escola's 1977 theme. KR Pip4 doc 49 (FJN, KRPIp4doc.34/52).

71. Metz, "Cultural Geographies." Recordings of three of Recife's afoxés, Alafin Oyó, Ylê de Egbá, and Filhos D'Ogundê, appear on the CD *Afoxés de Pernambuco* (Recife: Pernamhusica, 2002).

72. Roberto Benjamin, *Folguedos e Danças de Pernambuco*, 118–19; Valdemar de Oliveira, *Frevo, Capoeira e "Passo,"* 136–39; Katarina Real, *Eudes: O Rei do Maracatu* (Recife: Fundação Joaquim Nabuco), 2001.

73. "No carnaval do Recife cabe o samba também," *Diário de Pernambuco*, January 26, 1969.

74. Carneiro, "Caretas da Bahia," Centro Nacional de Folclore e Cultura Popular (Rio de Janeiro), Biblioteca Amadeo Amaral, Arquivo Digital: Arquivo Edison Carneiro, Documentos\Textos\Caretas da Bahia. Visible on a page of the essay is a typed date that appears to be 1940, although it has been marked through with black ink.

75. Ickes, *African-Brazilian Culture*, 172–80, 201–2.

76. Letter to Guilherme Santos Neves dated October 22, 1952, CNFCP DA: CNF\Assuntos Gerais\expedidias—1947 a 1959.

77. Ickes, *African-Brazilian Culture*, 181.

78. That date is taken from the closest thing to a history of midcentury Salvador carnival available, *Bahia, Carnaval* by Anísio Félix and Moacyr Nery (Salvador? Brazil?: s.n., 1993?).

79. Various advertisements in *A Tarde* early that month, such as and February 7 and 9, 1954.

80. "Evohé Carnaval," *A Tarde*, February 13, 1954.

81. "Rainha do Carnval de 52," *A Tarde*, February 20, 1952.

82. Ickes comes to that conclusion for the late 1940s (*African-Brazilian Culture*, 160).

83. "O desfile dos cordões, blocos e batucadas," *A Tarde*, February 13, 1956.

84. Antonio Jorge Victor dos Santos, "Raízes e Tradicões da Música Afro-Carnavalesca Contemporânea (A Importância da Música Baiana no Processo de Legitimação da Cultura Negra)" (Masters thesis, Federal University of Bahia, 1997), 161.

85. Cate, "The Brazilian Urban 'Carnival,'" 148.

86. "Juventude pronta para brilhar," *Jornal da Bahia*, Febuary 19, 1971.

87. According to period newspapers these were bateria (percussion section); coreografia (dance); efeito de conjunto (overall group effect); luxo, originalidade e bom gusto (luxury, originality, and good taste); alegoria (theme development).

88. Félix and Nery, *Bahia, Carnaval*, 62–65. Curiously, they also suggest here that some of Salvador's escolas used wind instruments, as in Recife.

89. "Escola de samba e afoxé têm diferenças básicas que marcam a catégoria," *Diário de Notícias*, February 13, 1970.

90. "Fracasso de audiência no 1. concurso de músicas de carnaval," *A Tarde*, January 12, 1970; "Juventude pronta para brilhar."

91. "Garcia quer ser campeã desta vez," *Diário de Notícias*, February 7, 1970.

92. "Médici sensibilizado com o carinho e homenagens de todo o povo baiano," *Diário de Notícias*, February 10, 1972.

93. Metz, "*Alegria*," 200–201; *Diário de Notícias*, Febuary 9–12, 1975.

94. Daniel Crowley, *African Myth and Black Reality in Brazilian Carnaval* (Los Angeles: UCLA Museum of Cultural History, 1984), 22.

95. Risério, *Carnaval Ijexá*, 43–44.

96. Antonio Medrado, "A república negra da Bahia," *Afinal* (São Paulo), February 9, 1988. Reprinted in João Jorge Santos Rodrigues, *Olodum: Estrada da Paixão* (Salvador: Edições Olodum, 1996).

97. Larry Crook, "Northeastern Brazil," in *Music in Latin American Culture: Regional Traditions*, ed. John M. Schecter (New York: Schirmer, 1999), 224.

98. "Orixás falaram mais alto," *Diário de Notícias*, March 8, 1973.

99. "Os Filhos do Morro têm samba enrêdo pronto para o carnaval," *A Tarde*, January 28, 1970; "Juventude pronta para brilhar."

100. "'Casa Grande e Senzala,' o samba dos Diplomatas," *Diário de Notícias*, February 22, 1974.

101. "'Ilê Aiyê', um bloco de raça aberto a gente de qualquer cor," *Jornal da Bahia*, February 24, 1979.

102. Risério, *Carnaval Ijexá*, 67–70.

103. Crook, *Brazilian Music*, 274.

104. "Apaches Uma festa de cores com 3500 homens na avenida," *Jornal da Bahia*, February 3, 1975.

105. "Juventude pronta para brilhar."

106. "Amanhã 23 blocos na rua: nosso carnaval é o maior," February 22, 1974; "Filhos do Tororó não saem. Falta Dinheiro," *Diário de Notícias*, February 16, 1974.

107. Goli Guerreiro, *A Trama dos Tambores: A Música Afro-Pop de Salvador* (São Paulo: Editora 34, 2000), 61.

108. Waly Salomão, *Folha de São Paulo*, May 13, 1988, reprinted in Rodrigues, *Olodum*.

109. "Juventude pronta para brilhar"; "Um prêmio pequeno," *Diário de Notícias*, February 13, 1970.

110. Gambling and other games of chance were prohibited in 1946, but they persisted in clandestine venues in Rio's poor suburbs where, increasingly, organized racketeers channeled part of their profits toward bribing policemen, and another part to escolas that were instructed in how to vote in elections. In this way, organized crime grew and diversified under protection while helping underwrite the expansion of Rio carnival's spectacle. Maria Isaura Pereira de Queiroz, "Escolas de samba do Rio de Janeiro ou a domesticação da massa urbana," *Ciência e Cultura* 36, no. 6 (1984), 893–909.

111. "Vadu é atração no Diplomatas," *Diário de Notícias*, February 2, 1973.

112. "Escolas: dinheiro magro," *Diário de Notícias*, February 25, 1976.

113. A fuller history of the trio elétrico and its role in transforming Salvador carnival is in Metz, "*Alegria*."

114. Trio Elétrico Dodô e Osmar, *Jubileu de Prata* (Phonodisc, 1975).

115. "Juventude pronta para brilhar."

116. Caetano Veloso, "Atrás do Trio Elétrico," on *Álbum Branco* (Philips LP, 1969), http://www.youtube.com/watch?v=sd99slI8Jzk.

117. "Nosso carnaval 'exportação,'" *Diário de Notícias*, February 12, 1972.

118. "A vez do rico samba das escolas," *ViverBahia* 29 (February 1976).

119. "Escolas de samba," *Diário de Notícias*, February 12, 1976.

120. "Até que ponto é viável a extinção das escolas de samba?" *A Tarde*, February 28, 1973.

121. "Sutursa é contra as escolas de samba no carnaval de Salvador," *A Tarde*, February 20, 1973.

122. "Escolas: Dinheiro magro."

123. Bahian carnival music was banned from some parts of the city and neighboring Olinda, while Recife's mayor begged local radio stations to ignore Bahian hits and "Play Pernambucan music." "Atrás do trio elétrico," *Jornal do Brasil*, January 29, 1989.

124. *O Carnaval no Passo do Tempo* (Sistema JC de Comunicação / TV Jornal), n.d.

125. "Os blocos de todas as ruas," *ViverBahia* no. 29 (February 1976).

126. By the late 1970s trio musicians began to synthesize other elements, starting with the rhythms of the afoxés plus other Caribbean rhythms, adding keyboards to the mix. *Axé music* (or samba-reggae), appearing in the 1980s, layered electric instruments atop a heavy rhythmic bed derived from blocos afros. Daniela Mercury was called "queen of axé" in the early 1990s. A detailed overview is Chris McGowan and Ricardo Pessanha, *The Brazilian Sound* (Philadelphia: Temple University Press, 1998), chap. 6.

127. Secretaria de Cultura, *Carnaval 2007: Uma Festa de Meio Bilhão de Reais* (Salvador: Secretaria de Cultura do Estado da Bahia, 2007), 5.

128. Binder labeled "Samba 2009" at SalTur, Salvador's metropolitan tourism department.

CHAPTER 10

The Opera *Manchay Puytu*

A Cautionary Tale Regarding Mestizos in Twentieth-Century Highland Bolivia

E. Gabrielle Kuenzli

The history of opera in Latin America dates back to at least the early eighteenth century when the earliest known opera performances were performed in the country of Mexico. It is within that nation that the first indigenous opera composers of Latin America emerged, with Manuel de Zumaya (ca. 1678–1755) considered as the first and most important early Mexican opera composer. Outside of Mexico, opera was slower to gain a foothold, and it wasn't until the early to mid-nineteenth century that other nations in Latin America began producing their own opera composers. Many of these nineteenth-century operas focus on the historical conflict between Europeans and indigenous peoples and were influenced by the *zarzuela*, a form of Spanish opera. In the twentieth century, many nationalist operas were composed across Latin America, with particularly thriving opera scenes in Mexico, Argentina, and Brazil.[1]

While indigenous protagonists often prevail in Latin American operas, the question as to why we should expect an indigenous presence, especially in the late nineteenth- and twentieth-century productions, goes unanswered. In addition, while indigenous opera in Mexico might be expected, given the twentieth-century postrevolutionary promotion of a mestizo identity that recognizes a glorified Indian past, the other two countries recognized for Indian-themed opera are countries with relatively small indigenous populations that have been marginalized in national narratives, namely Argentina and Brazil. I discuss the importance of the historical context during which operas were written and produced through my analysis of the opera *Manchay Puytu: El amor que quiso ocultar Dios* in Bolivia, a country often overlooked in terms of operatic production. *Manchay Puytu*, originally a novel written in 1977, was performed as an opera in the city of La Paz in 1995.

Cover of the novel *Manchay Puytu*, written by Nestor Taboada Terán (1977) and based on the legend.

The opera represents a break with the 1952 revolution and its promotion of *mestizaje*, illustrating instead the social isolation associated with being mestizo in highland Bolivia. *Manchay Puytu* served to bolster the Indian-based political parties and movements that played a central role in Bolivia in the late twentieth century.

In part, opera in Bolivia has been overlooked because twentieth-century production of opera as been limited. Bolivia boasts three operas. The first, *Incallacjta*, was composed by Ailiano Auza in 1980. In 1995 Alberto Villalpando wrote *Manchay Puytu: El Amor que quiso ocultar Dios*, the focus of this chapter, and was based on Nestor Taboada Terán's 1977 novel, *Manchay Puytu*, which was influenced by popular legend and *yarawis*, an indigenous poem or song. The third opera, *El Compadre*, was written in 2011 by Nicolas Suárez. While Bolivia has seen limited operatic production, the shows were met with enthusiasm and the topics and methodology of the productions were innovative. *Incallajcta* deals with Inca history and protagonists; *Manchay*

Puytu is about the tragic story of a mestizo protagonist; and *El Compadre* highlights a radio personality-turned-politician who was famous in Bolivia. To write *El Compadre*, the collaborators engaged in extensive interviews, privileging oral sources in writing the opera. These Bolivian operas feature oral sources and indigenous languages in their operatic production.

Manchay Puytu tells of the tragic love story between an indigenous man from Chayanta, Bolivia, who becomes a priest—a cultural mestizo, who does not fully belong to nor is fully separate from the Creole and the indigenous societies, and his Indian servant. *Manchay Puytu* is a well-known legend in the Andes, and four different variations on the tale exist.[2] Bolivian scholar Jesus Lara included the poem *Manchay Puytu* in his anthology of Quechua poetry, identifying one version of the story with Bolivia.

Alberto Villalpando, who wrote the opera, was born in La Paz in 1940 and grew up in Potosí. He learned to play the piano and in 1958 he left for Buenos Aires to study at the National Music Conservatory. He was recognized for his compositions, receiving the National Prize for Bolivian Culture in 1958. He has written compositions for several productions, including for Javier Sanjines's movies, *Ukamau*, *Yawar Mallku*, *Mi Socio*, and *Los Andes no Creen en Dios*.[3]

The story is set in eighteenth-century Potosi and features the unraveling of the unfortunate mestizo priest, who wanders about playing on the bone of his loved one. Though written primarily in Spanish, the author interjects a significant amount of Quechua throughout the opera. Using the genre of opera to tell the story reflects the solitude of the mestizo in highland Bolivia. Antonio, the mestizo protagonist, belongs to neither the Creole nor Indian musical traditions. If Antonio plays an Indian flute, in his hands, the hands of a mestizo, the music is unnatural, unsettling. Antonio inserts the flute into an earthen pot, attracting stares from indigenous people and Creoles alike who had seldom heard such an eerie sound. The truncated repertoire of Bolivian opera, as a musical genre, serves to represent the unusual plight of the mestizo. Operatic production has struggled to find a home in Bolivia as a means of musical expression, as has the mestizo and his mixed cultural past in the highlands.

The place of the mestizo in Bolivian society is a complicated theme in national history. In the late nineteenth and early twentieth centuries, during the era of eugenics and nation building, highland Bolivian intellectuals rejected rather than embraced the mestizo, saying that he represented the worst qualities of both the Indian and the Spaniard.[4] The promise of the nation-building project rested on "educating" and "civilizing" the Indians rather than on the mestizo population. An attempt at a nationwide celebration of the mestizo identity emerged later in Bolivia as part of the revolutionary platform of the *Movimiento Nacionalista Revolucionario*'s (Revolutionary Nationalist Movement, MNR) 1952 revolution. This arguably more inclusive revolutionary project was received with unequal regional popularity, but was cut short by several decades of dictatorship that commenced in the late 1960s and ended in 1982. Taboada Terán's novel *Manchay Puytu* was published in 1977 toward the end of dictatorship rule in Bolivia. Why did he take up the unfortunate plight of the mestizo?

Bolivian sociologist Silvia Rivera Cusicanqui describes the emergence of resistance to the dictatorship expressed through the revisionist anticolonial historical narrative that revalorized the Indian—especially the Aymara—referred to as Katarismo: "In the late 1960s there emerged a new generation of young Aymaras, who felt they were 'foreigners in their own country,' despite their formal inclusion in the citizenry, since they experienced the daily phenomena of ethnic discrimination, political manipulation, and humiliation."[5] This generation of Aymara scholars and activists formed Indian-based cultural centers and engaged in a revalorization of Aymara history. Organizations established during this period include the 15th of November Movement (late 1960s); the Julian Apaza University Movement (late 1960s, UMSA), made of up students who demanded recognition of the anticolonial efforts of Tupaj Katari; and the Center for the Advancement and Coordination of the Peasantry (MINK'A) worked in education and organization in both countryside and city. These separate efforts culminated in the signing of the Tiwanaku Manifesto of 1973, the founding statement of Katarismo, which was signed by members of the Tupac Katari Peasant Center, the National Association of Peasant Teachers, and others, clearly states the common struggle of indigenous peoples in Bolivia: "We the Qhechwa and Aymara peasants, like those of other indigenous cultures in the country, say the same thing. We feel that we are economically exploited and culturally and politically oppressed."[6] The central identity to this revalorization of Aymara history was Indian, not mestizo or based on a class or worker identity. The focus on Indian history and politics in the late 1960s and 1970s responded not only to the dictatorship but also to the mestizo project of the 1952 revolution, which these activists viewed as a failure and as a form of state marginalization that again sought to demote the Indian population and past. Taboada Terán, who had not been an MNR supporter, emphasized the tragedy of a mestizo identity through Antonio's decision to leave his place of origin and become a priest and culturally mestizo.[7] As his tragedy unfolds, Antonio seeks his Indian past, through his love for the Indian servant, through his playing the indigenous instrument the quena flute, and through his increased expressions in Quechua as his misery mounts. If the Katarista intellectuals developed Indian-based political parties and discourses in the late 1960s and 1970s, Taboada Terán's novel complemented their position through his graphic illustration of the unfortunate mestizo and the problems of cultural identity associated with the mestizo. Far from being an inclusive identity, as Taboada Terán illustrates, the mestizo suffered from the constant attempt to navigate multiple spaces, which more often than not resulted in social rejection. In this sense, *Manchay Puytu* symbolizes a break with the mestizo project of 1952 and the coming of a new era that would center on Indian politics.

The opera is comprised of three scenes. It opens in a jail, where a Spanish man is being punished for the deaths of 360 indigenous women, who all killed themselves lovesick for him. The second scene takes place on the outskirts of the city, and involves a meeting between the Indian priest Antonio, who has fallen in love with his Indian servant, and the Indian sage Nauparuna. The final scene turns to the core of the city, taking place on the colonial streets of Potosí, colonial silver capital of the world. As the priest Antonio moves from the outskirts to the center of the city playing the flute he fashioned out of his loved one's bone, projecting the sound into a clay pot to produce the most melancholy of sounds, Antonio occupies the heart of the city. As he plays in the heavily trafficked space, indigenous people and creoles alike turn to stare, wondering at the strange sound and at the musician. For a brief minute, it seems that the mestizo flute player might serve to unify the indigenous and Creole populations, but instead he is ostracized by both because he is a cultural mestizo, of Indian blood but living and working in the church, outside of his indigenous community. In the opera, Indian and non-Indian worlds stand in stark contrast, perhaps in order to heighten the case of the mestizo caught in between. Antonio's profession as a member of the clergy, which grants him some authority within colonial society, is now a source of further condemnation of his behavior, as he has flagrantly violated all codes of priestly conduct through his love affair with his Indian servant and his fabrication of the bone flute from her leg. It is interesting that in the novel and the opera the indigenous population is the most critical of Father Antonio. When a group of indigenous people who are rebelling approach the city of Potosí, they call Father Anotonio a traitor and an oppressor, and tell him to go home to his mansion in the suburbs. Throughout the tale, the Indian population is most critical of Father Anotnio; however, the Indian woman is Antonio's great love, and the Indian sage will give him advice throughout the story. Through these actions, indigenous protagonists are the priest's main base of support. Through the performance of high culture, opera, Villalpando places the question of a mestizo identity at the heart of Bolivian society and history.

If Antonio occupies the center of colonial Bolivia, the great city of Potosí with his flute playing, Villalpando occupies the center of La Paz, and by extension, the center of Bolivia, with his lyric opera. Villalpando presents the question of mestizaje again to the Bolivian public in the heart of La Paz, occupying the municipal theater to force Bolivians to consider the plight of the mestizo identity. In a city where many residents of indigenous descent live, work, and study in the urban center of La Paz, the question of cultural mestizaje is most relevant. Should this population be considered less Indian? Are they able to better keep a foot in each world, or is the cultural mestizo rejected by both? How many viewers identify with Antonio's plight, yet would not self-identify as a mestizo? As the translated title of the book and the opera reads, Manchay Puytu: The Love that Even God Wanted to Hide, begs the question of the role of the historically undesirable mestizo identity in Bolivia.

In 1995, when the opera was performed, the question of mestizaje and, moreover, cultural mestizaje was paramount. People of Aymara origin not only lived in the cities but also occupied professional, political, and intellectual posts. Katarismo as a political and cultural Aymara-based movement permeated Bolivian politics.

Why, then, select *Manchay Puytu* as the third opera written in Bolivia? If we can contextualize and understand one of the main messages of the novel *Manchay Puytu* in 1977, why would it resonate with the public as an opera in 1995? The year 1993 marked an important election in Bolivia. Gonzalo Sánchez de Lozada was elected as president, along with Victor Hugo Cárdenas, the first Aymara vice-president. This unlikely alliance between a University of Chicago trained neoliberal and an accomplished Aymara intellectual from the Revolutionary Tupac Katari Liberation Movement (formed in 1985) introduced important changes, such as the redefinition of Bolivia in the Constitution as multiethnic and multicultural and also introduced the first articles in the Constitution that recognized indigenous rights. Gonzalo Sánchez de Lozada also introduced the Ley de Participación Popular, or the Popular Participation Project, which gave municipalities greater regional autonomy, and also developed programs to educate Bolivian children in indigenous languages. This legislation in certain ways increased and legitimized indigenous culture and citizenship within urban spaces. The servant Maria's death due to abandonment by the mestizo figure of Padre Antonio served to underscore the injustice of her role as a domestic servant, dependent on a mestizo master. The desolate end of the mestizo priest serves as a cautionary tale; perhaps he should have never left his Indian village and distanced himself from his community or origin to suffer such sadness as a mestizo in an urban center. Antonio's turn to quena playing on a flute made of his beloved's bone represents his longing for indigenous culture, underscoring the loneliness of the mestizo within society. This opera, then, bolsters the promotion of an indigenous identity that shaped Bolivian politics in the 1990s, through legislation passed by Sánchez de Lozada and Cárdenas.

Notes

1. See, for example, Horacio J. Sanguinetti, *La opera y la sociedad argentina* (Buenos Aires: MZ ediciones, 2001); Maria Elena Kuss, "Nativistic Strains in Argentine Operas Premiered at the Teatro Colón 1908–1972" (PhD dissertation, University of California, Los Angeles, 1976); Rufus Clement Hopkins, *Malinche: An Opera of Mexico* (Tuscon: Office of the Arizona Star, 1881); R. J. Planché, *Hernando Cortez, or the Conquest of Mexico: An Opera in Three Acts* (1823).
2. A different version of *Manchay Puytu* was performed at the Musem of Modern Art's sound garden concert series in 1995 by an Argentine composer, Alejandro Iglesias Rossi.
3. "La opera Manchaypuytu de Alberto Villalpando," *Presencia* (La Paz), December 12, 1995.
4. For highland Bolivia see Brooke Larson, "Redeemed Indians, Barbarized

Cholos: Crafting Neocolonial Identity in Liberal Bolivia," in *Political Cultures in the Andes, 1750–1950*, eds. Nils Jacobsen and Cristóbal Aljovín de Losada (Durham, NC: Duke University Press, 2005), 230–52. For the contrasting promotion of a mestizo identity in lowland Bolivia, see Paula Peña Hasbún, *La permanente construcción del Cruceño: Un estudio sobre la identidad en Santa Cruz de la Sierra* (La Paz: PIEB, Universidad Autónoma de Gabriel René Moreno, 2003); Hernán Pruden, "Santa Cruz entre la post-guerra del Chaco y las postrimerias de la revolución nacional: Cruceños y Cambas," *Historias: revista de la coordinadora de historia* 6 (2003), 41–61; Nicole Fabricant, "Performative Politics: The Camba Countermovement in Eastern Bolivia," *American Ethnologist* 36, no. 4 (2009).

5. Silvia Rivera Cusicanqui, *Oppressed but not Defeated: Peasant Struggles Among the Aymara and Qhechua in Bolivia, 1900–1980* (Geneva: United Nations Research Institute for Social Development, 1987), 149.

6. Ibid., 116–17.

7. "Manchay Puytu: Los códigos disperos," *Presencia* (La Paz), December 13, 1995.

CHAPTER 11

Sounding Modern Identity in Mexican Film

Janet Sturman and Jennifer Jenkins

From the beginning the film industry set out to mirror popular culture, to reflect its achievements, its myths, its prejudices, its tastes, its attitudes to fiestas, to the search for Mexican national identity.

—CARLOS MONSIVÁIS[1]

According to Carlos Monsiváis, arbiter of twentieth-century and millennial Mexican culture, the film industry and national identity developed together as paired protagonists of the modern nation. If cinema reflected popular understandings of national identity, it also shaped them. Intentionally and unintentionally, across the twentieth century, cinema productions mirrored and occasionally challenged the social agendas of the leaders of the moment.

Whether the focus of the government was land reform, education, nationalization of industry and natural resources, or fiscal independence from hemispheric corporations, Mexican cinema addressed such issues in comedy, melodrama, and other genres. Whatever the issue and whatever the period, cinema taught what it means to be Mexican, a habit born in the *época de oro*. As Andrea Noble argues, the Golden Age "was a mythical moment of cinema consumption: a moment at which 'all the people'—or, at least, more than before and since—went to the movies and in doing so, participated in the everyday rituals of belonging to the modern nation."[2] Often overtly, and sometimes nearly subliminally, films' musical scores furthered that process, offering songs of hope and mournful ballads in equal measure as a reflection of national temperament.

Here we examine films that represent three periods of Mexican history and identity: the revolutionary 1930s; the post–World War II época de oro; and the post–NAFTA millennial period. We do not contend that these films are exclusive representations of the cinema of their respective eras; indeed, they are not. Nevertheless, these films provide notable representations of national identity through both sight and sound. They offer insight into the formation over time of national identity to "cinematically enfranchised citizens"[3] their particular combinations of visual narrative and musical score.

Águila o Sol (1937) in its title evokes two motifs of pre-Hispanic iconography: the eagle and the sun. Both definitive for Mesoamerican Nahua culture, they function as comically intended surnames in this comedy vehicle for the rising star, Mario Moreno (Cantínflas). Only the third film in which the *pelado/lépero* appeared, this film establishes Cantínflas as a cinematic emblem. The grand historical implications of the title are immediately undercut by the fact that Águila and Sol are the names of abandoned children. Their names together also carry the slangy sense of "heads or tails," derived from the obverse and reverse images on the peso. Like much of Cantínflas's rapid-fire nonsense talk, this double meaning both links the orphans to the exalted pre-Hispanic history and hints at a how-the-mighty-have-fallen political statement. Both would be appealing to the cinema-going audience of the day, whose identification with a noble past and present misery would be palpable. This dialectical existence, as Octavio Paz has shown, shapes the national sense of self.[4] It also provides space for comedy in the disjuncture between the two modes of existence.

Like Chaplin's Little Tramp character, the feisty but sweet bum or lowlife character that Moreno developed in *carpa* (tent-shows) functions as a *pícaro*, the scrappy underdog who emerged in eighteenth century European literature to challenge class structure and entrenched notions of privilege. The Cantínflas character is utterly oblivious to social rank and moves freely among the spaces that demarcate identity, a freedom reinforced by the medley of songs ranging from folkloric to cosmopolitan embedded in the film's soundtrack. Because Cantínflas comes from the lowest of the low, he is not expected to achieve or understand anything; this condition affords him a freedom to move up and down the social ladder without regard for rules or conventions. His occupation of the cultural interstices allows for an identity that transcends most structures. He is neither, both, and, not.

The film's prince and pauper story follows three orphan children, Polito Sol (Jesús de la Mora) and siblings Adriana (Margarita Sodí) and Carmelo (José Girón Torres) Águila, left as infants on the steps of a convent on the same day. The children make their way from street entertainment to stage performance as the Trio Águila o Sol. The girl sings and the boys do a slapstick *carpa* routine. Directed by Russian émigré and Eisenstein protégé

Arkady Boytler,[5] this film is notable for its comic set-pieces by Cantínflas and Medel, a team at the time.[6]

From a historical distance, we can see that its rags-to-riches motif clearly mirrors the rise of the former carpa performer, Mario Moreno, into his internationally known clown persona as Cantínflas. As such, it reflects the rising national belief in social mobility after the Revolution and contributes to Cantínflas, born one year into the Revolution, as the emergent voice of the pueblo:

> The political theater became an [*sic*] vital part of Mexican civil society, as Mario Moreno and other actors portraying members of the lower classes publicly discussed governmental scandals that print journalists dared not mention. By defusing their critiques through humor, comedians and their audiences intervened in political debates while avoiding the worst effects of censorship.[7]

As a nascent form of social critique, the comic carpa routines on the screen allow for bold statement; the films place such issues as social mobility and criticism of the status quo within a narrative framework that affords audiences a fable to live by. The inclusion of popular song reinforces the message: if the film's theme song is stuck in one's head, inevitably its social message will be, too.

After the children run away from the orphanage, they enter the "real" world through a brief montage of carnival images [08:59–09:11],[8] suggesting not only the wheel of fortune but also the theatrical world that will absorb the children. At a traveling circus, they first hear what will become their signature song, the tango-canción "La Mariposa Negra,"[9] offered by a chanteuse who lends a bit of class to the vaudeville. Like other music heard in the carpas and populist theater revues of the era, this song, composed by the film's musical director, Manuel Castro Padilla, matches memorable melody with a fashionable dance rhythm, here the tango that Mexicans had recently adopted from Argentina.[10]

The three children soon begin performing the canción on the streets, outside a theater that headlines the iconic bourgeois religious melodrama, *Don Juan Tenorio* [13:00]. The fashionably dressed middle-class audience leaving the theater barely notice the children, although a few drop coins in Adriana's outstretched hand as she croaks along to the accompaniment of the two boys on rudimentary guitars. A cross-dissolve condenses time as we meet the adult Adriana (Marina Tamayo) singing inside a theater—clearly a step up socially and artistically [13:40]. Moreover, the adult Adriana sings in the correct register for her voice and exhibits a trained voice. From the cross-dissolve, the camera pulls back to reveal the proscenium stage, with Polito (Cantínflas) and Carmelo (Manuel Medel) on guitars and dressed in motley. The first of a series of three medium shots captures Polito, right, earnestly playing his guitar; Boytler cuts to Carmelo, left, who twirls his guitar and occasionally strums it with a feather-duster. The final medium shot in the triptych is of Adriana, center, now a beautiful young woman with a full, rich voice. A close-up profile of her, cut on the line, "Sin embargo mi negra mariposa, si adoré la mujer y acabé se matar." The legend of the mariposa negra, the black butterfly, as a symbol of death seems a fitting backstory in a song for Adriana and her fellow orphans.[11] The metaphoric lyric referents to a femme fatale seem to presage the anguish that Pollito will seek to extinguish in the later bar scene with his buddy Carmelo, when he fears that Adriana may succumb to attentions of the wealthy club owner and leave the trio.

This number is followed by a comic *apache* dance to an instrumental rendition of "La negra mariposa," with gender reversals and comic vying between the men to lead the dance. The dance of the underdog is one of Cantínflas's leitmotivs, seen in these early black-and-white films all the way through his later Technicolor color work with M. M. Delgado. The pelado character dances with enthusiasm and concentration, hampered only by his rags and his natural lack of talent. These scenes of the trio in their first theater engagement reveal performers who are still somewhat awed by audience appreciation: they exhibit a natural modesty and deference that shows their likeability and also their awareness of their place in society. While instructive to a point as a model for upward mobility, this performance behavior could be quite limiting. Discovery by a theater angel solves the problem and allows for a more exalted performance of Mexicanness.

The culminating spectacle of national identity occurs three-fourths of the way through the film, in a cabaret number that displays women in Tehuantepec costume [46:00]. Adriana is now fully absorbed into café society as a headliner, and the men have taken subordinate roles to her public visibility. At this point in the film narrative, Adriana has risen above her birth to such a degree that her performance of a Tehuana is neither parodic nor true, but simply a show-biz projection of a visually stimulating and nonthreatening aspect of indigeneity.

Less dramatic than the folkloric presentation, but equally relevant to Boytler's projection of modern national identity, is the contemporary mix of *danzones*, *boleros*, and *chachas* provided by the club orchestra, directed by Rafael Hernández, the second compositional partner in the film score. Cosmopolitan dance music drew patrons to the club and it is the music that viewers hear as Pollito enters the club and edges his way along the crowded dance floor toward the stage area. The cabaret show interrupts the music provided for the couples on the dance floor, and the scene opens with the bright sound of the marimba. Two lines of chorines enter the frame from the right rear, crossing the checkerboard dance floor on the diagonal to separate and fill the frame space with parallel but oppositely costumed Tehuanas. Frame left is filled with dancers in dark *huipils*, modified to show midriff, and lace headdresses off the face. Their counterparts wear more modest Tehuana skirts, the lace headdresses around the face and covering the torso: thus modern and traditional regional costume meet in the cabaret, each affording the other legitimacy.[12] As the two complementary lines of chorines part, Adriana moves forward, in the more modest costume, to sing a *son de marimba*, that opens with the words "Por los palmares bien secos" (by the well-dried palms) with a refrain, "Donde canta, la marimba," (where the marimba sings, where my love stays). Thus, begins a medley of Oaxacan dance tunes in a stage show that will culminate in an updated version of the song "Sandunga." This signature melody of the isthmus of Tehuantepec in the state of Oaxaca appears earlier in the film as part of the overture of melodies that precede the first scene in the film when the children are left at the orphanage. The lyrics, which would be well known to Mexican viewers, mourn the loss of a beloved mother. This choice is also notable since director Boytler's mentor Sergei Eisenstein dedicated a full chapter of his iconic 1931 film *Qué Viva México* to Tehuantepec, and titled it "Sandunga." The song was also sung by the smoldering screen star Lupe Velez in another contemporary film, *Zandunga* (1938), directed by Fernando de Fuentes and Miguel Delgado.

Oaxaca and its indigenous people became important emblems of postrevolutionary conceptions of national identity. The public displays of the archaeological treasures of Monte Alban between 1922 and 1933 helped "prime the public" for an interest in the indigenous people of this region and aided national initiatives to draw upon regional and indigenous identities to establish the postrevolutionary Mexican identity.[13]

The stage show in the club scene blends indigenous tradition with cosmopolitan frames in a cabaret format designed to signal multicultural inclusiveness. We can recognize here the importance of the cabaret as a space for trying on identities that are, in the words of Marilyn Miller, "easier to simulate than to integrate."[14]

As Adriana sings in center stage, the chorines perform simple moves from *folklorico* dance, dipping and twirling outspread skirts. The second song in the medley is purely instrumental, and at that point the camera cranes up to an overhead shot, and the dance sequence commences in the mode of Hollywood director-choreographer Busby Berkeley, as the musicians shift to the song "Dios no muere" (God doesn't die), considered an unofficial national anthem of Oaxaca. Upon the canvas of the checkerboard dance floor, the women move through a sequence that suggests the mechanistic infinite repetition that marks Berkeley's futurist set-pieces. This combination of ultra-modern (circa 1938) staging and cinematography with Tehuana costuming presents a somewhat surreal hybrid of colonial and postcolonial Mexican imagery. It is worth noting that Polito only truly realizes his love for Adriana after seeing her perform as a Tehuana, historically the most independent and self-reliant women in Mexico. As aspirational types, or demonstrators of national identity, these picaresque figures—male and female—define modern youth. The show projects an idealized blend of cultures formerly separated by region, time, social status, and race (albeit underplayed), now united in the modern nation.

Boytler intercuts the dance sequence with cutaways to the band and the marimberos, to Polito's dumbfounded reaction, and to the enthralled stylish café society audience, returning to the overhead shot of dancers moving in precision, alternating black-and-white costumes and inward and outward motion centered around Adriana. A few close-ups of chorines reveal *not* indigenous features, but aquiline noses and light-skinned beauties swathed in the Tehuana garb. The finale culminates in a dramatic presentation of the "Sandunga" waltz melody, and the show ends with a concluding orchestral fanfare.

Immediately following the stage show, the sound of orchestral strings and flute signal a shift to a *charanga* style dance number as the musicians resume performing the popular Caribbean dance music adored by cosmopolitan patrons of the era.[15] Pollito approaches the conductor, a cameo role played by composer Rafael Hernández himself, who brushes off his advances. Pollito shifts his glance to watch Adriana conversing with the club owner and when he again turns to the conductor he finds the dark-skinned maestro transformed, dreamlike, into his friend Caramelo—or did Caramelo assume the identity of the famous Afro-Puerto Rican musical star? The transformation reinforces Pollito's confused state, but it also mirrors the integration of the Puerto Rican–born Hernández, who, like his polished compositions and arrangements of Afro-Caribbean music, was adopted by Mexicans. Hernández moved to Mexico in 1932 when he was forty years old and stayed until 1947, when he returned to Puerto Rico. He earned acceptance and fame in Mexico as a composer, orchestra director, film score arranger, and actor. Even today, residents of the state of Puebla view Hernandez's song "Que chula es Puebla" as a state anthem.[16]

The conscious amalgam of traditional and shifting national tropes in *Águila o sol* serves as a prelude to the plot resolution. Polito's father, having won the lottery, appears on the scene to reclaim his son into wealth and position, offering at the last minute to take the Águila siblings into the family as well. Clearly the performance of modern national identity in the Sandunga cabaret medley sets the stage for the reunion of fathers and sons and the reconciliation of poverty and wealth. As such, it presents a convenient narrative of assimilation and aspiration that rewards the scrappy pelado and the pure-hearted and -voiced young woman. The film concludes back in the cabaret, with an overlay montage of champagne bottles as the two young couples celebrate their good fortune—fully underscoring the message that modern Mexico is modern, indeed.

Nosotros los Pobres (1948)

Ismael Rodriguez's overt adaptation to cinema of *costumbrismo*, a Spanish literary, theatrical, and visual trope seen in the expressive arts of the Americas in the eighteenth century, constructs a popular cinema of realism in the Pepe el Toro trilogy. *Nosotros los Pobres* (1948) is the first in a serio-comic melodrama trilogy focused on the daily lives of Mexico City's working poor.

Starring Pedro Infante as carpenter Pepe el Toro—a characterization that mirrored Infante's own biography—the film gives face and voice to the lowly populations who migrated to the cities, most particularly Mexico City, after the Revolution.[17] It showcases the people's hero, Infante, as a relatable character who faced the same tribulations as cinemagoers.[18] As an expression of national identity, then, *Nosotros* speaks to the many rather than the few. The film's plotline is inextricably intertwined with Infante's biography, and both celebrate the underrepresented working poor who struggle and endure, in this case with a song in their hearts. The musical numbers incorporated into the film's very structure overtly reinforce themes of personhood and identity.

The opening sequence of *Nosotros los Pobres* subscribes to the cultural discourse of upward mobility through urban migration that became reified in the postwar period. A dedication to the "simple and good people" of the urban underclass self-consciously plays to the audience, ennobling these pobres in a melodrama of identity. Rodriguez's focus on the arrabal in which his characters live, love, and lose directly imports daily life, lowly characters, and indigenous into a musical vehicle for Pedro Infante. Like Gershwin's similar focus on the lowly in *Porgy and Bess*, Rodriguez opens his film with a survey of characters and activities unique to the people of the *vecindad*. More significantly than class, perhaps, this community is bound together by song, and song that allows for individual variation and collective refrain. Thus, the form, as well as the performance of the songs, reflects the social structure of the world of the film.

After a pan shot left to right across the tidy plaza of the arrabal as the community enjoys a stroll, the film opens, famously, with two children pulling a book, titled *Nosotros los Pobres*, out of a trash bin.[19] In a device commonly used in Hollywood films of the era, they open the book, accompanied by the opening chords of the orchestral overture, thereby initiating the film narrative. As the children leaf through the opening pages of the book, lyric string melodies and harp accompaniment establish the transition into storyland, while the interjections of brass instruments allude to conflicts along the way. An over-the-shoulder shot reveals drawings of the cast of characters, mainly stock types drawn from carpa shows and popular adaptations of *commedia del'arte*. The resulting survey of the inhabitants of the neighborhood presents a horizontal view of the lowest level of Mexico City society at the time, in a format accessible to even the least literate among the audience.

National identity is defined as the pueblo or arrabal, writ large, in this "poor-but-happy barrio saga."[20] The mixture of mestizo and indio, artisan and laborer, noble and comic, sober and drunk, chaste and debauched (within period standards), male and female in the opening number creates a spectrum of representation that gives visible presence and voice to the capital's often invisible or underrepresented working poor. The very fact of dedicating screen time to the urban underclass defines identity to Mexicans and outsiders as diverse, both culturally and economically, and accessible to all.[21]

The array of neighbors in the arrabal ranges laterally across the lowest social stratum: Pepe el Toro, the carpenter, and his little girl Chachita; the paired opposite women, La Tisica and La Romántica (later called La Chorreada); villains Don Pilar and Licenciado Montes; La que se levanta tarde (she who awakes late) and La Paralitica, all of whom inhabit the melodramatic narrative; and the paired low characters who function as comic relief and a kind of Greek chorus or voice of *la gente*, the perpetually inebriated La Tostada and La Guayaba, and their male counterparts Topillos and Planillas.

We meet these characters in the jaunty opening musical number set to a polka beat that showcases the types, functions, and jobs in the arrabal. Rodriguez pans right from a departing truck into the plaza, to catch strolling musicians, the famed Trio Cantarrecio (really a quartet), who walk right to left, tracking back into the center of the plaza as they sing the opening lines, extolling the values of laughing, loving, and living, "*Que bonita es el reir, que bonita es el querer,*" each statement closing with the refrain "*¡Ni hablar, mujer!*" an idiomatic phrase that roughly translates to "There's nothing more to say!" The meaning changes with the context: it can be an expression of enthusiasm but also might be used sarcastically. On the surface, the exclamatory expression of wonder fits the film's setting for this catchy song where the neighborhood members sing of genuine joy, but a thoughtful viewer can't help but notice that these same people face genuine privation as well.

As in a staged musical, the leads are joined by comic characters, one and then two tipsy couples who proclaim the joys of desire and a good plate of beans. As the camera moves further left, a group of newsboys enter from left rear, whistling the chorus and pulling the camera to the door of Pepe el Toro's shop, where the first edit is a jump cut to Pepe discoursing on beautiful women as he planes boards in his carpentry shop. The shop door frames Pepe like a proscenium and effectively sets him apart from the characters seen thus far: he is working, he is indoors, and he is shot in medium close-up. To the extent possible in this very horizontal social world, Pepe is at the top, and Rodriguez's lateral camera movement subtly reflects that distinction. The carpenter moves rear to open the window, and Rodriguez cuts to a reverse shot showing Pepe, now framed by the window, looking out into the courtyard. As Celia (Blanca Estela Pavón) takes up the song, the camera tracks her across the inner courtyard to the well where laundry is in progress. This is a female domain, and men are barred by architecture and topicality, save for a drunk who slurs the refrain, "Ni hablar, mujer." The containment of (nice) women around the *fonda* also signals gender roles at this time: occupied with domestic labor, the women in the inner courtyard of the film represent appropriate models of femininity.

When Rodriguez cuts back to the plaza—with the musicians picturesquely arrayed like Picasso's—they move offscreen right to make way for the tall and energetic "La que se levanta tarde" (Katy Jurado), who enters from the rear along the sidewalk to blow a kiss to Pepe (apparently late-rising is worth it). This gesture prompts Pepe's solo line about being a lowlife ("Nací pelado, si Señor") as he continues to measure and cut, working in the frame of a shop door, until Chachita (Evita Muñoz) enters with laundry to interrupt the flirtation. There follows a cutaway to extreme close-ups of the drunk women in the outer plaza slurring "*Ni hablar mujer*" to a 2-shot and then a 4-shot of the drunk couples, as locals two-step about the plaza, ending on a final shout of the refrain.

While this description might seem excessively labored, it is worth looking at this establishing sequence to scan the representation of national identity. As noted, the social world of the film is broad but not deep: this is the lowest level of urban existence, in which Pepe refers to himself as a pelado—the figure that Cantínflas parodied as the essence of the urban male a decade earlier.

The exterior placement of "La que se levanta tarde," in her low-cut, tight dress trimmed with lace, and the tipsy women in their *rebozos* and shredded *huipiles*, indicates their less domesticated and less constrained sexual identities. Notably missing from this survey of the neighborhood is the acknowledged fallen woman La Tisica (Carmen Montejo), who only comes out at night and would have nothing to contribute to the up-tempo *canción*. Nonetheless, she plays a significant role in the melodrama and her backstory reflects that of countless young women seduced and abandoned in the federal district.

Shot on a soundstage, *Nosostros* stands in stark and safe contrast to Luis Buñuel's 1950 cinéma vérité masterpiece, *Los Olvidados*. For every sunny song and cheerful act of endurance in *Nosotros*, Buñuel offers privation, lack of redemption, and footage of actual colonias in the rapidly expanding federal district. Rodriguez's choice to shoot on a soundstage contains the action in an imaginary world, a fantasy diegesis apart from the harsh realities of Mexico City. Still, his focus on this sector of the population is notable in its diversity and realism—within studio constructs. Susan Dever rightly notes that "Mexican urban dramas [of the Golden Age] challenge the indomitable spirit of the other prominent genres of the era," within the confines of musical melodrama, and *Nosotros* joins the sterner genres in engaging "viewer complicity."[22] The fact that most of the cinemagoers who saw themselves onscreen were enfranchised *only* by cinema is worth remembering.

The bolero, "Amorcito corazón," pairs Pepe and Celia in a charming duet between carpenter and laundress across the courtyard. Composed by Manuel Esperón with lyrics by Pedro de Urdimalas (who also plays Topillo, one of the local drunks) as a vehicle for Infante, its range and sentiment are particularly well-suited to Infante's talents. The song entered popular culture almost immediately, and was reprised in *Ustedes los ricos* (1948) and *Pepe el Toro* (1952), the second and third films in the trilogy. The modest dreams and aspirations of this couple are reflected in Pepe's continuing to work as he sings (and smokes), as Celia responds, whistling countermelodies as she cooks, echoing the coded manner of whistling communication in which she and Pepe engage in an earlier scene when they didn't want others to follow their conversations.

Rodriguez uses familiar conventions of Hollywood musicals, cutting between the two principles on emotional lines and dollying in to close-up on Infante's sustained notes. The duet shows a modern Mexican couple in a relationship of equality, each joining in from his and her distinct space in a distinct musical register (voice and whistle). This sequence indicates a new role for women: while Celia lives with her mother, she still controls her own money, love life, and future. She debates the future of her relationship with Pepe, and decides at one point to break off their courtship. She has her own means of support and does not relish being hostage to the ghost of Chachita's mother, so she takes the somewhat radical step of halting the relationship (with Pedro Infante!). This characterization of a modern woman, shot the year after female suffrage was enacted, is more radical than it might first appear.

Whistling is not limited to clever exchanges between lovers in this film score. Throughout the film whistle- and flute-like sounds are important signals of status, mood, and identity. At meaningful moments in the film, Manuel Esperón uses the breathy tones of clay vessel flutes (ocarinas), oscillating between the tones of a minor third to signal trouble ahead. We heard the mournful motive in the nondiegetic background music when Pepe encounters the band of men who will take him to jail and when the La Tisica stands dejected and alone in an alley facing the rising fog at dawn on her daughter's birthday. Typically, the ocarina is heard when the most humble residents, los pobres, are on-screen.

The tones of this ancient indigenous instrument (known as *huilacapitztli* to the Aztecs) evoke the persistent yet unsettled indigenous legacy. It is one of the instruments with which the nation's classically trained composers, notably Carlos Chávez and Silvestre Revueltas, experimented in their efforts to reconstruct pre-Hispanic music as a foundation for revolutionary identity. These experiments in musical *indigenismo* contrasts with prior musical treatments of indigenous heritage of *indianismo*, where composers' emblematic references to indigenous people were cast in the language of European classical music with little attempt to re-create native musical sounds.[23]

In the course of a melodramatic plotline drawn loosely from Dostoevsky's *Crime and Punishment*, Pepe el Toro ends up in jail, falsely accused of murder by a richer, predatory romantic rival, the lawyer Montes (Rafael Alcayde), for Celia. When the neighborhood joins to serenade Pepe's adopted daughter—really his niece—Chachita (Evita Muñoz) on her birthday, the centerpiece of the film emerges to the strains of "Las Mañanitas." Chachita is experiencing teenage doubts about identity, having heard rumors that her adoptive father Pepe murdered her mother (her actual mother, La Tisica [Carmen Montejo], is the local prostitute and Pepe's sister). Chachita also struggles with Pepe's conviction for murder and the contemporaneous theft of her savings by the scurrilous Don Pilar (Miguel Inclán). Thus, the communal serenade of "Las Mañanitas" evokes a series of complicated emotions for Chachita. A turning point in the film narrative is marked by this song, which is known to all

Mexicans and functions as the national birthday song. An *aubade*, the morning love song speaks across class and wealth lines. It is not difficult to imagine cinema goers singing along in the theater, and in fact Infante is credited with popularizing this version of the song in Latin America and the Philippines.[24]

The sequence begins in a long shot of Pepe backed by a band, the singers and guitars of the Trio Cantarrecio now augmented by violin and a modern flute, singing the opening verse in unison in the courtyard surrounding the community well [41:38]. Rodriguez cuts to a medium close-up reaction shot of Chachita in bed, listening woefully to her song. After a brief return to the band, the camera pans far left to Celia's window, where she appears in a slow zoom as she recognizes Pepe's voice. Pepe's reaction shot registers dejection when Chachita does not come to her window, and a cutaway to La Tisica reveals the tearful femme fatale's one weakness: the love for her daughter. Not until he sings a solo verse does Chachita recognize that her father has returned and all is forgiven. She struggles with whether to open her window, but finally sings a responding verse thanking the singers for their serenade. Her sweet voice contrasts with the tipsy *indias* who quaver out the chorus. As a morning song, "Las Mañanitas" offers hope and redemption on one's feast day; played as a mourning song in this sequence, it evokes all of the loss of loved ones experienced by the inhabitants of the arrabal. Even Celia warbles along, but cannot join the reunited father and daughter framed in the window. The narrative is not yet ready for the *sagrada familia* to be reestablished, for happiness in this neighborhood must be earned.

When Pepe is incarcerated on false charges, Esperón uses music to introduce the prison setting. As Pepe sits alone reading a letter from Celia [131:37], the orchestral background music recalls the song "Amorcito corazón." The camera shifts to another section of the prison where four prisoners sit with guitars singing a ranchera inflected bolero opening with the lyrics "Dicen que soy cacomistle . . . *Soy ladrón*," (They say I am a raccoon, meaning I am a thief, using a term of indigenous origin for raccoon, not the Spanish term *mapache*.) Calling someone a mapache is common slang for a thief that Mexicans frequently use either to charge politicians of graft or corruption.[25] Esperón's decision to favor the Nahuatl word is a nod to *Mexicanismo*, and not likely to be recognized by non-Mexican Spanish speakers. Like the indigenous whistle sounds, the *cacomistle* is an insider reference steeped in historical implications. The musicians (once again, the members of El trio Cantarrecio) wear vertical striped uniforms like the other prisoners. They sing until a riot breaks out, centered upon a vengeance dispute between Pepe and another prisoner, the actual killer whose sentence he bears. This prison fight is followed by a cutaway to a scene back home with Celia's father that moves the melodramatic narrative and provides a thematic bridge between the thief in the cacomistle bolero and the thief at home who has threatened Pepe's very existence.

As Pepe sits in solitary confinement, the quartet plays a reprise of "Amorcito corazon" (heard in an earlier moment in the prison scene, [131:37] as background music when Pepe read a letter from Celia) over a montage of prison scenes. A prisoner drinking from a fountain moves out of frame to reveal the quartet of musicians [1:41:40]. The camera pans left across the prison yard, then tracks in toward the gates, only to cut to a reverse shot from outside the gates that pans fairly fast then tracks to the interior alleyway leading to Pepe's cell. The quartet finishes their verse, and Celia appears top left in a vignette overlaid upon the image of Pepe in his cell. For the first time in the film, she is singing, if only in his imagination. After the first two phrases, Pepe chimes in and the two finish the duet in harmony as the scene dissolves to a silhouette of them together, turning as on a wedding cake (although in their humble street clothes) as they pledge to be *companyeros en el bien y el mal* (friends through good and bad).

Chachita joins them for the final bars, and the *sagrada familia* is restored, albeit in Pepe's imagination alone. As the image fades and the melody recedes, the camera pulls back from Pepe to reveal his face framed by the hatch in the cell door. Stark reality replaces the dream.

The melodramatic plot demands an O. Henry–style exchange of selflessness: Celia takes a secretarial job with the predatory licenciado Montes to earn money for Pepe's defense, while Pepe is smuggled out of prison to visit his mother who is critically ill after a beating by the paranoid and thieving Don Pilar. An overwhelming number of plot elements resolve as La Tisica is reunited with Chachita, Pepe's mother and sister die, Pepe is apprehended and returned to prison after a tearful reconciliation with Celia and Chachita, only to beat a confession out of—and blind—the real murderer and find his exoneration. The film ends a year later at the *panteón*, over the graves of Chachita's and Pepe's mothers. Pepe, Celia, the new baby Torito, and Chachita stand together as the new family for a new day. This resolution is commented upon by the two drunken couples, who salute the happy ending and fertility of Pepe and Celia. As the voice of *la gente*, these comic characters place the seal of approval on the comic resolution of the plot. Now that the unsavory elements—the prostitute, the usurer, the thief, the murderer, and false witness—have been excised from the neighborhood, marriage and family define Mexican identity. The diversity of the arrabal has receded in favor of the elevation of the modern family. Rodriguez does offer a nod to reality and urban cynicism by giving the final frames to the two urchins who opened the film by opening the book: they close and toss it back into the trash bin, walking off while shaking their heads. This glimpse into cinematic costumbrismo offers much to entertain, but as a realistic portrayal of postwar urban existence, it would need to defer to *Los Olvidados*.

The relative homogeneity of the arrabal in *Nosotros* fulfills what Néstor García Canclini defines as the modernist socio-spatial identity: "territorial and monolinguistic."[26] Although we hear references to indigenous words and instruments in the film, they occur within the context of a blended, homogenizing mestizaje and reinforce monoterritoriality. While the film and its score hint at diversity with passing references to African and indigeneous ancestries, it is all presented within the larger embrace of mestizaje, the official political narrative of idealized blended identity. Similarly, despite the way that Rodriguez's film has transformed well-known tropes of costumbrismo from music theater by merging them with more realistic issues, in the end the reigning sentiment of the production remains a romanticized idealism. García Canclini contends that postmodern identity is "transterritorial and multilinguistic," often using the term "deterritorial" to describe what is essentially a globalist identity that exists outside of linguistic and nation-state definitions. No Mexican filmmaker better inhabits that condition than Guillermo del Toro.

El Laberinto del Fauno: What Is the Sound of Magical Realism?

The Spanish-Mexican co-production *El Laberinto del fauno* (2006) exemplifies the millennial revival of Mexican cinema as a world genre. The paradox of that last clause speaks to the postmodern condition that García Canclini proposes. After the 1998 kidnapping of his father in Guadalajara, Guillermo del Toro moved to the United States and became a cinema citizen of the world just when the industry—even the Hollywood industry—was becoming more international and collaborative across geographicand linguistic boundaries.[27] Del Toro's first feature in wide release, *Cronos* (1996), signaled its NAFTA–era production by using a polyglot, multivalent Mexican city as the backdrop for an apparently simple vampire narrative. *Cronos* probes the ways in which, under persistent cultural and economic colonialism, Mexico becomes strange to itself and strange to others. The baroque Cronos device, a product of Spanish alchemy, offers eternal life in exchange for human blood. This hybrid mechanical parasite transforms its host into a voracious hematophage, mimicking the Spanish quest for domination by making its subjects consumers of their own subjugation. Released two years after the then-vaunted NAFTA agreement, *Cronos* presented a cautionary fable of globalism gone wrong.[28]

Globalism is fully embedded in *El Laberinto del fauno* (Pan's labyrinth), a fairy tale set in the aftermath of the Spanish Civil War and filmed in Spain with a mixed Spanish and Mexican crew. While overtly a Spanish narrative about Spanish history, populated by characters who speak with Iberian accents, the film nonetheless can be seen as a revisiting of Mexican cinematic themes. Oppression by a powerful elite, the pathos of *la gente*, and magical realist escape from present woes all populate Mexican war films to some degree, and appear as well in *El Laberinto del fauno*. Simply put, Mexicans cannot stop telling the story of their own Revolution.[29] Del Toro's choice to situate this story in a similarly fraught period of Spanish history allows Mexican audiences to recognize the tropes and motifs of their national cinema and to thus identify with the Spanish characters in roles familiar from Mexico's cinematic imaginary. The fairy tale is the means by which del Toro can achieve this global synthesis—"deterritorialization" in García Canclini's terms—by anchoring its devices in magical realism, a definitively New World response to Spanish presence.

The historical prologue of the film commences in black, underscored by a faint lullaby, first hummed and then joined by an orchestra. The haunting melody composed by del Toro's Spanish collaborator, Javier Navarette, anchors an ineffable blend of nostalgia and premonition in the scene, and its motives give birth to nearly all the music in the full score. The camera pans left to reveal the vertical image of Ofelia (Ivana Baquero), panting and with blood around her nose. As the camera pivots 45 degrees, the blood recedes into her nose, and we are in the realm of magical realism. The vocal (human) timbre of the lullaby ceases as the voiceover announces, "Cuentan que hace mucho, mucho tiempo" (They say that a long, long time ago) and the camera zooms into Ofelia's left eye, a portal to the underworld kingdom that hosts the backstory: a fairy tale of a princess, love, loss, return, and redemption. The instrumental lullaby scores the remainder of the voiceover as a sound bridge into the present time of the film, 1944, and the arrival of Ofelia and her mother, Carmen (Adriana Gil), at the disused mill occupied by Capitan Vidal (Sergio López) and a detachment of Franco's fascist military. Given the horrors to follow, the lullaby frames the narrative with a necessary safety zone of imagination.

After replacing a stone in a stele along the road and unleashing a fairy, Ofelia discovers a world of magic to counter the unremitting cruelty of Capitan Vidal, her new stepfather. The spiral-carved stone represents an eye, and this is a film much about looking, the seen and the unseen. Del Toro uses point of view and over-the-shoulder shots to emphasize the need for Ofelia to parse the visual narrative in a situation of competing dangers. Shot through the blue filters that were ubiquitous in millennial cinema productions, the color palette of the film is desaturated to browns, greens, ambers, and gray tones, save for the scenes of mortal threat, which are hued in reds and oranges: the all-consuming toad in the fig tree; the Tantalos-like pale man at a perpetually uneaten feast; and Capitan Vidal in his attic room, shaving. The recurrent motif of the spiral links eyes, the labyrinth, staircases, and, of course, history.

Navarette draws on a similarly defined palette of musical colors as a guide through the blend of fantasy and real life. The timbral palette of the film score highlights bowed and plucked strings, particularly the violin with piano or harp, enriched at crucial moments by hummed voices. When Navarette includes woodwinds and brass, the orchestration portends danger, as evident in the scores to scenes such as "The Three Trails," "The Moribund Tree and The Toad," "Not Human," and "The Waltz of the Mandrake."

While not overtly about any kind of identity other than that of a young girl testing boundaries, the portal scene evokes a number of motifs central to the Mexican psyche. Not only does the labyrinth itself invoke Octavio Paz's definitive trope of the *laberinto del soledad* (labyrinth of solitude), but Ofelia's experience in it is precisely that of the orphan whom Paz characterizes as the essential Mexican: "The past has left us orphans as it has the rest of the planet and we must join together in inventing our common future. 'World history' has become everyone's task, and our own labyrinth is the labyrinth of all mankind." This presciently postnational view of identity is precisely what Ofelia must negotiate as she moves between 1944 Spain and the eternal present of Princess Moanna's underworld realm.

One view of films about the US–Mexico border signal larger issues about nationhood: "Neither should we underestimate the ways in which Mexican culture and cinema are caught up in broader, transnational configurations of culture and power."[30] This discussion is limited to literal national borders and juxtapositions of nation-states rather than extending the metaphor to states of being such as are explored in *El Laberinto del fauno*, but such ontological questions have been at the heart of del Toro's body of work from his beginnings in Guadalajara through his own crossings to the United States, Spain, and, more recently, New Zealand. For Ofelia, the borders are those between childhood and adulthood, good and evil, myth and reality, family and self. Identity is nascent for her in the world of the film and will never be one fixed thing. She does have to choose, however, among alternatives offered by the various authorities in her life, from Vidal to the faun, and her mother to the housekeeper Mercedes.

Ofelia's entry into the labyrinth [20:00],[31] led by the fairy (*hada*), is accompanied by a variant of the same suspenseful harp and piano motives that introduced the fairy-like insect. A chorus of humming women, punctuated by a bassoon obbligato and a responding clarinet, establish the undertone of danger, as the eye-level camera tracks then leads Ofelia in head-on, tail-on shots; where she is going and where she has been are subtly alluded to in these editing choices and reinforced by the interplay of instruments in the musical score. Clearly, Ofelia is on the brink. As she moves deeper into the above-ground maze, the chorus acquires a monastic quality with the addition of male voices when del Toro cuts to an overhead shot. This addition of lower tones denotes Ofelia's approach to darker regions, and the overhead, or "eye of God" perspective indicates a kind of surveillance by unseen forces. The camera cranes down, leads and then tracks Ofelia in a pan shot that shows her turning the final corner in the above-ground maze. The choral strains recede as strings and winds fill out the soundscape when Ofelia approaches the lip of the underground labyrinth: all human intervention is behind her.

The camera cranes up to include the omphalos of the labyrinth in frame as Ofelia descends on the rim steps. The dark circle mirrors Ofelia's eye in the prologue, and we enter this dark spiral with her as we entered the film narrative through her iris. Choral voices lay in the lullaby theme, bolstering the melody in the violin, as Ofelia moves lower into the underworld and into the center of the labyrinth where, inevitably, a monster awaits. He arrives in silence, without musical accompaniment and in response to Ofelia's calls for an echo. The aural vacuum is punctuated only by his creaky movements and the anxious fluttering of the hadas' wings.

In its height, lankiness, and angularity, the faun visually counters the circular motif of containment—sonically defined by the recurrent motives of the lullaby—that protects and comforts Ofelia. The mother's belly, the navel into which she tells stories to her fetus brother, the bathtub, even the labyrinth, all of these are round places of security. The faun rises vertically from the verdant world inside the labyrinth, covered in lichens and leaves like the central stele in the spiral. He addresses Ofelia in the *vos* form, the archaic honorific due the princess he believes her to be; she answers with *tu*, indicating a familiar and populist attitude toward the world. As he hands her the *Libro de las encrucijadas* (Book of crossroads), telling her that it foretells her future, a faint musical motive underscores his gesture. We hear three descending pitches, a half-step followed by a minor third, played by the low bowed strings. The sound quickly fades away as the perplexed Ofelia opens the book and realizes that each page is blank.

Immediately the scene shifts to Capitan Vidal's self-reflexive act of shaving, alone, in his private quarters in the wheel room of the mill; this man is the real monster and the soundtrack offers subtle supporting clues. His ablutions are accompanied by a lively foxtrot, "En los jardines de Granada," emanating from the record player beside him. The jaunty, jazzy tune that accompanies his morning routine would seem to humanize the sadistic Vidal, but even the way he shaves contains menace. The opening shot of the record spinning initiates a pan into a series of head-on and over-the-shoulder shots that create a 360 effect in the mill room. This, too, is a labyrinth with a monster at its heart. (Certainly, careful viewers may begin to wonder at this point about the faun's true nature as well.) As the record plays and the camera moves around Vidal, the focal length shifts from long shot to close-up, establishing Vidal's cold view of his own face in the mirror, as well as his military stance and command of the empty stone room. When he polishes his boots, the record player cues a new song. Rafael Medina, a popular singer of the 1920s, can be heard faintly singing the flamenco *pasodoble* "Soy un pobre presidiario" (I am a poor convict). The lyrics express the sentiments of a man enslaved by desire, like a caged bird, suffering from lack of love, but intent on flying again, ready to sing about pain, in freedom. It was a favorite song of the so-called Blue Division of Spanish soldiers who volunteered to fight with Hitler's army on the Eastern front against Russia.[32] The irony of this particular love song playing as the Fascist polishes his jackboots signals a tortured link between passion and fascist resolve. The inclusion of these songs connects the common language of Navarette's contemporary film score to songs grounded in time and place, yet marked at points by the shared international tropes of jazz and torch song that were also familiar to Spanish and Latin American audiences from the earliest circulation of sound recording.[33] Over his shoulders we can see the massive gears and wheels of the mill, which recall the gears and springs of his father's watch that stopped at the time of his death. Vidal obsessively adjusts the watch, oblivious to his surroundings and unaware that he, too, is a cog in a larger mechanism. This fascination with mechanical devices has been evident in del Toro's work from the beginning, and indicates a baroque sensibility that unites the old and new worlds.[34]

Ofelia is given three tasks by the faun: retrieve a golden key from the belly of a giant toad; enter the chamber of the Pale Man and retrieve a special dagger; and bring her baby brother to the faun. The Pale Man sequence takes Ofelia deepest into the labyrinth world and tests her obedience and intelligence. The Pale Man presides over a table set for a feast, although he himself is skeletal and hampered by sagging folds of flesh. The image of Famine, the Pale Man's only food is children, and he gobbles up two of Ofelia's fairy guides like Saturn in Goya's painting. His eyes, like those of Santa Lucia, rest in a plate before him.

Ofelia enters this world by drawing a door with special chalk given her by the faun [56:11]. That device creates a frame, literally and figuratively, for her adventure in this Tantalos kingdom. Despite being warned by the faun not to eat anything, Ofelia cannot resist taking two grapes from the table. This theft awakens the Pale Man and precipitates Ofelia's flight. Among the rich implications of this scene, it surely stands as a metaphor for the risks and temptations facing migrants who venture uninvited across the borders of modern nation-states.

What is notable in this sequence is the strategic use of silence. Just as Paz invokes the "dialectic of solitude" to describe the profound ambivalence at the heart of Mexicanity, so del Toro places score and silence in counterpoint to emphasize the interstitial nature of Ofelia's existence as "the general collective memory of the Spanish Civil War serves as a vitally important axis of nostalgia for del Toro."[35] Del Toro offers this embrace of in-betweenness as a quintessential quality of modern existence, essential to contemporary Mexican national identity, yet universal. The tremendous success of *El Laberinto del faun* with viewers worldwide who identify with its story and themes confirms the resonance of del Toro's vision.

Ofelia's failure and then refusal to do the faun's bidding, to sacrifice her baby brother, leads to a final confrontation in the labyrinth. Flanked by the faun and Capitan Vidal, Ofelia is trapped in a maelstrom of power as the two dominant figures vie for control of the future, represented by the baby. Two underworlds—the fantastic and the fascistic—compete, and ultimately, they are indistinguishable. Neither Vidal with his pistol nor the faun with his dagger will hesitate to sacrifice Ofelia to his designs. It is simply a matter of which reaches her first. Throughout this final scene, in which Ofelia's several worlds and states of being collide, the instrumental score underscores the tension. The soft, caressing melody is absent during the chase scene; instead, we hear a fragmented, pounding theme with rising strings, punctuated by dissonant and chaotic bursts from the full orchestra, the brass portending the moment of crisis, sounding danger and urgency. The tempo matches Ofelia's quickened breathing, until a gunshot breaks the pattern. The simple piano accompaniment and human voice returns as Mercedes hums the lullaby, Ofelia's breath eases, and the palette brightens to a golden glow at her apotheosis. While clearly a direct allegory about Spanish factionalism, such tension over the struggle to reconcile myth and history is definitive in twenty-first-century global identity. In this Spanish and Mexican co-production about the political and personal forces that shape modern being, del Toro opts for ambiguity rather than a clear answer. National identity is no longer a function of place or time.

Conclusions

While the cinematic themes, musical score, and soundtrack to *El Laberinto del faun* may seem to be a departure from the films that characterized the Golden

Era of Mexican cinema, we can find common strategies for conveying the complexities of Mexican identity. First among them is the directorial focus on essential human struggles, shaped with special resonance to unite viewers in Mexico, but also to reach audiences beyond the nation. Musical collaborations signal how national and state boundaries insufficiently represent the cosmopolitan nature of even the most humble Mexican experience. So well-absorbed was the Argentine influence in the tango-canciónes sung by street urchins in itinerant theatrical shows that its importation may not have been noticed by some Mexican viewers. These same viewers considered the bolero, foxtrot, and other imported popular dance rhythms as to belonging to Mexican music. Manuel Castro Padilla's collaboration with Puerto Rican composer Rafael Hernándezon, *Águila o sol*, presages that of the Spanish composer Javier Navarette with Mexican director Guillermo del Toro. The trajectory marked by these three collaborative films and musical projects marks three stages in defining Mexican national identity in a shift from cosmopolitan to global.

Anthropologist Thomas Turino identifies a shared trend of increasing inclusiveness in nationalist discourses across Latin America. Beginning with movements of independence at the beginning of the nineteenth century, he notes an increased willingness of Latin American nations to include distinct social groups as belonging to the nation. What we might today call a "multicultural project" gained momentum in the twentieth century when the cosmopolitan nation became aligned with capitalist expansion.[36]

In our examinations of Mexican film, we see music as a critical tool in the stage of defining Mexico's project of cultural nationalism, which Turino defines as "the semiotic work of using expressive practices to fashion the concrete emblems that stand for and create the nation, that distinguish one nation from another and most importantly serve as the basis for socializing citizens to inculcate national sentiment." [37] In *Águila o sol* Manuel Castro's integration of Oaxacan music, once viewed as outside the sphere of genuine Mexican national identity, matched political concerns of the era. Moving beyond integration, in *Nosotros Los Pobres*, the project shifts more squarely toward the issue of the individual and the nation, inviting Pedro Infante's projection of one man's integrity and identity to stand for the many. Leaving overt cultural nationalism behind entirely in *El Laberinto del faun*, Navarette and del Toro offer metaphoric themes that address identity beyond national borders. The film's signature lullaby belongs to a shared dreamlike world rather than to any specific person, time, or place.

Reception and Influence

We have focused largely on matters of directorial motivation and compositional design, but equally important is how audiences have received and responded to the films and their music. In its heyday, Mexican cinema operated as a regional industry; it exerted powerful force well beyond national boundaries. Mexico's film industry supplied films to all of Latin America and was second only to oil production in the nation's economy.[38] Like melodrama itself, movie theme songs open the opportunity to explore contradictions.[39] Songs, and sometimes other aspects of the film, score as well, regularly acquired a life beyond their association with the film. Within and beyond its original cinematic context, film music indexes the complex nature of identity. Each of composers discussed, Manuel Castro Padilla, Manuel Esperón, and Javier Navarette, drew upon regional practices of music, drawing existing traditional and popular songs into their film scores. In the process, they also created new songs. Esperón (1911–2011) is credited with composing more than 950 songs, and many of these songs were quickly adopted as lasting favorites. A tribute to this dynamic appears in a hit tune currently (2014) popular on Mexican radio stations, "Época de Oro" (Golden era) sung by Los Cuates de Sinaloa, which speaks directly of the lasting legacy of the songs promoted and created expressly for the Golden Age of Mexican cinema.

Certainly, iconic film images also persist in the minds of viewers, entering the collective consciousness, often because of how they came alive through music. *El Laberinto del faun* exemplifies this bond of sound and image.

That bond also signals a shift in cinematic representations of Mexican identity. No longer must the music be exclusively Mexican in origin or conception (which as we've seen has never been exclusively the case), but as in the best of Mexico's early films, the score and soundtrack must speak to modern Mexican realities and accommodate the contradictions of lived realities. Music offers cues to viewers for understanding lived experience, and even in the early days of Mexican cinema, that experience included collaborations that expanded viewers' and listeners' conceptions of Mexican identity. The trajectory continues, but clearly, Mexican film, once a product delivered to the world, is now, like Mexican music and identity, inseparable from it.

Notes

1. Carlos Monsiváis, "Mexican Cinema: Of Myths and Demystifications," in *Mediating Two Worlds: Cinematic Encounters in the Americas*, trans. Mike Gonzalez, eds. John King, Ana M. López, and Manuel Alvarado (London: BFI, 1993), 140–46.
2. Andrea Noble, *Mexican National Cinema* (New York: Routledge, 2005), 91.
3. Susan Dever, *Celluloid Nationalism and Other Melodramas: From Post-Revolutionary Mexico to fin de siglo Mexamérica* (Albany: SUNY Press, 2003), 104.
4. See Octavio Paz, "Mexican Masks," in *The Labyrinth of Solitude and Other Writings*, trans. Lysander Kemp (New York: Grove Press, 1985).
5. Sergei Eisenstein was a primary force in the development of Russian montage. He met Diego Rivera at the tenth anniversary celebration of the Bolshevik Revolution and soon traveled to Mexico to stay with Rivera and Kahlo. With funding from Hollywood, engineered by socialist novelist Upton Sinclair, Eisenstein spent 1930–1931 in Mexico shooting footage for what would become Qué Viva México. In 1979, the raw and unseen footage was located in the Museum of Modern Art archives and edited together by Grigori Aleksandrov. For more, see Masha Salazkina, *In Excess: Sergei Eisenstein's Mexico* (Chicago: University of Chicago, 2009); and Inga Karetnikova, *Mexico According to Eisenstein* (Albuquerque: University of New Mexico Press, 1991).
6. For a fascinating study of Cantínflas, see Jeffery Pilcher, *Cantínflas and the Chaos of Mexican Modernity* (Wilmington, DE: Scholarly Resources, 2001).
7. Pilcher, *Cantínflas*, 4.
8. Timecodes refer to *Águila o sol*, directed by Arkady Boytler, with music by Manuel Castro Padilla; Laguna Films, 2003 [DVD].
9. The film's musical director, Manuel Castro Padilla, is credited with defining the nine aires that comprised the official jarabe for Russian ballerina Anna Pavlova's 1918 homage to jarabe, *Fantasía Mexicana*. See Gabriela Mendoza-Garcia, "Bodily Renderings of the Jarabe Tapatío in Early Twentieth-Century Mexico and the Millennial United States: Race, Nation, Class, and Gender" (Unpublished dissertation, University of California–Riverside, 2013), 18.
10. Jorge Sareli, *El Tango en Mexico* (Mexico City: Editorial Diana, 1977).

11. John Rosenberg, *The Black Butterfly: Concepts of Spanish Romanticism* (Oxford: University Press of Mississippi, 1998).

12. Frances Toor describes these lace headdresses and their curious origin: "To cover the head for church a different type of huipil is used; this is made of lace and starched to form a frame for the face. When worn for adornment it hangs from the top of the head down the back. This huipil grande, or the one for the head, has tiny adornments attached to it that look like the sleeves of a baby's dress. There is much speculation as to its origin but nothing more definite has been discovered than that it may haven been copied from a lace baby dress that was found in a trunk of a wrecked vessel off the coast at Salina Cruz." *A Treasury of Mexican Folkways* (New York: Bonanza, 1957), 79.

13. Zahra Moss, "The Golden Treasures of Monte Alban: Mexican Representation and Exhibition Controversy, 1933–1936" (PhD dissertation, Tucson, University of Arizona, 2012).

14. Marilyn Miller, "The Soul Has No Color But the Skin Does: Angelitos Negros and the Uses of Blackface on the Mexican Silver Screen, ca. 1950," in *Global Sountracks: Worlds of Film Music*, ed. Mark Slobin (Middletown, CT: Wesleyan University Press, 2008), 241–57.

15. Crespo notes that Caribbean popular music, particularly Cuban music, owes a debt to Mexican film for promoting it throughout Latin America and the world. Francisco Javier Crespo, "The Globalization of Cuban Music Through Mexican Film," *Musical Cultures of Latin America: Global Effects, Past and Present—Selected Reports in Ethnomusicology* 11 (2003), 225–31.

16. "Rafael Hernández," Fundación de la Cultura Popular (Foundation for Popular Culture) (San Juan, Puerto Rico, 2014), accessed March 2, 2014, http://www.prpop.org/biografias/r_bios/rafael_hernandez.shtml.

17. "For those metropolitan spectators who had recently abandoned the close-knit security of rural village life, the cinema offered a form of collective public experience that provided a refuge from the alienating effects of urban life," Noble, *Mexican National Cinema*, 76.

18. For an assessment of Infante's position as icon of national identity, see Sal Acosta, "*En el corazón del pueblo:* Pedro Infante's Funeral, the *Pueblo* Motif, and the Contest over this Legacy," in *Latin American Popular Culture Since Independence: An Introduction*, eds. William H. Beezley and Linda A. Curcio-Nagy, 2nd ed. (Lanham, MD: Rowman & Littlefield, 2012), 229–46; and Anne Rubenstein, "Bodies, Cities, Cinema: Pedro Infante's Death as Political Spectacle," in *Fragments of a Golden Age: The Politics of Culture in Mexico Since 1940*, eds. Gilbert Joseph, Anne Rubenstein, and Eric Zolov (Durham, NC: Duke University Press, 2001), 199–233.

19. Timecodes refer to *Nosotros los Pobres*, Dir., Ismael Rodriguez; Perf. Pedro Infante, Katy Jurado, Miguel Inclan. Producciones Rodríguez Hermanos, 1948. Warner Bros, 2007 [DVD].

20. Dever, *Celluloid Nationalism*, 103.

21. For a useful discussion of cinema-going behavior, see Carlos Monsiváis, "All the People Came and Did Not Fit onto the Screen: Notes on the Cinema Audience in Mexico," in *Mexican Cinema*, ed. Paulo Antonio Paranaguá (London: BFI, 1995).

22. Dever, *Celluloid Nationalism*, 104.

23. Alejandro Madrid, *Sounds of the Modern Nation. Music, Culture and Ideas in Post-Revolutionary Mexico* (Philadelphia: Temple University Press, 2009).

24. Laura Vázquez Blázquez, "Leyendas, historias, canciones e himnos populares," *Culturas Populares, Revista electrónica* 1 (January–April 2006), 1–25.

25. Luis Coronado Gruel, personal communication with the authors.

26. Néstor García Canclini, *Consumers and Citizens: Globalization and Multicultural Conflicts*, trans. George Yúdice (Minneapolis: University of Minnesota Press, 2001), 29.

27. Daniel Zalewski, "Show the Monster: Guillermo del Toro's Quest to get Amazing Creatures Onscreen," *The New Yorker*, February 7, 2011.

28. For an insightful reading of economic vampirism in *Cronos*, see John Kraniauskas, "*Cronos* and the Political Economy of Vampirism: Notes on a Historical Constellation," in *Cannibalism and the Colonial World*, eds. Francis Barker, Peter Hulme, and Margaret Iversen (Cambridge: Cambridge University Press, 1998), 142–57.

29. Unlike its neighbor to the north, which struggles to produce credible and marketable films about the American Revolution, Mexican directors have compulsively and effectively addressed revolutionary tropes in every decade of its cinema history. Jacqueline Ávila counts more than 250 Mexican films about the revolution, noting how the theme serves as a "smokescreen for current struggles." Jacqueline Ávila, "Resounding the Mexican Revolution: Music and Changing Conceptions of the Revolution in Contemporary Mexican Cinema" (58th Annual Meeting of the Society for Ethnomusicology, November 14, 2013).

30. Noble, *Mexican National Cinema*, 173.

31. Timecodes refer to *El Laberinto del fauno*, Dir. Guillermo del Toro, Perfs. Ivana Baquero, Adriana Gil, and Sergio López. Tequila Gang, Estudios

Picasso, Telecinco Cinema, Sententia Entertainment, Esperanto Filmoj, 2006; Warner Bros [DVD].

32. Foro Memoria Historica de la Division Azul, http://memoriablau.foros.ws/t1412/soy-un-pobre-presidiario-pasodoble-/ (site discontinued).

33. Jason Borge, "La Civiladada Selva: Jazz and Latin American Avant-garde Intellectuals," *Chasqui: Revista de literatura latinoamericana* 37, no. 1 (2008), 105.

34. For a useful discussion of Baroque reimagined in cinema, see Angela Ndalianis, *Neo-baroque Aesthetics and Contemporary Entertainment* (Cambridge, MA: MIT Press, 2004), chap. 1.

35. Christopher Hartney, "With Spain in Our Hearts: The Political Fantastic of Guillermo del Toro's *El Laberinto del Faun* (2006) and *El Espinazo del Diablo* (2001)," *Literature & Aesthetics* 19, no. 2 (2009), 187–201.

36. Thomas Turino, "Nationalism and Latin American Music: Selected Case Studies and Theoretical Considerations," *Latin American Music Review* 24 no. 2 (Fall–Winter 2003), 70.

37. Turino, "Nationalism and Latin American Music," 75.

38. John King, *Magical Reels: A History of Cinema in Latin America* (London & New York: Verso, 1990), 47.

39. Miller, "The Soul Has No Color But the Skin Does," 241–57. Jesús Martin Barbero, *Communication, Culture and Hegemony: From the Media to Mediations*. Trans. Elizabeth Fox and Robert A. White, intro. Philip Schlesinger (London: SAGE, 1993).

CONTRIBUTORS

William H. Beezley. Professor of Latin American history at the University of Arizona, William Beezley has a research interest in Mexican and Guatemalan cultural legacies expressed in fiesta forms, especially music. Recently, he has published *Problems in Modern Mexican History: Sources and Interpretations*. He is the editor-in-chief of *The Oxford Research Encyclopedia for Latin America*.

Alejo Carpentier (1904–1980). Born in Switzerland and reared in Havana, Alejo Carpentier achieved an international reputation as a novelist, journalist, musician, and musicologist. He became one of the first writers to incorporate surrealism and later magical realism in his fiction. He also gave much attention to Afro-Cuban society and culture, especially music. He had prominence among French and Latin American writers and intellectuals. He supported the Cuban revolution of Fidel Castro.

Jan Fairley (1949–2012). Jan Fairley, ethnomusicologist, writer, broadcaster, lecturer, DJ, and singer, began her career as a teacher in Chile and managed to escape with her husband following the 1973 coup d'état. Back in the United Kingdom, she earned an M.Phil in Latin American Studies at Oxford University, followed by a PhD in ethnomusicology at Edinburgh University, and soon began teaching, often at the Liverpool University, as she developed a writing career especially about world music. She became a tireless advocate for human rights, especially in Latin America. She sang and danced throughout her life. At the time of her death, she was interviewing Cuban female musicians for a book about them. A significant collection of her work is available as *Living Politics, Making Music: The Writings of Jan Fairley*, edited by Simon Frith and Ian Christie.

Jennifer Jenkins. Professor of English at the University of Arizona, Jennifer Jenkins directs the National Endowment for the Humanities–funded Bear Canyon Institute for Southwest Humanities, and the NEH-supported *The*

Afterlife of Film: Tribesourcing Southwestern Materials in the American Indian Film Gallery to repurpose mid-century educational films about indigenous peoples through narration of the films in either or both tribal or European languages. She is the author of *Celluloid Pueblo: Western Ways Films and the Invention of the Postwar Southwest.*

E. Gabrielle Kuenzli. Professor of Latin American history at the University of South Carolina, Gabrielle Kuenzli focuses her research on Bolivia, especially the topics of ethnicity, nationalism, and identity. This research resulted in the recent monograph, *Acting Inca: National Belonging in Early Twentieth-Century Bolivia*, which examines the ignored and forgotten role of the Aymara peoples. A recent Fulbright Fellowship has enabled additional research on this essential topic of the nation's indigenous peoples.

Carolyn Ryan Larson. In *Our Indigenous Ancestors: Museum Anthropology and Nation-Making in Argentina, 1862–1943,* Carrie Larson moves the analysis of nation building into the significant examination of museum exhibits and the anthropologists who collected and displayed them. Her evaluation of cultural objects led to her current approach to music in Argentina. She teaches at St. Norbert College in De Pere, Wisconsin.

Jerry D. Metz Jr. Parts of the essay in this book were adapted from Jerry D. Metz Jr.'s 2012 PhD dissertation, *Alegria: The Rise of Brazil's "Carnival of Popular Participation," Salvador da Bahia, 1950–2000s*, the University of Maryland. The author thanks Marc A. Hertzman. Currently, he is an independent scholar in Lawrence, Kansas.

Sonia Robles. Sonia Robles, with a PhD from Michigan State University in history, has taught at University of North Carolina–Charlotte and currently is a professor at la Universidad Panoamericana in Mexico City. Her research, building on her dissertation, centers on radio broadcasting of music during the 1920s and 1930s in Mexico.

Robin Sacolick. Besides a position as world music and musicology instructor at San Jose State University, she has diverse intellectual interests that mirror her educational background with a BA from Pomona College, MBA from UC Berkeley Haas School of Business, and a PhD from University of California–Santa Cruz. Her recent dissertation is titled *Transcendence and Son Jarocho as Practiced in the San Francisco Bay Area.*

Janet Sturman. Musician, musicologist, director of productions including *TzinTzunTan*, and author of *The Course of Mexican Music*, Sturman has wide ranging interests throughout Latin America in the region's musical legacies and performances. Currently she is the Associate Dean of the Graduate College at the University of Arizona.

Ketty Wong-Cruz. Ketty Wong-Cruz expresses internationalism based on her education with university degrees from Ecuador, Russia, and the United States, her interdisciplinary scholarship in history, performance, and musicology, and her interests in Latin American art, folk and traditional music, history, and Chinese ballroom dancing. She currently teaches in the Department of Music, University of Kansas. Her recent book, *Whose National Music? Identity, Mestizaje, and Migration in Ecuador*, received several international awards, including one from Cuba's Casa de las Américas.

INDEX